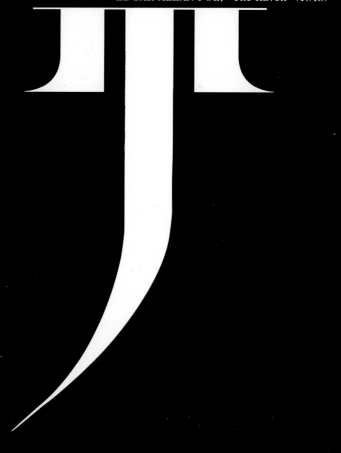

*"Prophet!" said I, "thing of evil! – prophet still, if bird or devil! –
Whether Tempter sent, or whether tempest tossed thee here ashore,
Desolate yet all undaunted, on this desert land enchanted –
On this home by Horror haunted – tell me truly, I implore –
Is there – is there balm in Gilead? – tell me – tell me, I implore!"
Quoth the Raven, "Nevermore."*

EDGAR ALLAN POE, "The Raven" (1845)

NOVELS BY
JAMES HERBERT

THE RATS
LAIR
DOMAIN
THE FOG
THE SURVIVOR
FLUKE
THE SPEAR
THE DARK
THE JONAH
SHRINE
MOON
THE MAGIC COTTAGE
SEPULCHRE
HAUNTED
CREED
PORTENT

JAMES HERBERT

BY HORROR HAUNTED

EDITED BY

STEPHEN JONES

BCA

LONDON · NEW YORK · SYDNEY · TORONTO

This edition published 1992 by BCA
by arrangement with New English Library,
a division of Hodder and Stoughton Ltd,
Mill Road, Dunton Green, Sevenoaks, Kent TN13 2YA
Editorial Office: 47 Bedford Square, London WC1B 3DP

CN 6615

Photoset by Rowland Phototypesetting Ltd,
Bury St Edmunds, Suffolk

Printed in Great Britain by
Butler & Tanner Ltd, Frome and London

EDITOR'S NOTE

James Herbert: By Horror Haunted was conceived as an exploration and tribute to Britain's bestselling horror writer.

Through the presentation of interviews, essays, articles, reviews and artwork by and about Herbert (culled from a wide variety of books and magazines or original to this volume), the book is designed to give the reader a general overview of the author's phenomenal success over the past seventeen years and hopefully a better understanding of Herbert's past and where the future is leading him.

However, this is *not* a biography, nor is it intended to be a definitive work. *James Herbert: By Horror Haunted* is a mosaic of comments and opinions that will perhaps allow the reader an unbiased insight into Herbert's (often unjustly maligned) talent.

As with any collection of disparate material, there is an overlap of certain information; however, except for some minor editorial tidying-up, I have elected to leave most of the pieces to stand by themselves. This is a volume to be dipped into, rather than read from cover to cover in a single sitting.

Obviously a book of this size and scope could not have been compiled without the involvement of a great number of people. So besides the many contributors listed on the contents page, I would also like to thank all those individuals and periodicals we have quoted extracts from, as well as the following people: Jo Fletcher, Kathy Gale, Tony Hammond, Tony Mulliken, Nick Sayers, Carolyn Caughey, Lisa Tuttle, Dave Taylor, Sara Tracy, the Herbert family: Eileen, Kerry, Emma and Casey, and by no means least, Jim Herbert, for opening up his home and his life to me.

I hope the result does him justice.

STEPHEN JONES
London

CONTENTS

Editor's Note   STEPHEN JONES   5

ONE   James Herbert: Introduction   STEPHEN KING   9

TWO   A Category to Himself   STEPHEN JONES   19

THREE   A Life in the Day of James Herbert   VICTOR OLLIVER   33

FOUR   Bowled Over by the Beast: Me and My Car   JAMES HERBERT   39

FIVE   At Home With James Herbert   DAVE HUGHES   43

SIX   Doing It With Style   DOUGLAS E. WINTER   47

SEVEN   Comic Relief   JAMES HERBERT   65

EIGHT   Castaway   MIKE ASHLEY   69

NINE   My Ten Favourite Books   JAMES HERBERT   75

TEN   The Craft   NEIL GAIMAN   79

ELEVEN   Breakfast   JAMES HERBERT   93

TWELVE   Season of the Rat   ADRIAN COLE   99

THIRTEEN   Horror of The Rats   JOHN GILBERT   105

FOURTEEN   The Fog   JAMES HERBERT   109

FIFTEEN   The Curious Case of The Spear   JO FLETCHER   113

SIXTEEN   Maurice and Mog   JAMES HERBERT   123

SEVENTEEN   James Herbert and Science Fiction   MICHAEL A. MORRISON   137

EIGHTEEN	The Dark Domain	*JOHN FRASER*	151
NINETEEN	Breaking the Mould	*STEPHEN LAWS*	161
TWENTY	The Eidetic Image	*MICHAEL A. MORRISON*	165
TWENTY-ONE	A British Phenomenon	*DAVID J. HOWE*	169
TWENTY-TWO	Herbert, *Haunted,* and the Integrity of Bestsellerdom	*STEPHEN GALLAGHER*	181
TWENTY-THREE	Haunted by Success	*JOHN GILBERT*	189
TWENTY-FOUR	Selling a Bestseller	*NICK SAYERS, IAN HUGHES, DAVID SINGER, TONY HAMMOND*	199
TWENTY-FIVE	In the Hall of the Monster King: Music and the Maestro of Horror	*EDWIN POUNCEY*	209
TWENTY-SIX	Hallowe'en's Child	*JAMES HERBERT*	217
TWENTY-SEVEN	Swamp Thing	*JAMES HERBERT*	231
TWENTY-EIGHT	The Devil You Know	*JOHN GILBERT*	235
TWENTY-NINE	*Creed*: The Advertisement	*DAVID J. HOWE*	243
THIRTY	Big Climaxes and Movie Bullshit	*STEFAN JAWORZYN*	249
THIRTY-ONE	From Rats to Riches	*DAVE HUGHES*	261
THIRTY-TWO	Jim Meets Gray	*GRAHAM MASTERTON*	267
THIRTY-THREE	Dark Dreamer	*STANLEY WIATER*	271
THIRTY-FOUR	They Don't Like Us	*JAMES HERBERT*	283
THIRTY-FIVE	Notes Towards A Reappraisal	*RAMSEY CAMPBELL*	289
THIRTY-SIX	James Herbert: Afterword	*CLIVE BARKER*	299
James Herbert: A Working Bibliography			302
Acknowledgements			318
Illustrations Acknowledgements			320

JAMES HERBERT: INTRODUCTION

Stephen King

ONE

"Don't know what I want, but I know how to get it."
– The Sex Pistols, "Anarchy in the UK"

"He knew that she was dead. But he wondered why her
tongue had been ripped out."
– James Herbert, The Spear

"I was very lucky.
I came along at just
the right time – like
the Beatles. It isn't
anything you can
study or plan for. It
just happens."

– JAMES HERBERT,
from "Animal Calm"
by Neil Gaiman,
Today, June 1, 1986

"Engage brain before grasping pen" is a pretty good rule to follow when writing essays, but in this case I might have overdone it a little.

I was first asked to write a piece for *By Horror Haunted* over a year ago, and have been thinking about James (Jim, to his friends) Herbert at odd moments ever since. Sometimes I found myself wondering how he has continued to write such delightful (strange word to use, considering his subject matter, but a true word nevertheless) and involving novels when so many of his contemporaries and imitators have either fallen by the wayside or into self-parody. At some later date I found myself wondering if I might be able to write about him in an evolutionary sense – because he has evolved – and realised that I had answered my original question by posing this second one.

James Herbert is still around and still prospering precisely because he *has* evolved. How much? Well, let's put it this way: someone who had not followed him from his first novel in 1974 to his most recent in 1992 would probably not realise they had been written by the same man. If there is any truth to the

STEPHEN KING

imperative "evolve or die", Jim Herbert is a pretty good example of the idea as it applies to fiction writers.

All good thoughts, but they took me no closer to truly engaging my brain, let alone grasping my pen. Finally I got a letter from Hodder & Stoughton, enquiring as to my progress on the piece I had promised them. It was a very polite letter, but reading between the lines, I sensed a certain impatience, as in "Say, mate – are you going to do this fookin thing or not?"

I decided that the time had come to write something, so I got Jim's newest novel and a couple of old favourites, settled in with them, and hoped for illumination. It eventually came, but from an unexpected source: my stereo. I was listening to Joan Jett's most recent album, *The Hit List*, as I read. This record (except they're really all CDs now, aren't they) is a compilation of cover versions, most of them quite well done, although for the most part without the flash and fire of the originals. The one that caught my ear as I was re-reading *The Spear* was Ms Jett's cover of "Pretty Vacant," originally done (one doesn't quite like to say "performed" in this case) by the Sex Pistols. And the question that finally got me down to business was simply this: *I wonder how close James Herbert and the Sex Pistols were to being contemporaries?*

I dug out my ancient copy of *Never Mind the Bollocks, Here's the Sex Pistols* to see if I could find out, but the time-tattered inner sleeve didn't really answer my question, being an American reissue of the original EMI recording. I was, nevertheless, electrified by the songs when I slipped the record, which I hadn't listened to in some years, on my dusty, disused turntable. The one which particularly caught my ear and returned my thoughts to James Herbert was the furious and threatening "Anarchy in the UK". I flashed back to the first time I ever heard that song; at the time I felt as if I had been stabbed in the ear with an icepick made out of pure rage.

A little research showed me that Herbert and the Pistols had burst upon the English pop culture scene at roughly the same time. Herbert's first novel came out in 1974; the Pistols were in the studio, recording "Pretty Vacant" and "Anarchy in the UK", less than a year later. By then I was not surprised; my original intuition had taken hold with the force of a conviction. And why not? If *The Rats*, with its scenes of gruesome horror and its blasted East End landscape, is not a literary version of "Anarchy in the UK", what is?

I don't want to belabour this point, but I do intend to make it as clearly and as persuasively as I can. The Sex Pistols showed up on the pop scene (by slithering out from under some

"Perhaps the best way is to compare my early stuff with punk music. When it first came out it was a bit rough and ready but, as the good musicians among them learned their craft, so their music became more sophisticated and professional.

"They got good, honed their skills and started to impress. The same should apply to a writer."

– JAMES HERBERT, from "Herbert's Not Such a Horrible Hack" by Keith Newbery, *Portsmouth News*, June 19, 1986 muck-encrusted rock, many of their critics implied or actually said) at a time when rock and roll music was, for the dozenth time in as many years, being pronounced dead. They shocked an established bunch of ageing rockers who thought they were still rebels and thus unshockable; they blew the doors off a coterie of pompous rock critics who had not predicted them and were totally unprepared for them; in America they called a whole broadcasting format, known as AOR (for "album-orientated radio") into question, and they quickly spawned a host of imitators. Longer-lived groups such as The Clash, The Stranglers, and U-2 formed a vital connective sinew between such "old fogey" groups as the Rolling Stones and the Who and such current supergroups as Guns n' Roses, Metallica, and Inxs.

"I do get recognised occasionally. But not enough to be a nuisance, just enough to feel pleased about. There's no great invasion of my privacy, just enough to make me feel good – and that's the way I like it."

– JAMES HERBERT, from "Quiet Man Behind the King of Horror" by Angela Carless, *Northampton Chronicle & Echo,* August 15, 1989

On the print side, James Herbert did almost exactly the same thing with such early novels as *The Rats, The Fog,* and *The Survivor.* One of the best examples of just what Herbert was up to in those days comes early in *The Rats,* when an infant is menaced by the nasty little monsters. The year-old girl, Karen Blakely, is with her loyal mongrel pal, Shane, when the rats show up. In a conventional horror novel of that time, good old Shane would have saved his tiny mistress from germ-laden meanies, although he would probably have been forced to give up his own life in the process of doing so – salvation for the kid, and a nice, comfy cry for us.

James Herbert, however, was having none of this tired old tripe from the very beginning. It's not that he doesn't understand the patterns and movements of conventionality, one comes to believe; it's just that he doesn't really give a shit. Karen's dog does the best he can, but it's not enough. His throat is torn out, and when Karen's mother rushes in to see what all the fuss is about, she sees only "a small white shape. A tiny hand quivering above the mass of black."

That's all, readers of the time must have thought. Surely that has to be all, doesn't it?

The answer is no. Like the Sex Pistols, recording "Anarchy in the UK" mostly in order to get to the *really* appalling stuff like "God Save the Queen", Herbert is only getting warmed up. "The little body came up, but with two of the monsters clinging," Herbert writes. "The two rats fell away, not from the blows, but because the soft flesh of the child separated from her body."

And there it is. James Herbert has spoken the unspeakable, has made the outrages of William Peter Blatty's *The Exorcist* look almost tame by comparison, and dramatically upped the ante in the old gasp-and-groan business; *The Rats* is a couple of light years from the pallid delicacy of Oliver Onions and M. R. James, certainly. If the Sex Pistols created punk rock at a stroke with *Never Mind the Bollocks*, then I think it could be argued that James Herbert created the entire splatterpunk genre at a stroke with *The Rats*. I wouldn't argue it, however, because I don't have much use for the splatterpunks. I'd rather think of James Herbert as a kind of late twentieth-century Road Warrior, ushering the horror genre into a radioactive post-nuclear age full of fleshy horrors and 3-D nightmare creatures that do not relax their jaws even when the sleeper wakes.

Of course the comparison between Jim and Britain's proto-type punkers eventually breaks down, as all such comparisons eventually do. Although they were the creative equivalent of a hurricane wind blowing fresh air into a previously closed and stuffy room, the Sex Pistols were a commercial dead end. Johnny Rotten, visibly despondent about the critical catcalls which had greeted the group's first and only American tour, called it quits. A bleary and aptly named Sid Vicious apparently killed his girlfriend during what the police like to call a "domestic disturbance" and then died of a heroin overdose shortly there-after. I can't remember the exact details or chronology, and the whole business is too depressing to look up. In a very real sense it makes no difference, anyway. The obituary might have said that the Sex Pistols suffered a head-on collision with the real world and detonated on impact.

"Everyone expects to see Christopher Lee standing here, I can't believe what I read about myself . . . I rarely wear black and I don't carry skulls around."

– JAMES HERBERT, from "Herbert – The Writer Who Brings Horror Down to Street Level" by Caroline Lynch, *Irish Press*, August 5, 1989

James Herbert, however, is very much alive and still hard at it. His sixteen novels have been so successful he need never grasp his own pen again (or engage brain either, for that mat-ter), but he is hard at it just the same; like most of us who write stories, making the living is really just a side-effect. One does it because it's fulfilling and entertaining, not because it puts bread on the table and pays the electric bill. The reason he's still around, however, goes back to the "evolve or die" thing I talked about back at the beginning. And that's a fact worth mentioning – perhaps even celebrating – because there was a time when I really didn't think Jim Herbert would be around for the long haul. I didn't think he'd o.d. on sex, drugs or fast cars, but I *did* believe he was at risk, just the same. I thought a total creative flameout was a very real possibility.

In his interviews, Jim has expressed impatience with the idea that many horror novels gain their power from their subtexts – things felt and experienced but not actually set down in the words of the story – and he's quite entitled to his opinion. Yet I don't think even Jim would argue the idea that his early novels burn with rage and its slightly more cerebral counterpart, outrage.

"I go to parties, people ask me who I am and I tell them I'm James Herbert and I'm a writer, and they say, 'What name do you write under?'"

– JAMES HERBERT, from "Streetwise, and a Master Craftsman" by Gerald Bartlett, *Publishing News*, June 19, 1987

In *Danse Macabre*, my informal overview of the horror genre published in 1981, I wrote: "Herbert rarely finesses and never pulls back from the crunch; instead he seems to race eagerly, zestfully, towards each new horror." I stand by everything to the left of the semi-colon, but I have come to wonder if I was correct about the stuff to the right of it. Is it eagerness when the baby is eaten alive by the rats? Or when, in *The Fog*, a crazed bus driver castrates his old enemy with a pair of garden shears? Is it zest when, in *The Spear*, Harry Steadman finds his business partner and ex-lover crucified to his front door with her tongue cut out?

I think there's something else going on here, and that something else is closely akin to the primal scream I hear on those early Sex Pistols recordings. It is a mixture of anger and exuberance I hear in the voice driving those novels, a combination which offers a uniquely exciting experience for the reader or listener, but one which is remarkably tough to maintain over the long haul. Energy runs out, that's the thing. Energy runs out.

Yet for every crash-and-burn story like Sid Vicious, there are a hundred other stories like James Herbert's – stories of talented people who first impinge on our consciousness not because they are particularly artistic or cultured but because they are screaming at the tops of their voices in a kind of pissed-off speed-rap Godhead ecstasy. These voices all say the same thing: *I'm having the time of my life, Sammy, but I have to get rid of this thing before it kills me.* Bob Dylan was one of these jive shouters; before he got fat and stupid and pompous, Norman Mailer was another. Yet a third, and one who clearly learned his lessons at Jim Herbert's knee, was Clive Barker. Barker's *Books of Blood* were received with mostly ecstatic critical notices, but few of Barker's analysts failed to note the debt such stories as "The Midnight Meat Train" and "Pig Blood Blues" owe to *The Fog, The Survivor*, and *The Dark*.

But the job of making things up doesn't get easier as you do it; on the contrary, it gets harder. Yet you find some way to do it just the same, you have to, if that's what you were made for. And in the end, I suppose, it makes no difference whether you're looking at an empty notepad on which you hope to begin a novel, a blank reel of tape on which you hope to record a song, or a blank canvas on which you hope to paint a picture and capture a bit of the world as it looks to you on the inside

STEPHEN KING

of your eyes, in those dark places where you think and feel. In the end, the old rule – so cruel and yet so practical – remains the same: grow or die. Put quite simply, James Herbert is still around because he has continued to grow.

Has he quit screaming? Good God, no. If there's one thing both horror writers and rock singers need, it's a good set of leather-lined lungs. If you can't raise a good scream from time to time, you might as well turn in your Horror Writer's Membership Card and your eight-by-ten glossies of He Who Must Not Be Named and go to work writing soap ads or, even worse, romances. No, Jim can still scream with the best of them, but when he found out he could no longer scream his way through an entire book, it didn't kill him. And don't laugh, please; it *does* kill some writers to find out they can no longer maintain the pitch they were able to achieve so effortlessly at sixteen and twenty-one and even thirty-five. Given that relentless choice, grow or die, some of them simply flip up their trenchcoat collars and go slinking away into the rain.

In America, baseball pitchers are divided into two categories: throwers and pitchers. The throwers are usually talented young kids with rocket-launchers buried in their arms. Pitchers, however, are an older, craftier breed; they have learned to throw a variety of pitches, and some of their best stuff is barely hard enough to break a pane of glass. And, it goes almost without saying, a thrower who cannot learn how to be a pitcher doesn't stay up in the major leagues for long. Because youth runs out. Because formerly tight tendons eventually stretch and grow loose. Because the old rule – so cruel and yet so practical – is still the old rule: grow or die.

The key books in James Herbert's sea-change from thrower to pitcher are *Fluke* (where Herbert first shows a heretofore unexpected ability to vary both his pitch and his formerly fevered pace), *The Spear* (where plot for the first time remains paramount over incident), *The Magic Cottage* (which is a fabulist work despite Herbert's own dislike of the word), and *Creed*, where Herbert displays a fresh, sassy and satisfying wit. Some of the other books have amusing moments, but – and this happens without sacrificing horror – *Creed* is often hilarious.

This is how a good writer – and James Herbert has turned out to be a very good writer indeed – constantly re-invents himself, coming not out of the one single cocoon but a whole series of them. He doesn't do this because he wants to (based on personal experience and personal observation, I'd say that most writers would like nothing better than to dig a rut and

"People think I have got a strange mind until they meet me. I think I'm fairly well balanced . . . after all any strange thoughts I've got get into the books. I don't need a psychiatrist."

– JAMES HERBERT, from "Fear That Haunts Top Author" by Lynne Powell, *Birmingham Daily News*, June 13, 1986 furnish it) but because he has no choice. It isn't just grow or die, you see; it's change or die.

The last lesson to be learned from this odd comparison between the writer and the rockers is the simplest. The tabloids drive the dark side of this lesson home to us with clocklike regularity and jackhammer force. Only God may create with impunity, this part of the lesson goes. When His lesser creations attempt to go and do likewise, they often get so stoned with the joy of it that they either go mad or kill themselves. Sid Vicious . . . John Belushi . . . Janis Joplin . . . Jim Morrison . . . Hart Crane . . . Dylan Thomas . . . the chain of names is endless, leading all the way back to Icarus and his silly wax wings.

The tabloids are less eager to point out the bright side of the lesson, and the reason is simple: we're a miserable bunch of vampires, for the most part, as addicted to tears as we are to blood. Happiness doesn't sell papers as well as the photographs of mourners at a funeral or those showing what happened after the bomb in the baby-carriage exploded, but happiness exists, just the same, and people quite often overcome the ordinary demons that lie in wait for all of us. The bright side of the lesson is that creativity and make-believe are not the great destroyers but the great healers. A good story, a good poem, a lovely picture . . . these things are not dangerous drugs but lifelines. The trick, I think, is not to change or lose heart when the going gets a little tough, or when the path starts to slant up again. It helps to remember that a lovely view may disclose itself around the very next turn . . . or the one after that.

If I have gone on about this at tiresome length and sounded a little Rebecca of Sunnybrook Farm-ish, I apologise . . . but I'm not going to take a word of it out, because my re-examination of James Herbert's work makes me believe that this point is also worth making. Jim was an unpretentious, down-to-earth man when his career took off like a guided missile back in 1974, and he is still an unpretentious, down-to-earth man these eighteen years later. His sharp-eyed face has filled out a little, but the expression of cautious, curious intelligence is the same. There's still wit and good humour in the eyes, and the mouth is still that of a man who does not suffer fools gladly, or for long.

I'm just a storyteller – he says it over and over again in his interviews. *Just a storyteller*, and that's fine with me. Yet the interviews – and, more importantly, the books – of the last few years make it clear that the process of becoming a storyteller is still going on inside Jim. The cauldron is still bubbling, the loom still shuttling. Herbert has got enough better, in fact, to make me wonder with real excitement what he might be up to in the year 2010, and that is a long way from thinking he might flame out or blow up.

It's enough to make you wonder what the Sex Pistols might have become if that silly clot Sid Vicious had managed to stay away from needles.

A CATEGORY TO HIMSELF

Stephen Jones

TWO

"I REALLY don't know what started me writing," admits James Herbert. This is an unexpected confession from an author who, since his first novel appeared in 1974, has had sixteen consecutive bestsellers published, easily making him Britain's most successful horror writer.

In December 1989 the *Daily Mail* newspaper produced a survey of "The Singles, Albums, Films and Books of the Decade" and it is worth noting that James Herbert made the Top Ten paperback books with *The Magic Cottage*. While the *Guardian*'s guide to "1989's Top-Selling Softbacks in Britain" showed that Herbert is still the UK's bestselling horror author, regularly outselling such genre rivals as Stephen King, Dean R. Koontz, Clive Barker and Ramsey Campbell.

In real life James Herbert is to evil what Bela Lugosi is to break dancing.

– ANNE CABORN, from "Meet the Nice Mr Herbert, the Master of Horror Stories", *Express & Star*, July 9, 1986

Not bad for someone who, less than two decades ago, worked in an advertising agency and had no real ambition to write books.

"I was working with copywriters, although I was an art director, and it just occurred to me one day that all these copywriters had manuscripts they were writing to get them out of advertising.

"Now, I didn't want to get out of advertising," continues Herbert, "but one day I decided I was going to write a book – it was as simple and as naïve as that.

"I didn't speak to anyone about this idea of doing a book, and a couple of weeks later I was watching an old Dracula movie on TV, when Renfield sees a thousand rats staring up at him – I've told this story *so* many times – and the idea just clicked.

STEPHEN JONES

"The secret for me is that I didn't talk about it to anyone. Obviously my wife knew about it because I was working at home, but I didn't tell anyone in the advertising business because I think the more you talk about something you expend energy, and you need to keep your energy for the actual written word.

"So I shut myself away for nine or ten months and produced *The Rats*. Then I photocopied the manuscript six times (for any would-be writers this is one of the secrets: you must have a good, clean manuscript, never send anything hand-written or with crossings out, it must be well typed and well presented) and sent it to six different publishers on the same day.

"Within three weeks I'd received three replies: two saying 'No Thank You' (one from Gollancz and one from Michael Joseph) and the other from New English Library saying 'Yes Please'. And that was it."

So what made James Herbert think he could simply sit down and write a bestselling novel without any previous experience?

"I had absolutely no burning desire to write," he laughs. "This is a terrible thing to admit, because you really should be that committed. Art was my subject – posters and illustrations – that's what I loved, and it was something I needed to do.

"However, I was always good at telling stories. I was the kid at school who did the long essays, and in advertising I wrote copy headlines. So once I'd started it came very naturally, it seemed so right to be doing that. If the book had failed though, I wouldn't have done it again – it was too much like hard work!"

Back in the early 1970s, when James Herbert wrote *The Rats*, the horror market in Britain was going through one of its periodic declines, so why did he choose that particular genre to work in?

"I've always loved the good old ghost story," he replies enthusiastically, "and when I was a kid I was always being told ghost stories; it was just something that was very natural to me. It must have been ingrained in me from a very early age, and the moment I started to write that is what came out.

"It *could* have been a comedy and, in fact, there is a lot of humour in my books. It could have been a romance or," he laughs, "even worse, an historical romance!

"It had to be something, and it was horror with humour. It just came very very naturally. I always loved anything that was a bit creepy, but I was never obsessed by it. I'm still not obsessed by horror now: I don't read many horror books, I don't like 'video nasties' – I watch them, but a lot of the time it's under sufferance, because I know I should be aware of

It is unusual for an author to create an entire publishing category. James Herbert did. It is unusual for an author to gain critical recognition while already a bestselling writer. James Herbert did. It is unusual for an author to sell the first book he writes, have it become a huge bestseller, then to continue to write bestsellers, honing and refining his craft as he goes – growing up, as it were, in public. James Herbert did. And he's still doing it.

– NEIL GAIMAN, from "James Herbert: Growing Up in Public", *Gaslight & Ghosts* (1988)

what's going on in the field – and I don't want to be influenced by other people's books or films. I want to do what I do. I love it, but I'm not obsessed by it."

If he was writing his first novel in the publishing climate of the 1990s, would Herbert perhaps aim to produce a thick, commercial, mass-market novel as opposed to a genre work?

His reply is emphatic: "You should never look at it that way. You should always just sit down and do something that you want to do. It so happened that I wanted to sit down and tell a story. But if you say to yourself, 'I am going to make a great deal of money out of this', you become very self-conscious about what you are doing.

"In a way, it's why I hate this sort of thing – when I'm asked how I do it and why I do it. I don't like to investigate too much because then I'll be too sure of myself, I'll know what that secret is, and then maybe I'll start working to a format. You can't do that. And if you start writing you must never imagine that you're going to make a lot of money – that is the luck of the draw, it really is. Only write if you want to write, and you have to *persevere*."

However, James Herbert is the first to agree that, for him, success came quickly. Within weeks of the publication of *The Rats* the first printing of 100,000 copies completely sold out.

"The reason I was successful is because there was nothing quite like it on the market – the last big horror writer was Dennis Wheatley and he was dead, so he wasn't doing much any more! His kind of horror was a very snobbish, right-wing type of horror fiction. Although I loved it as a kid, it wasn't really all that accessible to the public; it wasn't 'streetwise', and the language was a little bit above what most people were used to.

"So that was the secret why *The Rats* actually sold so well to begin with: because it was very accessible, and because it was *very* explicit. That wasn't a deliberate ploy of mine, it's just the way it turned out. If I was going to write about someone being chewed by rats, I wanted the reader to know what it *felt* like.

"Of course, you've got to remember that I didn't know whether the book would even be published. I was really doing it for myself, which is another thing about writing – you must do it for yourself. You mustn't look at the market, you mustn't think you're going to have so many thousands of people reading what you're writing, because that's when you begin to think about it on a different level.

STEPHEN JONES

"It's like you've got a mother and father and they think their boy is very bright; then suddenly they pick up this book and there's sex, there's violence – very graphic violence – and they are going to be embarrassed. So you've got to discount all that. When I write now, I have to disregard my parents (who are still alive), my daughters, my wife – everyone!"

At the time *The Rats* was published, Herbert didn't have an agent, so what happened when his publisher wanted him to write the inevitable follow-up?

"Well," smiles the author, "their next move was they took me to lunch to get me drunk. They were on a loser there! I refused to actually sign another contract then and there because I didn't know what the publishing business was all about. I didn't know if I could do another book – as far as I was concerned, it could have been a flash-in-the-pan – I didn't even know if I had another book in me.

"Also, my advertising career was very busy anyway, and I didn't know if I'd have the time to write another book, so I said: 'Look, let me go away and write something; if you like it, then we'll talk business.' And I've always worked like that, until recently. I'd write a book, give it to them, and if they liked it they bought it. I would never sign a contract in advance, and I was never paid any money in advance.

"So we went to lunch, and the chief editor at that time said, 'Jim, you really *must* sign another contract; I mean, what do you want from us? What sort of royalty do you want?' Now you have to remember they had paid me £150 advance for *The Rats*, with 4.5 per cent royalties. Which was okay, because I would have paid *them* to have it published. But once I knew the book was selling well, I said that's not going to happen again.

"By the time that lunch was over, the editor was on the floor and I didn't sign anything."

The next book Herbert wrote was *The Fog*, which proved to be a more rewarding and enjoyable experience than *The Rats*, as he explains:

"I thought, 'Well, this seems good to me. I can write a story and somebody's going to publish it – this is wonderful!' I actually set out to knock back the barriers of horror in Britain, and with *The Fog* I did. It seems fairly tame nowadays, but at the time this kind of horror had never been done before. I submitted the manuscript, and they published it exactly as it was with hardly any editing at all. I couldn't believe it. Then everybody started doing the same thing!"

While James Herbert was pushing back the frontiers of horror fiction in the UK, another young writer was just getting

One of the world's most successful horror writers, James Herbert remains one of the least affected and most approachable . . . The Rats *and all of James' subsequent horror novels are* tours de force *of hit-you-where-you-live, out-and-out terror, and his enormous popular success is well deserved.*

– GRAHAM MASTERTON, from *Scare Care* (1989)

started on the other side of the Atlantic – his name was Stephen King.

"*Carrie* came out a few months after *The Rats*," recalls Herbert. "There was me in Britain and Steve over there, and we did different kinds of things, although I was much more explicit.

"It was something that the time was ripe for. People suddenly want something new, but they don't necessarily know what it is. Then someone comes along and produces it and they say, 'Yes, that's it.' It was the same with Elvis Presley and with the Beatles. Many people say to me, 'You were very fortunate that you tuned in to the public,' but it wasn't that way. I don't mean this to sound in any way arrogant, but the public actually tuned in to what I was doing and what Steve was doing. That's the way it works, and it's the only way it can work."

Herbert strongly believes that to be a successful writer, you must first write what you know about: "A lot of new writers extend themselves too much, they write about things they are not familiar with, and they fail because it doesn't look or sound authentic."

So has he ever considered writing an out-and-out fantasy, set on another world or in a different dimension?

"I did – years ago," comes the reply. "That would have been one of the books that would have been on the cards, probably after my fourth or fifth novel. The trouble was that everyone started doing it, and I don't get along with 'the crowd'. I don't want to do what everybody else is doing, and because that type of fantasy was getting more and more popular (and there was some great stuff being published) I didn't do it. I can see myself moving into fantasy – I do in the books now, anyway – but not the out-and-out fantasy. There's too much good stuff to compete with at the moment."

With sales of *The Fog* outstripping even those of his first book, Herbert decided it was time he found himself an agent. "The reason I decided to get an agent was because I didn't know enough about the business, I didn't know what was a good deal and what was a bad deal. I needed protection – every writer needs protection. However, as the years progressed I discovered that there's nobody better than yourself as an agent.

"You know what you're after, you know what you're trying to achieve. If you are not embarrassed about talking money, then you can demand certain figures. You get to a stage, of course, where they tell you the figures and you just say yes or no. It's something I can handle, but a lot of writers can't. Many

He has produced some of the most powerful horror fiction of the past decade – including a certain classic in The Fog . . . *Herbert is also, save for Stephen King, the most influential and widely imitated horror writer of our time.*

– DOUGLAS E. WINTER, *from* The Penguin Encyclopedia of Horror and the Supernatural *(1986)*

of them sit in their ivory towers and they don't want to know about that side of it, which is okay. The only trouble is that you're going to get ripped off if you adopt that attitude; it's inevitable, and I *hate* being ripped off!

"You've always got to be fair: you've got to be fair to the publisher, and you've got to be particularly fair to yourself. And I just found that I could do that. With agents I found that I was a lot tougher than they were. I've sacked about three agents, I'm sorry to say. I have an agent now in Britain, and one in America, because the business side of things became too much; it was taking over and it just became ridiculous. I don't like business that much, I'd rather write the stories. However, I still say yes or no."

Over the years, James Herbert has shown remarkable loyalty to his publishers – particularly in Britain; is this because he earns increasingly larger sums for each new bestseller?

"Money is important," he admits, "I make no bones about that. I mean, given my background, it is very important; it is a priority. But that doesn't mean, as one journalist put it, 'James Herbert only writes for money.' It's not like that. I write because I love writing. I had a really good job in advertising, so there was no need to write.

"I write purely for the pleasure of writing. Sure, the money is important and Hodder & Stoughton have always been good to me as far as money is concerned. But then, I only earn what the public buy. They are your salary masters, they pay your wages. Of course I get big advances, but they've got to be earned out. I've got to sell a certain number of books. Before, no publisher would pay you more than they were going to make back from you. Nowadays it's become a bit ridiculous: there are huge advances going round and you know the publishers are never going to get their money back.

"Hodders also listen. They listen about jacket design, they listen about the text of books – I've actually had books pulled because they'd made a mistake and the body copy was in the *wrong* typeface. In the new edition of *The Fog*, which celebrates the millionth copy sold, I wrote a little foreword in which I had a line that said that the book built up to a big climactic finale. But when I checked the copy, it said '*climatic*' finale – which is all to do with the weather! I couldn't believe it, so they actually pulped all those editions. They wouldn't do that for any other author.

"So they have been good to me, but you must always keep your publishers on their toes. You must never become part of the furniture. You must always have that threat in the air that

In its judicious use of colloquialism his style parallels Stephen King's, but his voice is authentically English. His work shows a growing stylistic deftness. Some of his set pieces are awesome (a conflagration and its aftermath in Shrine, *the opening chapters of* The Fog), *but more intimate scenes are equally powerful (the death of the priest in* Lair, *one of the most terrible in horror fiction; a drowning man dragged back from the relief of death to the devastated world of* Domain). *At its best his work is an important example of horror fiction as the opposite of escapism.*

– RAMSEY CAMPBELL, from *The Penguin Encyclopedia of Horror and the Supernatural* (1986)

you could leave at any moment, you must never let them become complacent, because they do.

"It's good for you and it's good for them, because they are going to do more for your book. It's also good for other authors as well, because the more you tell publishers how they should be doing it, publishers will treat you and other authors better. I'm not just in it for myself, I'm really in it for other writers as well. Because horror has become so big, they are all scrabbling around now for good new horror writers – so it's better for all of us. The more doors that I kick down so the benefit is there, not just for me, but for many many other horror writers."

Following his early success with such books as *The Rats* and *The Fog*, how difficult was it for Herbert to give up his regular job and become a full-time writer?

Herbert is held in great esteem by devotees of horror fiction, and rightly so. He is a skilful and imaginative storyteller . . . He's got strange ideas, and he gets right down to them.

– DAVID SHERMAN, from "Nightmare Library", *Fangoria* No. 38, October 1984

"I didn't make the decision," he laughs, "the taxman and my wife made it for me. I was working seven days a week, five days in advertising (with late evenings and often at weekends) and just writing on Saturday and Sunday. I did that for five years. Advertising's very hard work and I wasn't seeing the wife and kids. I realised it was killing me.

"Also, at the end of the day – this was in the days of 83 per cent in the pound – I was paying all the money over to the taxman anyway. So I had to make a choice. Now I liked advertising – there's a lot of bonuses in advertising and the social life's great, and I knew I was going to miss that. On the other hand, writing was so good, I enjoyed it so much, and you could play God – whatever you put on the page, that was *yours* and nobody, not even an editor, could interfere with that.

"With advertising, of course, everything gets changed, everything gets diluted, and that really bugged me quite a bit. All your best work gets reduced, it becomes less effective to sell a product, because they like to play safe. So at the end of the day the decision really was fairly easy: the fact that I was working too much, the fact that the taxman was taking all the money, and the main reason was that I realised that writing was what I was all about."

Herbert reveals that it was lonely becoming a full-time writer: "It still is," he adds. "But then there are two sides to me: I love social occasions, I love being in the bar having a drink, I love meeting people. The other side is that I also love to be on my own and have my own space, my own thoughts. That side is taking over more than the garrulous side and I'm now becoming something of a hermit!"

So is there a regimen to the way he writes each book? Does he set himself a schedule?

STEPHEN JONES

"It's not a game, it is a business, and when I say a business I mean a piece of work. So I start at ten in the morning and work through until one; at two I'm back in the study working again, and I'll go through until six or seven o'clock. That's on Monday – the rest of the week I don't do anything!

"Seriously, over the past few years it has turned into a seven-day-a-week job again for me because there are so many other things to do. Now I try to restrict my writing to five days a week and Saturday I spend answering letters."

Despite the growth of word-processors, and other similar devices to make the author's life easier over the years, James Herbert still writes a book the same way he did when he first started, almost twenty years ago.

"I started off with a jumbo pad and a Pentel pen that I had used in advertising. Now they don't make this particular pen any more, you can't buy it in the shops and that worries me. I had a stack of them, and now I've got about a dozen left. I figure when they run out, I'm finished! So I'm desperately trying to find these pens from somewhere. I did find some in Jersey and I bought the whole stock!

"So that's how I started off, and I still work that way – in longhand. It's the old artist in me: I draw the pictures on the pages. I love that contact with a blank sheet of paper and I hate the idea of a machine coming in between. I don't decry other methods, this is just what works for me. Steve King loves the word-processor because he can change things around, but for me I just find that the process from the brain down the arm on to the page gives me more time to think; by the time I've scrawled it out I'm thinking of the next sentence. I'm not going to change it. What happens is that my wife actually types it up on a word-processor and that's how it becomes professional-looking."

Perhaps even more amazing is the fact that Herbert admits to doing only one draft of his books, although he does now keep a small notebook next to his jumbo pad. "To get through that pain barrier, as I call it," he explains, "I write very tiny scrawl in this notebook and after a few pages I transfer it to the larger pad. So in a way I'm doing two drafts together. I've never done that before – it's always *been* the way I've first written it. Of course, I've occasionally gone back and rewritten, which is hard to do – the most painful thing for me – and I cross out and change and make it flow more smoothly, but that's it. I don't write, then rewrite, then hone it. I'd love to have the time, but I just don't do it."

He has also never had much editorial interference, although

Herbert's forte is the set piece on a Grand Guignol scale.

– ANNE BILLSON, Time Out, August 15–21, 1985

there was one incident very early on, as he explains: "I think two words were changed in *The Rats* – it should have been about 360,000 words!" laughs Herbert. "That's the way it works and I think the book was good because it was sheer energy there, sheer rawness.

"You see, an editor comes in and it's his or her job to change things, that's what they're paid to do and they don't feel they have any input unless they've changed something. Now that's fine. I'm very reasonable about this: I do listen to what they have to say, I just don't take any notice of it! I can actually argue why a certain thing should stay in and why a certain thing should come out.

"I've only included one major editorial decision, and that was in a sex scene in *Sepulchre*. It was a bondage scene and it is almost the one thing I swore I would never do: '. . .' You lead up to a climax (if you'll excuse the expression!) and then you '. . .' start to *imagine* what happens next. Now I did that with *Sepulchre* because it was different. It was the first time I had actually put in '. . .' but I left it to the reader's imagination because the editor – he wasn't insistent – said, 'Jim, please let's try it this time, it's more effective.' The whole scene was a bit perverted and there's nothing more perverted than the reader's imagination! If you see it actually in words in front of you or on a screen before you it loses its impact. However, if you can imagine what's happening, then there's nothing more perverted. So it actually worked in that context."

Jim Herbert has suffered from being labelled "prolific", a "writer of overt horror" – critical brickbats placing him in the same category as, for example, Dean Koontz, and a chap named Williamson. How is it, then, that prolific Stephen King admits his enjoyment of James Herbert books, or that a tasteful student of horror named Douglas Winter considers him brilliantly descriptive; original?

So do I.

– J. N. WILLIAMSON, from *Masques II* (1987)

STEPHEN JONES

Despite gaining an often unfair reputation – particularly early in his career – as merely a purveyor of visceral horror, Herbert is adamant that nowadays the one thing he wouldn't include in his books is the popular "child in jeopardy" theme.

"I did that in *The Rats* and it makes me cringe now to think that I had a baby shredded by rats! You get older and you get more sentimental and I now have three daughters . . . Even in *Moon*, where the hero had a daughter based on one of my own daughters, I built up the suspense to where you knew something was going to happen to this little girl; she was so sweet and the hero loved his daughter so much that you just *knew* something evil was going to happen.

"And I copped out!" he laughs. "It happened to her friend next door, who the reader didn't even get to meet! That way it wasn't so dreadful – not for me nor the reader. So now I hate any horror to do with children. We're hoping to start filming *Shrine* soon and of course that involves a child, and I'm being very very careful about what the film people do to that kid. I don't know how it's going to come out, but I'm watching it . . ."

To date, James Herbert has not had too much success with the movie adaptations of his work, and he is now intent on making sure that they are approached with the same care and attention that he brings to each of his books – even if that means getting involved personally.

"I don't know if you saw *The Rats*, it came out on video and it was terrible – but it was *nothing* to do with me! They filmed it in Toronto, which they disguised as New York, and used dachshund dogs (which they couldn't stop barking!) disguised as rats! The story made no sense, it had hardly anything to do with the book, and it was just *dreadful*.

"The next was *The Survivor* – they showed it to me in Australia where they made the movie, in Adelaide, in a cinema on a bright sunny afternoon. There was myself, an agent and the publisher – just the three of us in this huge cinema. And I fell asleep halfway through because I couldn't understand the story!"

After the disappointments of *The Rats* and *The Survivor*, James Herbert has been careful about committing his books to film again, although he currently has no fewer than three (possibly four) projects in development. But, as he explains: "It's okay to talk about movies and say we've got so-and-so, it's going to be wonderful, fantastic! But it doesn't mean a thing until it's on that screen, you're sitting in that cinema, the title's come up and your name's there.

"The first movie is *Shrine*, which we hope to shoot in

Dublin. We are trying to start a new scheme for investing money because, you know, the British film industry is nowhere. We're finding a new way for investment. We have two-thirds of the money already, and the last third – I can't say too much about it at the moment – but it's a different way of investing money, to get the public involved. There's a guarantee that they don't actually lose their stake, and that's unusual. If they take it a step further, and take a slight gamble, a risk, they earn interest.

"Then there's *Haunted*. It was going to be a project for the BBC, but they chickened out and a well-known actor bought the rights. I wrote it as a script and a book, so it's very filmable. The trouble with my books is that they have that huge climax at the end; but there's no money in the British film industry, so it would be very hard to shoot that kind of movie. With *Haunted* it had to be filmable, and it was an interesting exercise for me to contain myself and do it under a very tight structure.

"The third movie is *The Magic Cottage*. The producer wants to combine animation, for the magical sequences, with state-of-the-art robotics. I've seen the script, and it really is well done.

"The joker in the pack is *Fluke*, which I think is totally unfilmable! An Italian wants to make it in Philadelphia, which is pretty odd because the first couple of scripts he had were based in England. It's about a man who dies and comes back as a dog, and it is sort of his journey to discover why he became a dog. So in the book I have him moving through London, out through the suburbs and down to Kent where he is reunited with his family. However, the screenplay had him going through Lewisham, where he saw a fox being pursued by hounds and the guys in red jackets! And when he arrived at Camberwell he stopped at a farm! It was totally ludicrous, and I was relieved that they transferred it to Philadelphia.

"So there are three that seem pretty certain and the joker, which might just be the only one that happens. As I say, until you see them on the screen you just don't know."

For an author as successful as James Herbert, the pressure is always there – from publishers and readers alike – to top his previous bestseller. So how does he cope with this?

"It goes back to what I was saying earlier," he said, "when I did the first book and then they wanted a second and I honestly didn't know if I could write a second book. I still feel that way today. At the back of my mind I always have this feeling with every book I do, and I always seem to win through in the end."

And once that book is written, how important is it for him to involve himself in all aspects of its publicity and promotion?

"You have to. That's the other aspect about writing: you have to work for the publisher. It's not a matter of sitting there and writing your stories any more. You've got to get out there and help; you've got to talk to the reps, you have to meet the trade. It's not an easy business any more and you can't stay in an ivory tower. You have to help the publisher because their investment in you is huge. You can argue that you're paying that back by writing the books, but it goes beyond that. You have to help a bit more."

Yet despite the year-round hard work involved in writing a new bestseller, Herbert is positive that he'd never want another full-time occupation.

"I'd never go back to advertising. I'd like to be involved a bit more in music, but I see myself as a writer now. It becomes a vocation, and if I didn't earn another penny from writing I'd still have to do it. I've been asked a number of times in interviews 'Why do you continue writing when you don't need to write any more' and the answer is – the same as Steve King's answer – do you think I have a choice?

"There is no choice, it's something I have to do. The times when I hate it – and of course there are days when you do hate it, when you're stuck and you really do detest it – are far outweighed by the times I love it. A good day's work in writing has nothing to beat it – there's nothing more satisfying. The joy I have at the end of the day that I've done a good few pages and some good ideas have gone on that page is wonderful.

"At the end of a good week, if I have hit my target for that week, I've earned myself a drink. And at the end of seven months or a year (however long it takes) and I have that completed manuscript, then there's nothing on this planet to beat that. Once you've done it it's a wonderful achievement. It's your life's aim to finish that one book, but once you've done that it *is* an anticlimax the day afterwards, and you start thinking about the next one.

"I get very itchy. I keep promising my wife that I'll take a few months off the next time round, but you can't. I'm okay for a few days, but then I say 'I'll just pop up to the study, I won't be long' – and that's it for a year! It has to be that way."

So how does he reply to that perennial interviewer's question, "Where do you get your ideas?"

"Ideas are no problem for me at all," replies Herbert, "I already have ideas for the next four books. The problem is that it's not just sitting down writing stories any more, there are so many other demands that are made on you that you dissipate your energy. As soon as I sit down and break through that

Cecil B. de Mille once said that a good film would be to start off with an earthquake and build up to a climax – James Herbert is the literary equivalent of that.

– Greater London & Essex Newspapers, May 9, 1980

everyday block that all writers have, then the ideas just bubble."

James Herbert is Britain's bestselling horror writer and is displayed in bookshops in a category by himself. By his own admission he is more than comfortable from the money his books earn around the world, he is a well-known TV chat show guest and his signing sessions attract record crowds. So how does he feel about being a celebrity?

"I don't feel that way at all," he admits, "I really do not feel that way because I'm alone with my work. If I have become a celebrity it's only from that work, and that's many, lonely, hard hours in that study – don't feel sorry for me because I'm not complaining – but it *is* a lonely profession.

"I get letters and they're lovely, they're smashing, but they are talking about James Herbert, they are not talking about *Jim* Herbert and that's who I am – Jim Herbert. James Herbert is the author who's fairly well known, but I'm not. I don't think I've changed that much over the years and I don't want to change."

A LIFE IN THE DAY OF JAMES HERBERT

Victor Olliver

THREE

THE alarm goes at 7.30 a.m. But I just lie there dozing – I'm terrible about waking up in the morning because I'm so exhausted. I dream very heavily. For me, going to sleep is like going to work: vivid. There's a different story every night, so getting up is really like a resurrection. When I first moved here, I thought I'd be slick and jog every morning. Then it started to rain after three days, so I stopped.

Eileen gets the girls up. She brings me some tea which I drink very grudgingly, but it revives me a bit. And when the mad-house has settled down about nine o'clock, I get up. It's a nice thing about being a writer, you don't have to shave if you don't want to.

I listen to programmes like *Start The Week* while I'm shaving. If it's a Monday, I've usually got fan letters to answer. I get about a dozen a week but Eileen says it's more. I always answer them personally. Eileen types up my scribbled replies. I've only had two nasty ones. One letter-writer tried to save my soul, saying I was a child of Satan.

Sometimes in the morning there are business matters to deal with. I'm a member of Lloyd's Insurance. They send me a lot of things to read, which is all a bit beyond me but you feel you've got to be involved. I also have a company called Scribble, which basically means I work for myself – any music I write, artwork, etc. Tax-wise it works out better. I'm single-minded. I designed the *Shrine* book-jacket – I took the photograph and used a friend's kid. I also handled the advertising. A lot of authors would like to tell publishers what to put on the book-

"There is also a great fascination with death – not so much with death itself, but what happens after. In a weird kind of way you are giving people encouragement that when they die it's not the end."

– JAMES HERBERT, from "Chill the Spine" by Christine Day, 19, November 1985

VICTOR OLLIVER

James Herbert and his home swimming pool (circa 1991)

James Herbert relaxing at home (circa 1987)

James Herbert signing The Dark *(circa 1980)*

A LIFE IN THE DAY OF JAMES HERBERT

jacket but haven't the technical knowledge – which I have. They can't bullshit me.

I always aim to get into the study by 10. I work till one, have lunch and read a daily paper which is usually the *Daily Mail* – got good writers, a bit too right-wing. I've no politics really – I just hate extremes of any kind. I am still a Catholic – more in spirit though. I'm not one for organised religion although my wife and kids still go to church every Sunday. I go now and again.

I listen to *World At One*. I love Robin Day. He's a professional and that's what I like. I'm very much into listening to news programmes and current affairs because it's stimulation for me. So I'm back in the study by two and I work till six. If it's going well I'll go on to seven. I never count words; I hand-write. I suppose it's the artist in me. I always use the same thing – a big jumbo pad from Smith's and pens I used when I worked in advertising. Writing words on a page for me is like drawing a picture – it's almost like a ritual. I reckon if I've done ten pages, that's a good day's work. That's about six book-pages.

When I've finished a book, I usually have about four to five jumbo pads which I have to read through because I never read through when I'm writing. Eileen does the typing.

A lot of people think if you're a writer, you've actually retired. They pop in: "Are you coming out for a drink?" And it's very tempting.

Some days I do research; I nearly always use real locations. For *The Jonah*, I went to Suffolk for a couple of weeks' mooching around air-bases. I wanted to find a way of smuggling drugs into the country. I found a perfect way to do it.

I enjoy going to remote places whether it's an old graveyard or whatever. It does give you ideas; you sink yourself into an atmosphere.

That's another thing that happens with my books: things happen afterwards. I mean in *The Dark*, for instance, I had these 38 people committing suicide in this one house. I thought that was over the top. But two weeks later, 900 people committed suicide in Guyana. Then in the book, I had one of those A10 American planes crashing into the North Sea; a few months later, an A10 from one of these Suffolk bases crashed into the North Sea. In another book, I have a man who falls into one of these grain silos and somebody opens the funnel and the guy sinks, like in quicksand, and drowns. A few months later, one of these workers in a grain-mill fell into a silo and drowned. It's strange. It's beginning to make me wonder.

VICTOR OLLIVER

In *The Survivor*, I had a church in Eton High Street and it was possessed by demons – sent the vicar mad, y'know. Just two years back, this same church was closed down by the vicar – he said it was possessed by demons.

During the day I might be doing the advertising or designing the book-jacket. Quite often I go up to town and see the publisher. In my spare time I play guitar, piano and I paint. I enjoy football and collect old movies.

In the evening, if I'm working, I never plan anything social; I can't work with a hangover. I watch a movie on TV or video. But if it's not a working day, I may pop out to the pub. Quite often I get phone calls. My agent is in New York. I got a call from Yugoslavia last night – somebody wanted me to work on a project which I turned down flat. I've been asked to do screenplays from my books and I won't get involved. It would be like being back in advertising, with too many fingers in the pie.

Weekends are very hectic. We have a very wide circle of friends. I still see contacts in advertising, photographers, old school friends from East London. We had a weekend free once, with nothing to do; but when it actually came, we were so bloody bored. We get to bed about half-twelve during the week, three to four at the weekends – sometimes not until nine o'clock in the morning.

"Some people think life on earth is Hell. I think it's our Purgatory. I think Heaven is one huge ephemeral mass where we float around."

– JAMES HERBERT, from "If It's Horror You're After, Jim's Your Man" by John McEntee, *Dublin Evening Press*, July 3, 1987

James Herbert in Jersey (circa 1984)

BOWLED OVER BY THE BEAST: ME AND MY CAR

James Herbert

FOUR

I'M one of those people who just wants a car to get me from A to B. However, I like to get there in comfort, and often I like to get there fast.

I don't spend weekends cleaning, polishing and tuning; but I do appreciate the mysterious logic of the engine and the sleek lines of aerodynamic bodywork. I also like the smell of cars.

My first real experience of the automobile was when, with three friends aged 19 and 20, I travelled to Monte Carlo and back in an ancient Ford Popular that cost £8. We had more adventures in that old banger than most people have in a lifetime.

My first car arrived with my first daughter, though from different sources, naturally. The vehicle – The Monster – was a 56 Hillman Minx, one of those big square jobs, constructed in the image of a tank. It cost £25, had a wheel-column gear shift, and I had to reach out of the window to unstick the right-turn direction indicator (for left turns, I had to flap my arm outside in swan-like gestures).

After eight months I discovered the accelerator pedal was not attached to the floor: the metal beneath had rusted away so that when I pushed down, the base of the pedal almost scraped the roadway. A mechanic bolted in a new metal plate for me and from then on, it was as though the engine had been souped-up.

The nice thing about it was that when the Hillman wouldn't start (this was every other day), I could step out, lift the bonnet and resuscitate the engine by pressing a rubber button inside.

Don't be deceived by the tidy and methodical air to James' hands, he may take life seriously but I'm sure he has a little flippancy there which could creep out and surprise you!

– SUE ARMSTRONG, Star Palms (1988)

JAMES HERBERT

The day after I sold it for £15, the brakes failed and the new owner drove it into a brick wall. Luckily nobody was hurt . . . nobody but the Hillman, that is, and the wall.

My next car was one of the first Ford Capris. "From the ridiculous to the sublime," as my local petrol-pump attendant commented. In those early days, the model had ridged sides like a Mustang; I flattened these due to the narrowness of my garage walls.

A Toyota Celica followed. I altered its body shape even more than the Capri's through various crashes. Mercifully, I didn't alter my own shape one bit.

Eventually I became less of an insurance risk. I left the world of advertising to become a full-time author. It was then that I bought my first Jaguar XJS. Unfortunately it was not a good Jaguar XJS.

The worst fault – and well worth mentioning – was that all power cut out when the car hit an unexpected bump in the road. Without power steering, the Jaguar's course became inflexible. I soon mastered the art of coasting along, switching off the ignition and turning it on again. Power would return immediately.

No garage I tried could correct this fault and, as they say, I decided to let the car go. But I wrote to Sir Michael Edwardes asking him to convince me first, to buy another XJS, and second, not to write about my current one in my next novel. His response was swift and excellent: John Egan (without the Sir then) had taken that part of Leyland by the scruff of the neck and forced it to shape up.

The company contacted me and made a promise: a superb new model, with any specifications I desired, and if still dissatisfied, my money back or a different car.

My specifications? Nothing grand. Just metallic black bodywork and black interior as opposed to the usual tan. And no flashy gold stripe down the side. The car looks moody and magnificent (a self-image I've tried but which invokes only derision). Every inch beneath that long, graceful bonnet is filled with fuel-injected 5.3-litre V12 engine, a joy and a wonder to behold. I've taken it up to 133 mph before running out of road, but I'm informed the XJS can manage 150 with ease. Nowadays (are you listening, officer?) I only use high speed to get away from dangerous traffic clusters. Without doubt, it's a mean machine; which is why my publisher has dubbed it The Beast.

For a runaround I use an Austin Mini, automatic and also black (the colour is almost a job requirement – not a fetish – it is horror fiction I write). I bought it when I was working in the

Channel Islands for two years and it was ideal for the narrow lanes and low speed limits. I use it for buzzing around Brighton or trips to the village pub. The reverse-snob in me also likes turning up in it to dinner parties where I know the drive will be full of Bentleys, Rollers and Ferraris.

For shopping and general ferrying of our daughters, my wife, Eileen, and I drive a Granada Scorpio.

So there you have it: three cars for specific purposes (and all British-made). My greatest affection, naturally enough, is for the XJS. Not just because it's a superb machine but more, I think, because of a certain gratifying smugness at having graduated from a Monster to a Beast.

AT HOME WITH JAMES HERBERT

Dave Hughes

FIVE

AUTHOR of a dozen bestsellers, including *The Rats* and *The Fog* (of which more than a million copies have been sold in the UK alone) and *Creed*, James Herbert seems like a good subject to kick off this series of informal interviews with genre personalities.

I met him, not strictly at home, but at his apartment in the Queen's Gate area of West London. His Brighton home is being extended "so I can keep my guitars plugged in all the time!" and he is staying alternately in London and at a rented Sussex cottage which, he quips, is "magic".

When I arrived James was as relaxed as ever, sitting in his luxurious living-room and wearing jeans, desert boots and a suede waistcoat. He's busy working on his new book, which concerns Joe Creed, a paparazzo photographer, and *three* feature films – not to mention the publicity for the reissue of *The Fog* and the launch of *Haunted* in paperback – yet he expends time and enthusiasm showing us around the seven rooms of his city residence.

The apartment is carpeted throughout in the uniform horror-writer cream deep pile (both Clive Barker and Brian Lumley share James' taste in carpets). What is it about that colour, I ask? Is it so that everyone can see that the floors aren't soaked in blood? "It was here when we moved in," he demurs. "The place was bare, but painted . . . I love the colour, but it's terrible for picking up the dirt." James is having his Brighton home recarpeted a similar colour. "I like white," he says. "My study will probably be all white. I like to clear my

"A psychic told me recently it's not me who writes these books, it's an ancient spirit that possesses me and wills me to write. It's funny because when I do sit down, it's as though I'm taken over. The story flows, it tells itself, like someone else is writing it."

'– JAMES HERBERT, from "Meeting With a Man of Horror", by Suzanne McDonnell, *Melbourne Sun*, October 31, 1987

DAVE HUGHES

mind, like Kline in *Sepulchre*, who had this big white room. I like white around me, so I've got no real distractions."

James Herbert's considerable wealth (he recently earned $2 million for two books) is hardly in evidence, aside from the high-security video and audio entryphone system which give some clue as to the other inhabitants of the building. The furniture is luxurious but unpretentious and the apartment has the air of a second home: it is unbelievably tidy for someone as busy as James (who is "Jim" when he's at home), and the study is virtually empty, with no typewriter or computer on show. The simple two-piece phone rings infrequently and the uncharacteristic confidence with which he answers it shows that he knows everyone who has the number.

Jim's wife, Eileen, a youthful-looking woman who, incredibly, has three children (all girls), pops in and out, organising his schedule of meetings, photographic shoots, launch parties and dinner engagements (not to mention coffee for myself and the photographer). James talks little about his personal life, although casual remarks about "Gordon the chauffeur" and the architects working on his real home in Sussex give an indication that he and his family live fairly comfortably: "I always wrote to feed my children. Now they need clothing as well!" is, he says, his glib answer to questions about money.

I ask him if Stephen Jones' forthcoming book will be a revealing biography of James the author. "It's more of a scrapbook than a biography. It's reviews – good and bad – articles and anecdotes and so on." How does he feel about doing it? "I hate it, I'm not looking forward to it at all. But then, Steve's gonna do all the hard work. I'm just gonna give him files and things and say 'get on with it'. I think there's nothing more boring than going back over old ground. I mean, it's lovely to talk about yourself, but it can get monotonous!"

But James confesses to an enjoyment of reading about other writers, mentioning Stephen King and Ramsey Campbell as particular favourites. "Steve says the things that I would say if I was articulate enough!" he jokes.

He hopes that his new book will shake off the label he has worn constantly of "the guy who wrote *The Rats*!" and tells of how he recently tagged along with paparazzo Richard Young while researching *Creed* and was spotted by another publisher, who surmised that he'd done a book on rats, a book on slugs, and now he was doing one on photographers! "But life's too short to bear grudges," he says, philosophically.

The mystical air implied by the many small crosses in both palms suggests that James' writing techniques are due to a force greater than his own . . . James belongs to a spiritual framework, with certain obligations to the unseen hierarchy.

– SUE ARMSTRONG, *Star Palms* (1988)

"I've talked to a lot of people involved in the occult: psychics, ghost hunters and psychic researchers . . . When I meet these psychics they always say to me, 'You're obviously very psychic' and I always deny it because I'm not. Certain things have happened to me but I can usually explain them . . ."

– JAMES HERBERT, from "Oh Rats! It's Herbert's Horrors" by Lesley Bendel, *Writers' Monthly*, October 1987

James Herbert and Fluke (circa 1984)

James Herbert signs for a very unusual fan (circa 1987)

DOING IT WITH STYLE

Douglas E. Winter

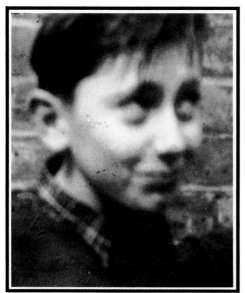 

James Herbert aged 16

SIX

"You can forgive virtually anything – any perversion, any nastiness – if it's really done with style."

J AMES HERBERT was born on April 8, 1943, in the East End of London, the third son of street traders. His family lived at the back of Petticoat Lane in Whitechapel – once the stalking ground of Jack the Ripper – in a house that had been condemned as part of a slum clearance scheme. Bombs had ravaged half of the street during the Second World War, and only gutted shells of houses were left standing. The ruins were alive with rats.

My train ride south from London into the heart of the Sussex countryside is uneventful but telling. The greys of the urban centre soon transmute to the greens of forests and rolling hills, and for miles, the railroad is the only vestige of human life in an otherwise unspoiled landscape. James Herbert's surroundings have changed since his youth; but he has never escaped the rats that once besieged his home. They have helped make him Britain's bestselling writer of horror fiction – and also one of the most maligned and least understood horror writers working today. From his first novel, *The Rats*, to his most recent one, *Haunted*, Herbert's fiction has been identified so closely with violence that he is often accused of writing solely for the sake of violence.

At Hassocks station, Herbert waits behind the wheel of a shining black Jaguar XJS. He stalks forward to greet me, in

"The incidents usually go in threes, graduating in violence. First I was at a conference with a film man when a can of beer I was drinking slid slowly over to the other side of the table. Yet the table was absolutely flat.

"Then we went for a drink at a Kensington club and the entire bar collapsed.

"I knew then we shouldn't have gone on holiday. But I did, to the Algarve. And there the entire kitchen blew up because of a gas explosion. Fortunately, Eileen, my wife, had just left the kitchen."

– JAMES HERBERT, from "James – The Devil of a Chiller" by Peter Grosvenor, *Daily Express*, May 16, 1980 jeans and leather jacket, moving with the graceful wariness of a bantamweight boxer sizing up his opponent. "I don't give interviews much any more," he tells me. "But this is different. You're not one of these newspaper types down to do a job on me." We repair to the nearest pub for a pint of bitter, then travel across winding roads to his isolated country home.

There, we talk of his youth, drinking vodka and lime in an enormous living-room that is a study in restrained elegance. He gestures self-consciously to the *objets d'art* that surround him as he evokes his East End upbringing.

"It's very hard to tell about my background without getting very clichéd. It was poor. Very poor. My old man was an old pisspot – a gambler and a brawler – and he still is at seventy. He had a stall in a market called Brick Lane, and another at Bethnal Green. A stall is like a glorified barrow, with its own walls and a roof. And he sold fruit and vegetables.

"What we lived in was a slum. It was a very narrow street, cobble-stoned, only gas lighting in those days. Two doors from our house was a little alleyway where Jack the Ripper cut up one of his victims. Behind us were stables where they used to keep their fruit and veg, and it was alive with rats. We had two monster cats to keep the rats down.

"We moved into this slum because it was due for clearance, and we thought we would get a nice council flat. Well, they didn't knock it down until fourteen years later. So I spent fourteen years in that place."

But he is quick to dismiss any sympathy for the poverty of his youth. "Look, as a kid you don't notice such things. Everyone around you is living under the same conditions, and many are far worse off. It was great. I loved it then; I love it now, on reflection."

His first reading experience – and his first exposure to horror fiction – came through comic books.

"My eldest brother used to come home with these horror comics from American army bases. Now in England you didn't have colour comics in those days; they were just black and white. He used to get these terrific colour comics – *Tales from the Crypt, Frankenstein*. And he used to hide them under the floorboards just outside his bedroom. He would take me to see all these old horror films, Bela Lugosi, and we used to sneak in the back way and sit under the seats and watch them. So it was kind of ingrained in me, all this horror stuff.

"I used to draw, because that was what I wanted to be – an artist. So I would spend most of my time just drawing and painting – and reading, of course. I used to draw comics – like

"In fact, lots of people, having read my books assume that I must be afraid of rats, but the more I wrote about them the less I found they bothered me. I haven't really got many phobias, like spiders or that kind of thing, although I must admit I'm still not keen on flying!"

– JAMES HERBERT, from "The Horror Books of James Herbert" by Jonathan Cook and David Whitehead, *Book and Magazine Collector*, No. 62, May 1989

"When I moved to Sussex I bought a tracksuit and ran around the garden three times. On the third day it rained and I thought bugger this for a lark and gave the tracksuit to Oxfam."

– JAMES HERBERT, from "From Rats to Riches" by Val Hennessy, *You Magazine*, July 13, 1986

DOUGLAS E. WINTER

Frankenstein and cowboy comics – and I would charge the kids at school to read them. My great hero was a cowboy called Casey Ruggles, in a comic by a brilliant American artist named Warren Tufts. It was violent, it was sexy – the hero in it even married his own sister by mistake. And it was very advanced for its time and beautifully drawn. I learned more about drawing by copying hands and feet and heads from this guy than I did in four years of art school. And what I was also picking up at the same time, though I didn't know it, was writing, because he used to write very succinctly and amusingly – very dry humour, this guy had. And I really did not learn just about art and writing, but a kind of attitude towards life, so that was one of my biggest, earliest influences. H. G. Wells was also a big influence on me, and Edgar Rice Burroughs. Then, when I started really getting into horror and science fiction, it was Richard Matheson and Robert Heinlein.

"What I used to do was to tell the other kids stories. Just sit in the playground and tell them stories. And, in fact, they used to pay me to do that, too."

He shrugs and laughs. "I guess this is where it comes from."

We talk about the seemingly relentless need to explain the genesis of a horror writer, as if that will explain away his writing.

"I think people have to theorise about somebody who is in a category, whether a comic or ballet dancer or horror writer. They have all had this shock as a kid. I had none at all; I had a very good childhood.

"The house we lived in was creepy though. I was left alone a lot as a kid. My brothers would be out, my parents would be in a pub, and so I would be there alone, sitting and painting. It was a very narrow, tall house, three floors with a cellar where the coal was kept – and we had a meter down there for the electricity, a shilling meter.

"At times I would be sitting there and the house would creak around me. It was very old; I mean, it was collapsing into itself. It would creak, which is scary enough if you are a kid. You're there on your own, and you're on a sinister street any-way, and you know there's rats at the top of the street, old stables behind you, and then, the lights would go out. And I would have to get a shilling, if I had a shilling, and go down to the basement, into the cellar, grope around in the dark and put the shilling in and twist the thing till the lights came on. There were no lights down there, anyway. So when the lights came on, nothing happened down there. And there were all sorts of things in this cellar. You know, a lot of rats. I mean, it must

"My wife, Eileen, bought our fairy twenty-one years ago, when we were first married, and it was on the tree in our first flat. It is about 6in high, with a starred wand and a billowing ballgown. It has a gold tinsel crown, which is now looking a bit tarnished, but, like our marriage, it has stood the test of time. We have one tree on the front porch and one in the lounge. I used to have an unusual centre-piece – a giant rat which was used in the film The Rats. *About 2ft long with a great 18in tail, it sat under the tree, among the presents, wearing a little hat."*

– JAMES HERBERT, from "Fairy Tales" by Clare Colvin, *Telegraph Weekend Magazine,* December 24, 1988 have had my imagination rioting – it was all getting ingrained down there, it must have been.

"Our toilet was out in the backyard. The yard was cone-shaped, with half a corrugated roof and a toilet at the far corner, next to this eight-foot-high wall. And it was so scary, no lights. There was this heavy back door down a flight of stairs to the open basement area. And when I was alone, I used to creep down there, just open that door, and pee out of it. I wasn't going out there in that yard. I mean, it was scary.

"But it was not an unhappy childhood. We had our rough times. My father, he was kind of rough to live with, although he was never bad to us as kids. He was a good man. Never bad – though he did take an axe to my mother once."

Herbert chuckles and assures me that we could spend the day with stories of his youth. "If you start from the bottom, you can go through all these things and live them and experience them and that way you actually know them. If you start at the top, there is no way you can go down and find out what it's really all about. You can only go up. So for me, as a writer, it's been great."

Leaving me in wonder about his mother and the axe, he launches into his schooling. After attending a local Catholic school, he passed a scholarship examination, allowing him to attend St Aloysius College in Highgate, "a rather plush grammar school run with strict discipline by priests. At that time they were taking pity on the East End kids – you know, 'We've got to get these kids out of that environment, and get them into these grammar schools.'"

At sixteen he went on to Hornsey College of Art, studying graphic design, print and photography; it was there that he became interested in advertising as a career. "Seems I was always in trouble there, but after the harsh regime of a Catholic grammar school, I guess I had to run a little wild. The good thing was that I was moving through a broad spectrum of people, still living among East Enders but mixing with old college friends and the art school crowd. It opened up my eyes and mind.

"I sang in a band in art school; I was the poor man's Ricky Nelson. I played a gig there, at the art school dances. I sang all these nice rock-and-roll numbers – Chuck Berry's things – and then a week after me, this unknown band called the Rolling Stones played. They made me look pretty sick."

After graduation Herbert had a difficult time finding work; eventually, using the name and résumé of a friend who had job experience, he found employment in a small advertising studio "as a paste-up artist, paint-pot washer, and general dogsbody.

DOUGLAS E. WINTER

It was a crazy place, just four of us in a loft area around the corner from the main agency. I learned more about advertising in six months than I did in four years at art college."

Two years later he joined a leading London advertising agency as a typographer. "I did tell them my real name this time – and it was great, I never looked back. From typographer, they made me into art director. And then, at twenty-six, they made me a Group Head. I was handling about five million quid's worth of business in those days, flying all round the world. I loved it. But after a few years I found the challenge had gone. I wanted to do something to expand whatever I've got inside me."

It was then, at twenty-eight, that he decided to write a novel.

"When I started writing, I didn't tell anybody. Because I thought, well, it's never going to be published, and I'm going to look like a jerk, like all these other people in the office look, talking about books they are doing and not actually getting them published. So I never said anything to anybody in that year that I was doing the book. But once it got accepted, I really rubbed it in. I walked into the office and said to the copywriters, 'Morning, Hacks.'"

He worked then, as he works now, entirely in longhand, writing in a series of notebooks. "I can type a little bit, but I always think of myself as a drawer and painter, and therefore, that I am actually drawing words on paper. The connection from the brain down the arm on to the page is a good connection for me.

"I don't do drafts. I write through without ever looking back. Every book I have done, I've always wished I had the time just to sit down and write the whole thing again, because you can always improve. But I don't. When it's done, the baby is born and that's it. I read through it all once – the term I use is 'crossing out'. I make it flow a bit more, cut out the countless repetitions, and then it's done. The only thing I go on when I am writing is whether it feels good.

"When I'm writing, I'm not sure what's going to happen. Once I've done it and I am reading through, I know exactly what's going to happen and it's a bloody bore. So that's the painful part."

His novel was a pilgrimage to his childhood, and a confrontation of its paramount image: rats.

"As I told you, the street I lived in was overrun by rats. Big ones – monster rats. I mean, my cat actually came home bald once; he had been in a fight with a rat. And I used to watch

"Two streets away from where I lived, Jack the Ripper spliced one of his victims. And I remember where we lived had a hook on the wall outside the door. I was told that was where the decapitated heads of criminals were stuck after they were caught. I was only six at the time."

– JAMES HERBERT, from "Meet Herbert the Horrible" by Jeremy Smith, *Bath Advertiser*, July 1987 them out of the window. We always had a window open in the summer, and one day the cat jumped in with a big rat in its mouth, so that obviously stuck with me.

"I came back from a Friday night drinking session, and I switched on the TV and *Dracula* with Bela Lugosi was on – where the madman, the one who eats spiders, said he had had this dream, this vision of a thousand rats looking up at him, staring at him, with red eyes. And for me, as an art director, that was very visual. I could see myself looking out of the window, and a thousand rats staring up at me. And it all clicked."

The Rats, published by New English Library in 1974, depicted London under siege by monstrous, flesh-eating rats, their origin unknown, but their meaning clear: they were a personification of neglect, and indeed, of the political and economic system that allowed the slum of his childhood to exist.

"The whole idea was a kind of allegory of one man against a system, and this is what I do with nearly all my books. It is one man against the system. Now it's a system that we all know, that we have all come up against, whether it's political or the tax man or your boss. It's a system that's eternal and you are up against it all the time. I've always been up against it and I've quite enjoyed the fight. The rats represented that big system, which is not necessarily evil – but to me, it is, because it's invulnerable, we can't actually beat it. And that's why *The Rats* was open-ended: the hero won his individual battle, but the system still marched on. It still won. He didn't get rid of it. It still went on."

One day, in the midst of a heated business meeting at the advertising agency, a co-worker walked to the window. "And I thought, 'What would happen if you jumped out?'

"And then I thought, 'What if everyone, all over London, started jumping out of windows for no accountable reason?'"

Working nights and weekends, he wrote *The Fog*, chronicling the effects of the escape of an insanity-inducing nerve weapon; it was one of the most powerful horror novels of the 1970s, brilliant in its dark ironies and its breathless depiction of random violence.

The Fog was published by New English Library in 1975, and Herbert began to think of writing full-time. "Naturally, they wanted another book, then another . . ." After completing *The Survivor* (1976) and *Fluke* (1977), he left his advertising position, then moved his family to Sussex in 1978. Novels like *The Spear* (1978), *The Dark* (1980), and *The Jonah* (1981) established Herbert's reputation as a rough-and-tumble stylist whose

"There's a lot of myths about the East End and a lot of romantic views about it: the worst thing I experienced when I went to art school in Hornsey was one of these girls from a middle-class family said, 'And where do you come from, James?' And I was always called Jim in those days, and here she was calling me James! And I said, 'The East End, Whitechapel.' She said, 'Ooh! How colourful!' That really pissed me off, you know, and that is just how they see it."

– JAMES HERBERT, from "Haunted by Rats" by Dave Hughes, *Skeleton Crew* II, 1988

DOUGLAS E. WINTER

novels delivered hard-hitting and bloody confrontations between good and evil; his readers adored him as passionately as certain critics, typically those who had read little of his fiction, reviled him. With the publication of his eleventh novel, *Moon*, in 1985, his worldwide sales totalled nearly twelve million copies; by the close of the decade, with *The Magic Cottage* (1986), *Sepulchre* (1987), and *Haunted* (1988), and an increasing American readership, he had doubled that amount. But that immense popularity has been shadowed by the extreme violence that admirers and critics alike have found in his work.

That link with violence began even before his first novel was published, when New English Library deemed *The Rats* as a "Nasty" horror novel, thereby creating an entirely new marketing category in England.

"Publishing was so tame in those days. Fifteen years ago, it was all James Bond, and the next spy novel, and another spy novel after that. But no gutsy stuff.

"*The Rats* was gory – it was doing things that had not been done before in the publishing scene over here. And Bob Tanner, being a very shrewd and commercial man, said, 'How can we categorise this?' Soon every other publisher in London jumped on that bandwagon and brought out all these other 'Nasty' horror novels. For Bob, it was a shrewd move; for me, it was something I have had to live with ever since. I didn't even know he was doing it – if I had known at the time, I would have taken the book away, even though I knew that *The Rats* was nasty. There was nasty stuff going on – the same is true with *The Fog* – but there was a lot more going on as well."

By the 1980s, the term "Nasties" had become pejorative in England, and the focus of a raging controversy about the censorship of films and video – and, some are concerned, books – in the country. Herbert roundly denies that his books exploit violence; he simply tells the truth.

"I think if you are going to describe an atmosphere, or a house, or a person, why fall short of the violence? Why don't you explain what happens if somebody hits you with a meat cleaver? Why shouldn't you explain exactly what happens and how nasty it is?

"It's the old cliché of Tom and Jerry: which is more harmful, the kind of violence that's in cartoons and John Wayne movies, or the violence that is explicit? To me, I think the Tom-and-Jerry syndrome teaches people that it doesn't hurt to hit some-body over the head with a mallet. You know, when John Wayne hits someone on the head with a rifle butt, there's no pain, they can be up in five minutes, drinking at the bar again. I think

"The teachers didn't like me too much. I'm not trying to build myself up into some kind of a rebel, but I did like to get my own way. They wanted me to join the Students' Union and stuff, and I said, 'I'm not joining anything.' They said, 'We can make things really tough for you as regards getting a job.' I said, 'That's showbiz' – and boy did they make it tough!"

– JAMES HERBERT, from "James Herbert: Growing Up in Public" by Neil Gaiman, *Gaslight & Ghosts* (1988)

you've got to show that it bloody well hurts and there's no getting up from it."

He wrote two of his best-crafted books, *Shrine* (1983) and *The Magic Cottage* (1986), in response to his critics.

"When I wrote *Shrine*, I included nursery rhymes at the beginning of each chapter. We have all been brought up with these mini-horror stories from nursery rhymes and the Brothers Grimm – so what I am doing is nothing different. In a way, I was trying to explain why I write violence, why I write horror, saying I am not doing anything different, anything new.

"It's just more graphic these days. We have come to this period of our evolution where we need the reality to come to any truths. You can't fob people off with things like those shoddy old novels that used to get to the sex scene and cut away. And this is the interesting thing about the supernatural novel – that's why I think it's popular. Because the kids are thirsty for that knowledge. And if somebody comes along who tries to see beyond this life, to explain in some way what happens after you are dead, then they are interested – they want to know. *I* want to know. That's why I explore the possibilities. And the kids want the truth; they are grabbing for it."

Can the depiction of violence be too graphic? Are there limits that should be observed?

"I saw *Friday the 13th*, and it scared the hell out of me. I was really frightened – I had never seen anything quite like it. I liked it because it did scare me, on reflection. It was one of the first of the really nasty movies. And I was of two minds: is that film really bad, shall I just be disdainful of it; or should I be honest and say that it did grip me? But again, like the books, you get everybody jumping on the bandwagon and doing it badly. And that's the thing you can't forgive.

"You can forgive virtually anything – any perversion, any nastiness – if it's really done with style. And so many of these films have no style. So I don't like most 'Video Nasties'; I don't like films that can't involve the viewer – if only to the extent of having sympathy for the characters. I don't believe in showing blood just for the brilliance of the technique.

"It's an intangible thing with me, like looking at modern art. I like what I like. If a thing grips me, if I am involved, then I can appreciate it. For example, I think David Cronenberg works from the heart. He does some terribly gory things, but I think he believes in what he is doing, the same way that I believe in what I am doing."

The Rats has remained Herbert's best-known work; he has written two sequels, *Lair* (1979) and *Domain* (1984), but he

DOUGLAS E. WINTER

James Herbert and his mother (circa 1991)

*James Herbert's wife, Eileen, on their wedding day
(August 26, 1967)*

has also stimulated a menagerie of emulators and imitators, from the occasionally entertaining – such as the "Crab" novels of Guy N. Smith – to the increasingly ridiculous, including such titles as *Killer Flies* and *Slugs*. His reaction?

"I quite enjoy it, although I don't actually read them. I mean, there's enough room for all of us as writers. It worries me only when other writers are not as good. People will pick up a book that says, 'In the tradition of *The Rats*,' and they will say, 'Oh, *The Rats* is the same kind of book as this?' Now that is not true, and it does denigrate my work, if you like, and that worries me.

"In terms of sales, and being successful, I shouldn't have to worry about anything; but I do, you know, because I write seriously. I joke about it. When not writing – that's when I am on holiday – I like to joke about things. But when I am doing it, I am so intense, and so wrapped up in the whole thing, it hurts when somebody criticises, and you know that they are just judging you on the whole mess of 'Nasties'.

"My editor said the other week, 'You're an institution, so you've gotta take the knocks because you are there to be knocked.' I don't think I am. I am just this guy who sits in my study and writes all day. I don't believe the letters I get or the articles – that's some other guy."

Much of his success, as well as the wide-ranging imitation of his work, arises from the fact that his fiction has a unique voice.

"That's what makes me James Herbert – the books are written by James Herbert, nobody else. I am not influenced too much by film – not consciously. Books? My favourite book of all time – it influenced me first – is *The History of Mr Polly* by H. G. Wells. Current day: William Peter Blatty for *The Exorcist*. William Goldman. David Morrell's *First Blood* was a great influence on me because of its pace.

"Stephen King's words are golden to me. He doesn't influence me, because we have totally different styles, but I just admire his stuff so much. And I don't just admire it, I enjoy it. I get the same feeling from his books as when I used to go round Petticoat Lane searching out those Casey Ruggles comics. You know, there was a little bit of sunshine in my life when I got one of those comics. And it's the same when I get Steve's books."

Does he have an audience in mind when he writes?

"Only me. I can't think of other people when I write. I say to one person, 'Come on, I want to tell you a story' – this is it, very intimate. That's why strangers who have read the books

"In many ways I'm like a sponge. I absorb everything that is going around and it's a violent world. When I sit down to write, I release it and it trickles out on to a page.

"It's like a psychiatrist's couch. It's the same with the readers, it's a great release. When you're scared it tunes the senses, it puts you on edge, makes you more aware and because of that you feel alive. It takes us out of ourselves. It's like a good laugh."

– JAMES HERBERT, from "Meeting With a Man of Horror" by Suzanne McDonnell, *Melbourne Sun*, October 31, 1987

"As a purist, I'd like to spend my time writing, but I'm also a perfectionist, so I make a cross for myself by wanting everything exactly right."

– JAMES HERBERT, from "Something Nasty in the Woodshed" by Minty Clinch, *Midweek*, May 22, 1986

DOUGLAS E. WINTER

feel they know you so well, because it's a very intimate thing. You are sharing a lot of inner feelings with that person. And it's always a bit awkward, because they feel that you should know them as well as they seem to know you."

The prospect of being typecast as a horror writer has never disturbed him: "Over here, you see, horror is not quite respectable. It's not respectable and it's not respected. But I don't mind being called a horror writer, because that's what I do. That's what I enjoy doing. When I want to do something different, then I'll do something different."

After his early successes, Herbert indeed attempted something different: *Fluke*, a fantasy about reincarnation. It remains his favourite novel, albeit his least successful commercially; it was also a lesson in typecasting.

"My publishers nearly fell off their seats when they saw the script. This nice, easy, humorous book – no horror, very little violence in it, I mean, it's killing the golden goose. But I can only work that way. And I said, 'If you don't want to publish it, don't do it.'

"The editor took me to lunch one day, and he had my manuscript. He started going from page one and right away I was getting mad, and then he got to page two and I was nearly overshouting that poor guy. And on page three, he had to go to the toilet. And I grabbed the manuscript and looked through it – they were crossing out and writing all over it, trying to make it into a horror novel."

We discuss what the critics and the gorehounds have overlooked about his books: the humanity of his characters, the strikingly ironic sense of humour, the instinct for pacing and structure. There is also a thematic pattern to his work.

"But it's not something that I talk about too much. Because I know it's there – and it's for the reader to realise. Some readers are just going to like the gory bits or the exciting bits, and that's fair enough. It's their entertainment. They pay their money, they get what they want from their books. But lots of others have got the underlying message. I think the books are very moralistic.

"I had a discussion the other day with a local priest, who said, 'I'm a bit worried about your responsibility to the people who read your books. And we know a lot of young people read them, because they are into horror, the young.'

"I said to him, 'I bet if we were in a room with a group of teenagers, I could influence them towards goodness far more easily than you ever could, because they see me as an individual who is not too good, but he's not too bad – someone who seems

"I do take good holidays with the family. But most of the time I would rather be working. I'm not a workaholic, I just genuinely enjoy writing. I'd hate to sit around and do nothing all day. There would be no justification for my existence. I might feel differently if I wasn't interested in what I do though, I mean, how could you get interested in work if you had to sell toilets for a living?"

– JAMES HERBERT, from "Quiet Man Behind the King of Horror" by Angela Carless, *Chronicle and Echo*, August 15, 1989 to understand life.' They would listen to a priest, but there comes that turn-off point where they know that he's just there for goodness and goodness alone. He's not a man of the world.

"Now in my books, there's a strong moral tone. It is good against evil. But the heroes are not too good. The hero in *Shrine* is my favourite hero, actually, because he's a bit of a shit. My heroes are people you can identify with – they don't pontificate, they are not goody-goody, they're not wet, they are a little bit rough-and-tumble, but they do stand for the overall good. And they are the individual fighting for what is right. Whether it's against monster rats, a fog that drives people mad, anything, it is the individual fighting for his own peace of mind, if you like. Which is the right.

"What I did for a long time – I don't do it now – was never describe what the hero looked like. And that was always conscious, because I wanted the reader to be the hero, whether it was a man or a woman, I wanted them to be that hero. I didn't want to give the hero an image.

"It's right against wrong. I mean, it sounds very simplistic, but it's a bit more subtle than that, because my heroes are not goody-goody. And I do cry, I do get scared, and I do get hurt. So, yes, that's what I am doing, that's what I believe I am doing. And when people don't judge my books that way, that kind of gets to me – that annoys me."

He finds that horror fiction focuses too often on absolute notions of good and evil.

"In my books, some things are absolute, like the rats. They are absolutely vicious, nasty, horrible; but there are greys in between – nothing, ultimately, is that bad. A lot of horror writers don't realise that. With the trash horror writers, it's just either good or bad – mostly whatever is bad.

"There was an old dosser who used to take me to the pictures when I was very tiny, about five or six. He worked for my father. He used to sleep in my father's stable, where my father had a horse and cart. Now, to me, he was a really nice man, kind of crazy, but he used to take my hand, take me to the cinema – my old man used to give him the money just to get rid of me for the afternoon – and then bring me home. This guy was put in prison for life: he's one of the last guys to get the cat o' nine tails, and he was put in prison because he chopped a man up with an axe. I think it showed to me that even in the worst sort of evil there is still some grain of goodness. It makes you realise that nothing is absolute. Even Hitler loved his dogs."

In *Shrine*, Herbert explicitly tackled the theme of religious doubt that had been implicit in his earlier novels, examining the

"You gotta remember also that because I am an art director I envisage what's gonna look good on the page. A title for me is a piece of artwork. The short titles you can have large or small and it still looks good. What I did for this [for Haunted*] is invent a mnemonic . . . a symbol or logo. I've used this just to get some identification – we'll use it even more on the paperback, we'll have badges and T-shirts, the whole thing. I just wanted some logo that was instantly recognisable, like* The Phantom of the Opera *mask."*

– JAMES HERBERT, from "Haunted by Rats" by Dave Hughes, *Skeleton Crew* II, 1988

DOUGLAS E. WINTER

effects of an apparent visitation of the Virgin Mary upon a small English village. Is he still a practising Catholic?

"I *am* a Catholic," he replies. "And I am – in a funny way – very, very religious. But I don't go to church, because I can't stand it – it drives me mad.

"There is something higher than all of us. There is a God, there is an Immaculate Conception, there is a Virgin Mary. It's good to have that faith, because it actually works, and overall, it is true. It's not quite the way we understand it, because we will never understand it, but it's not bad, there's nothing evil about it. Being a Catholic introduces you to the mystique at a very early age. Almost from birth, you are taught about miracles and this man who came from the sky. You are taught about the supernatural. And one of the things I can't understand is why the Church is so much against the supernatural, when the whole religion is *built* on the supernatural.

"You could preface every one of my books with 'What if?' In *Fluke*, what if when you died, you came back as a dog? In *The Dark*, what if this thing that they talk about in the Bible, this darkness that befell the land, was a real physical entity? What if? That's all I do in my books. It doesn't mean that I believe in these things, although I do believe in life after death.

"After all," he repeats, "I'm a Catholic.

"The whole point about my books, the same as the religious bit in *Shrine*, is that it's all nonsense. The moment we, as men, think we can conceive what is actually happening out there, that's when we've got to be wrong, because it's too big for us. We don't understand it. We can't understand it. And I say that over and over again in the supernatural parts of my books.

"I believe there's something else going on and we are a very small part of it. I think we are going to go on to better things – I hope so. It's just a total conviction."

He pauses. "Well, yeah, we all have doubts. I mean, I believe in God. But, you know, I don't believe that this guy with a grey beard is watching every move we make and putting it down in his book and saying you're going to get your come-uppance. I don't believe in that. But I do believe we are all striving for something.

"I don't believe in the Church and what it teaches. I don't believe in the dogma of the Church. So you have got the two things: this great sort of naïvety of believing, of having faith, but the cynicism of not believing in what man actually tells you it's all about. And I think that kind of parallel feeling comes through in the books."

As evening draws near, we walk outside, preparing to leave

"It just happens – I don't get pretentious, for me the title is the idea. That's where the whole book springs from. If I'm writing a story about rats, it's gotta be called The Rats. *If it's about fog it's gotta be called* Fog. *It was never a conscious decision – in fact, I wanted* The Fog *to be called just* Fog, *but the publishers at that time thought it needed some preposition to say this is a certain fog, but if I can get away without a preposition, great. Like* Shrine, Haunted . . ."

– JAMES HERBERT, from "Haunted by Rats" by Dave Hughes, *Skeleton Crew* II, 1988 for dinner in Brighton. He gestures back towards the house, into the dark beyond the trees.

"We've got a big garden out there, which I don't get out to work on much, but I have gardeners who come in and do it. The only thing I do there, I've got a little tractor and I mow the lawn – and there's about three acres out there. And I hate mowing the lawn; it's very boring, so unproductive.

"But I sit there on the tractor, and I think about my old garden. It was about this size." His hands indicate a cone shape of roughly one hundred square feet, the size of a small bedroom. "That was my garden, all concrete. And I get some kind of satisfaction from just sitting there and thinking, 'This is great.'

"But how come? Even to this day I don't understand it."

He talks regretfully about the time spent away from his beautiful home when the onerous British revenue system, which at one time took eighty-three per cent of his income in taxes, and the need for peace and quiet forced him into two years' exile in the Channel Islands. As he reflects on the price of his popularity, he remains honestly bemused about the reasons for his success.

"I write for myself, for my own pleasure – what I want to read. And luckily for me, people feel like buying it. Somebody said to me, years ago, 'How did you tune in to the public?' It wasn't that way. The public tuned in to me, just as they tuned

"I'm so unprofessional, it's unbelievable. I never plan a book. I have the basic idea and mull it over in my mind for a while. As I'm researching the idea I put down 'one-liners' on paper. These are ideas of what possibly could happen or images that have struck me as particularly unusual or horrific. Usually I get about 120 'one-liners' and use about forty. The rest are dumped. The 'one-liners' are worked into the story and dictate the way the story's going to go so I have a rough idea of where I'm going (at the beginning of each chapter I have an idea of what could happen in it). But I never have an ending."

– JAMES HERBERT, from "Oh Rats! It's Herbert's Horrors" by Lesley Bendel, *Writers' Monthly*, October 1987

James Herbert at the Hornsey Art College dance (circa 1961)

DOUGLAS E. WINTER

in to Steve King, just as they tuned in to the Beatles and the Rolling Stones when they came along. And that's timing, lucky breaks, whatever you want to call it.

"The day I consciously sit down and say that I'm going to do this for money is the day I don't think I would be any good. That's what I worried about so often when I went into tax exile; I had to do a few books in that time. I was paid a hell of a lot of money to do those books. And I worried about how that would affect me.

"I am very insecure about being a writer. I don't understand why I am so successful. And the longer I stay that way, the better it's going to be, because that keeps me on edge, striving if you like. There are so many writers around who have made it, and they sit back and figure they can do it like clockwork, and the books become less good. They're not scared of it anymore. And I'm totally scared of the whole business. You asked what horrifies me – I should have mentioned sitting down and writing a book!"

The turf has changed – from a slum to the seclusion of leisured wealth – but for James Herbert, the rats that haunted his youth, and the system that they represent, have never relented.

"I am out of the rat race," he says, pausing to savour the pun. "I am out of working for others, out of advertising, I am just doing what I do and nobody can touch it. Then the old system comes along, and it infringes on your territory. That's what I mean. It's always there, the system. You can win your own individual battles. But no matter how safe you feel you are, it still comes around.

"Which is why I keep striving, I suppose."

COMIC RELIEF

James Herbert

SEVEN

"Every book I've done I get to that stage where I think, 'How the hell am I going to end this?' I've got characters about whom I'm thinking, 'What have they got to do with this?' or 'How can I get rid of them?' I get myself into such a tricky position and it's very worrying. That's why I don't recommend anyone writes without a plan. It's just that once, when I wrote The Spear, *I tried to work out a plan and I was so bored. When I came to write it, I knew exactly what was going to happen next. So I threw it out."*

– JAMES HERBERT, from "Oh Rats! It's Herbert's Horrors" by Lesley Bendel, *Writers' Monthly,* October 1987

I HAVE to own up. The book that made the deepest impression on me wasn't really a book at all. It was a comic-book. Gets worse. It was a comic-book about a cowboy. And his best pal was a scoundrel called Kit Carson. And his best gal was a villainess called Lilli Lafitte.

Our Hero's name was Casey Ruggles, and I discovered him when I was eleven years old and living in London's East End. Illustrated and written by an American artist named Warren Tufts, Ruggles was syndicated as a strip to major newspapers throughout the USA, but put together over here in comic-book form. I happened upon them on a market bookstall.

Nobody I know has ever heard of Casey Ruggles.

So what made him unique to me? Well, firstly, the stories themselves. No kid's stuff, these, although the initial issues dealt with the great Gold Rush to California, with Ruggles as an ex-dragoon sergeant leading a wagon train across the plains and mountains, fighting off Indians, epidemics and starvation. (Tufts won accolades from US historians for his detailed research.) But subsequent issues dealt with rape, incest and jealousy (mean but lovely Lilli is eventually shot dead by her rival in love). Violence was there, but never gratuitously. Stories involved Chinese mayhem along the Barbary Coast, a self-proclaimed Messiah, a despot who creates his own kingdom in the mountains. I could go on, but you get the idea.

But the humour. The drollery. Stories told with such style and – important this – such integrity.

Then the artwork itself. Exquisite hands and feet. Wonderfully rich characterisations – so many *real* bit-part players. The atmosphere and details of landscapes, perspectives without fault. But all drawn by a *human* hand, if you know what I mean. And great for me as a kid who couldn't afford paints. Pen and ink became my medium and four years of art college much later couldn't teach me more about form, expression and appreciation than those Casey Ruggles comics.

The point is, those stories carried me away from a fairly rough environment. I learned from them and, believe it or not, they instilled a moral code in me that still applies to this day.

Many years later, married, settled, and with my own kind of success as an author, I wrote my first and only fan letter. To Warren Tufts, naturally. He replied from California and we became firm postal friends. We both looked forward to the day we'd finally meet, and that time was drawing close. Invitations had been extended and were about to be taken up.

I'd just got back from Africa and a letter was waiting for me. It was from Warren's wife, Lynn, only now she was his widow. He'd been killed testing an aircraft he'd designed and built himself; a heart attack, they thought, as the plane was taking off.

Lynn later came over to stay with us for a few weeks, a way of getting over her grief.

She looked just like Lilli Lafitte.

"There is some male chauvinism in the novels because I'm a bit of a chauvinist. But I'm a great respecter of women and I do look at them as equals. From my old East End background I've still got it inside me that the man is the guy who goes out to work and rules the roost. When you've been married for a while, however, you discover that's absolute rubbish."

– JAMES HERBERT, from "The Darker Side of Fiction" by Victor Olliver, *Woman's Journal,* January 1984

Sample drawing from James Herbert's graphic novel, The City, *to be published in 1993*

CASTAWAY

Mike Ashley

EIGHT

FOR over forty years one of the traditions of British radio has been the programme *Desert Island Discs*. Devised by Roy Plomley, who for many years presented the series, the idea behind it is simple. Each week a guest is asked which eight gramophone records he would take with him if he were shipwrecked on a desert island. Between the records the presenter chats with the guest about his life, career and the significance of the choice of records. It's an opportunity for an insight into people that doesn't always surface in regular interviews or chat shows. Sometimes the guests are obscure, their lives uninteresting and their choice of music pretentious, but occasionally the castaway is down-to-earth with a life to which listeners can relate and a choice of music that evokes memories for most of us. One such guest was James Herbert, who was castaway on September 15, 1986. The discussion brought out many memories about Herbert's childhood, the influences on his writing, and his career in advertising, as well as his passion for fifties rock and roll music.

The programme's presenter, who took over after Roy Plomley died, was Michael Parkinson, a blunt, no-nonsense Yorkshireman. This was rather appropriate as one of the surprises that emerged during the interview was that Herbert had used Parkinson as the mental image of his hero when writing *The Rats*. Apparently Parkinson had the right attitude of mind and the right "craggy features"; he was, according to Herbert, "a man's man, the sort of bloke I want to be my hero". Parkinson was suitably embarrassed!

What came over most strongly in the programme was Herbert's childhood, one that today would be described as "deprived" and perhaps it's hardly surprising that James Herbert would turn to writing horror fiction in later years. But his youth had its lighter moments and music was a major part of that. Some of that musical freedom came when his elder brother, Peter, arrived one day pushing a wheelbarrow containing a huge machine which, according to him, the local youth club had discarded. "It had a heavy arm and a tin needle which you had to change after every second record. The arm was so heavy it used to eat its way through the record, but it had a loud thumping bass on it, so that the whole street would reverberate."

This provided the memories related to his first couple of choices, *Blueberry Hill* by Fats Domino and *Little Darlin'* by the Diamonds. "The street we lived in was so narrow that it acted like a funnel. Our house was at the bottom of the street, and I used to blare out these records, so that people came from miles around to see what the sound was."

Herbert didn't recall his formal education with quite the same fondness. He had a very strict Catholic upbringing, first at the school of Our Lady of Assumption in Bethnal Green, which was run by nuns, and then at the St Aloysius College in Highgate.

Then came the comparative freedom of Hornsey College of Art, and with it a chance to explore his passion for music. "The Art School was full of musicians. Everyone played a guitar. I used to sing in a group, on a casual basis. I learned the guitar – I'm a frustrated rock singer and player. That's why a lot of my music goes back to those rock and roll days. My idol at that time was Buddy Holly. I remember my first school dance, at St Aloysius. The band playing was stuffy but at the break on came a group playing all those Buddy Holly numbers, and the leader of the group was Mike Berry." That memory led to Herbert's next choice, which was Mike Berry performing the old Crickets' number *Please Don't Ever Change*.

Another choice from that period was *Summertime Blues* by Eddie Cochrane. "When I was about 19, three friends and I bought an old Ford Popular for about £8, and we drove all the way to Monte Carlo and back, and all I can remember playing in the car was *Summertime Blues*."

From Art College Herbert found employment in advertising. "This was the swinging sixties. I joined the agency just as they were expanding into the commercial market. It was great. I used to love the work and the people. I got early promotion at

"People ask me, 'How did you tune in to popular taste with your books?' I didn't tune in to popular taste. I wrote the books I wanted to write and people tuned in to my taste. I've never intentionally decided to change direction or appeal to another kind of audience, it's just the way it comes out of me. I never look beyond the book I'm doing – I think the day I sit down and plan a book I'll become so self-conscious that it'll fail."

– JAMES HERBERT, from "James Herbert: Growing Up in Public" by Neil Gaiman, *Gaslight & Ghosts* (1988)

twenty-six and I travelled all over the world – the Philippines, Malaysia, Singapore – but something was lacking.

"So I sat down and wrote *The Rats*. It took me eight or nine months at weekends and evenings with no thought of reward at the end of the day, as I had no idea that it would get published. The story came out of my childhood – it's a story about the environment of the East End."

Michael Parkinson reminded Herbert of one of the first reviewers who classified *The Rats* as 'Rubbish'. Herbert remembered the review. "It was so traumatic. I remember that very Sunday morning. I'd collected all the Sunday papers and found no reviews at all except this one in the *Observer* which said that *The Rats* was 'Rubbish'. I said to my wife, 'Well, that's it. I'm no good as a writer; I'll stick to advertising.' I really thought I was finished before I'd even started. Yet the following week the *Sunday Times* said the book was 'Brilliant', so I kind of lean towards the *Sunday Times!*"

It was some while, though, before Herbert had sufficient confidence to become a full-time writer. "I still felt insecure – I still do – so I didn't want to give up a good job. But I was working a seven-day week, not seeing much of my wife or children. The taxman was taking most of the money and I was killing myself. So one had to go and, after five books, there was no competition."

Parkinson levelled at Herbert the criticisms about the blood and gore in his books and the images of "messy horror". This gave Herbert the chance to defend horror fiction and to talk about some of the advantages of writing in that field.

"I hate violence, and I always believe that if you depict violence you've got to describe it in detail to show how bad and nasty it is. The reader has got to feel it. And that's why I decided to explore that territory. Unfortunately because of the success of these books a lot of other writers jumped on that bandwagon and exploited it. I took the rap for a lot of that. Yet if you look there are a lot of other elements in my stories. For instance, they've all got a very strong moral tone: there is, I believe, some good writing, some subtle writing, and there is a lot of suggested horror rather than overt description. It's a reputation I've earned unfairly because people read *The Rats* and *The Fog* and they forget about the rest. This is now twelve years on and you develop. In *The Magic Cottage*, for instance, there is no blood and gore.

"You see, the great thing about horror fiction is that you can write humour, romance, you can write almost anything and it can still come under the heading of horror. You can start a story in an ordinary way, and once you get fed up with the mundane aspect you can bring in something that's totally outrageous, so you get your own and the reader's interest and adrenalin flowing."

A couple of Herbert's record choices were related to his writing. One was "Mars" from *The Planets* suite by Gustav Holst. "This music sums me up. I'm pretty easy-going as a rule, but once I get worked up, this music sets the mood. *The Planets* suite gives so many characteristics of the nature of Man. Uranus the Magician and Neptune the Mystic are all part of the stories I write, and Mars the Bringer of War could sum up the last chapter of any one of my books."

The other was *I Guess the Lord Must Be in New York City* by Harry Neilson. This took Herbert back to the time he went to New York on a publicity tour. "Harold Robbins sent his car to collect me, a big, black limousine, with tinted windows, chauffeur-driven. He sent his press secretary along, just to show me the sights. We got cleared at customs with no problem at all, we just skipped through them, because of Robbins's influence. We drove into New York City on a Sunday afternoon, and I was laid out in the back, literally, and all the kids, teenagers, saw us passing by. We stopped at some lights and suddenly they were all round us, and they saw this youngish guy in the back, and they thought 'He must be somebody', and they were banging on the windows . . . it was like being mobbed. And I got a glimpse of how a film star or a pop star must feel. I had a pair of sunglasses in my pocket which I casually took out and slipped on, and that really got them interested. It was such a good feeling about New York and it carried through the whole two weeks I was there."

"I brought horror down to street level with men in the street in mundane situations and then something dramatic happens. I didn't leave anything to the imagination and this hadn't been done before."

– JAMES HERBERT, from "Herbert – The Writer Who Brings Horror Down to Street Level" by Caroline Lynch, *Irish Press*, August 5, 1989

Herbert's remaining two choices were related to the notion of being cast away on a desert island. *Love Letters in the Sand* by Pat Boone because it seemed to sum up the image of being on a desert island, and "Morning" from *Peer Gynt* by Grieg because although it was meant to represent Norway, the music was so evocative of England, it would inspire Herbert to try and get back. "Morning" was also the single choice Herbert made if he was limited to only one record.

The castaway is also given a choice of taking one book with him (apart from *The Bible* or the works of Shakespeare) and one luxury which can be of no practical use. For the book, Herbert selected *The History of Mr Polly* by H. G. Wells. Herbert had first read this when he was twelve. It steered him away from comic-books and was his introduction to serious writing. From that he read a collection of Wells' short stories which introduced him to science fiction and fantasy and opened up the horizons of literature. For his luxury Herbert first wondered if Hot Gossip – the erotic dance group – were out of the question! He set aside pencil and paper as a possibility as it meant he would still be working. He finally settled for a grand piano, which he hoped to learn to play properly and at least fulfil the role of frustrated musician within him.

The programme finished with Herbert looking to the future, although he confessed he did not look to the future too much. At the time the programme was recorded in 1986 Herbert was working on a television series for the BBC about a psychic investigator. This series was subsequently shelved, though it formed the basis for his book *Haunted*. Already he was fulfilling his creative talents by helping provide the art and design for his books, but he wanted to take this further. "I'd like eventually to do children's stories, and illustrate them, so I can combine the art and the writing." He also felt he'd like to see some good films made of his books. They were all things to look forward to, when he had the time!

MY TEN FAVOURITE BOOKS

James Herbert

NINE

MAKING a list of ten favourite books was almost as difficult as deciding upon eight gramophone records for that dreaded Desert Island. The only way to do it was to choose those that have meant something to me through the years, eliminate most of them, then cut the choice down to the final ten. The sheer pleasure of reading each one has been the test for including them on my list, but the genuine insight they've provided runs a close second.

"Holiday reading. That's about the only chance I get to catch up with my list. Certainly throughout the year I have at least two or three [books] on the go simultaneously, but it's not until the summer that I find time to devour great chunks at a sitting (or lying)."

– James Herbert, from "A Patch of Shade" by Neil Gaiman, W. H. Smith Bookcase (Summer Reading), 1988

THE HISTORY OF MR POLLY
by H. G. Wells

This "simple" man's quest for love and fortune, but ultimately for contentment, was the first school book that I took seriously. Although I loved Wells' science fiction novels, this became, and still is, a firm favourite of all the great man's work.

I AM LEGEND
by Richard Matheson

The first non-Gothic horror story I'd ever read, an allegory really of how the isolated normal becomes the abnormal among a world of mutants. The main character finds himself living in a land of vampires whose sole purpose is to "convert" him, to make him conform, to become one of them. Quite riveting, and one of Matheson's best.

JAMES HERBERT

COLOUR OF LIGHT
by William Goldman

An American writer who produced some of the most entertaining and moving novels of relationships and manners in the sixties and seventies, but known better now for his screenplays (*A Bridge Too Far*; *Butch Cassidy*; *The Princess Bride*). He's still the master of slick one-liners and sad humour, though.

ONE FLEW OVER
THE CUCKOO'S NEST
by Ken Kesey

A cult success twenty years ago, only the film version brought it mass appeal. It was then, and still is for me, a stunning tale of a misfit's rebellion against Establishment rule – and in this case, the strictures of a mental institution. Comically and tragically brilliant.

THIS TIME NEXT WEEK
by Leslie Thomas

The author's account of his own boyhood in an orphanage. Although Leslie Thomas' novels have been hugely successful over the years, I still consider him to be one of our most underestimated writers. A little classic this one.

THE SILENCE OF THE LAMBS
by Thomas Harris

The most gripping thriller so far this year. Beautifully plotted, immense tension – a pleasure to read. One of those with which you regret turning over the last page.

DRACULA
by Bram Stoker

Need I say more?

CHILDHOOD'S END
by Arthur C. Clarke

True science fiction can often be a bit too technically clever for its own good, but Arthur C. Clarke has the knack (unique, I think) of making the "science" of his stories both understandable and awesome at the same time. The fate of mankind when the Earth has run its natural course makes wonderful fiction.

"The books I'm reading are scattered all over my house. The novels I have beside my bed at the moment are Love in the Time of Cholera *by Gabriel García Márquez and* Freaky Deaky *by Elmore Leonard. The book I have in my library is a life of van Gogh,* The Love of Many Things *by David Sweetman. In my sitting room is* Dim White Phlox, *an autobiography by Terry Gilbert, and the book I've got in my loo is one mentioned in* Creed – Stephen Hawking's A Brief History of Time. *I usually keep short stories in my flat in London, and at present I am halfway through* Einstein's Monsters – *I love Martin Amis' way of cutting through emotion."*

– JAMES HERBERT, from "Who's Reading Whom", *The Sunday Times*, July 29, 1990

THE SHINING
by Stephen King

A deceptively simple plot of one man's degeneration into evil madness in an isolated and empty hotel, and the resulting terror into which his wife and son are plunged. The son has "the shining" – he's psychic – and ultimately it's this gift that saves him and his mother. Steve King's work never fails to impress.

THE OCCULT
by Colin Wilson

My bible. An incredibly perceptive and well-informed study of all things paranormal and supernatural. Mind expansion is one of its many themes and, in fact, the book itself provides a trigger for that very thing.

James Herbert and family at home, Christmas 1983

THE CRAFT

Neil Gaiman

TEN

W HILE James Herbert's life and work as an author has been extensively chronicled, interviewed and criticised, his time in advertising has not.

I first interviewed Jim in 1984, in Guernsey, and have interviewed him many times since for a variety of publications. In that time we have talked about his books, about horror, about life, about writing. Occasionally advertising would be mentioned – Jim has a few anecdotes of those days he uses to illustrate specific points. However, we had never actually discussed those days, nor had I seen Jim talk about them in print, so when Stephen Jones asked if I would be interested in talking to Jim about his time in advertising, I realised that yes, I would be. It would be something new for me.

It was also something new for Jim.

I asked a couple of questions, and a career came spilling out: a picture of the younger Jim Herbert in his days before success (literary success, at least). Not only that, but often an illumination of James Herbert the writer, from the actions and attitudes of James Herbert, the impostor, typographer, art director and group head.

Neil Gaiman: I remember you telling me back in Guernsey the story of how you broke into advertising, using someone else's name . . .

James Herbert: Yes, the name I used was Dennis Barker.

Dennis Barker was a very good friend, we went to Art School together – Hornsey College of Art. Dennis was brilliant

The nice thing about Horror is that it's a big umbrella to work under – you can do romance, you can do humour, you can do politics, you can do religion . . . you can go into other fields, and still bring it back to Horror at the end of the day.

– JAMES HERBERT, from *Danse Macabre*, No. 8, January 1986

and he got a job with Goya, in their packaging department, doing their perfumes. He was a very good designer. So he left the college before most of us did, two or three months ahead of us, because he had got the job, whereas most of us left Art School and then spent another year looking for work.

Now, Dennis had got two job interviews. He went to the first one and got the job, so he rang me up (I was out of work) and said, "Jim, I've got this interview, do you want to go along instead?" Now, because Dennis had worked with Goya, then moved on somewhere else and then gone for this other job, he had experience of graphic design in advertising whereas I had none at all. I was straight from Art School.

So I went along as "Dennis Barker", with his experience and I got the job. I actually worked under the name of Dennis Barker for six months before I was established and could actually say who I was.

Gaiman: Did they actually call you Dennis?

Herbert: No – I'd say "People usually call me Jim." Once I was established there – I'd feathered my nest there shall we say – I could do the job, then I announced who I really was and that was fine, no problem, and I stayed there another two or three years. (Interestingly enough, Dennis Barker is now Art Director for whoever does the Whitley Strieber books. He did that terrific cover for *Communion*. So we both got into publishing eventually.)

Gaiman: Where was that?

Herbert: That was at a very small studio agency at the back of Chancery Lane. Our studio was actually in a loft; there was me and three other guys. It was a crazy place, and I was sort of pot-washer, coffee boy, errand boy and you imagine, four years in Art School and you actually start right at the bottom again – paste-up artist, typographer, I did the lot, I was just a general run-around.

They were absolute maniacs, but interesting people. The owner was the type who should have actually been in the rag trade, everything was done on the cheap, *everything*. We did a lot of mail order and point-of-sale stuff, like those ads you see for Dixons with lots of hi-fis, cameras, the whole bit, and I used to do all these paste-ups. To do these shots . . . for instance we did a shot of a hairdryer one day, the Creative Director went round with the Managing Director, to a photo-booth in Woolworths, put the hairdryer in, took the shot and it was pasted down as a bit of artwork. They charged the client about 30 guineas for it.

That was the type of place it was – *crazy*, but I learnt so

"I've always loved horror stories since I was a kid. When your flesh creeps, and your heart starts to thump, it makes you feel alive. It takes the blandness out of your system."

– JAMES HERBERT, from "James – The Devil of a Chiller" by Peter Grosvenor, *Daily Express*, May 16, 1980

"If you watch people at a horror film when they come to the really scary moment they half jump out of their seats.

"Then they flop back and turn to each other with a smile or a laugh. After the scare comes a sense of relief. We all crave strong sensation. The beauty of the horror story is that it is excitement and escapism without actual danger."

– JAMES HERBERT, from"Thrills and Chills Galore from Best-Seller Herbert" by Peter Grosvenor, *Daily Express*, January 29, 1983

much there in six months, more than in four years of Art School.
I learned the basic parts of advertising, the donkey work if you
like: the paste-ups, the putting things together, the panics. It
was a great experience for me. I was on slave wages.

I stayed there two or three years. Now, the first ad I ever
did was for a Christmas tree. It was a one-inch column about
six inches deep and it was just a bit of artwork for a Christmas
tree that I had to stick down, do a little bit of Letraset headline
and stick a bit of printed copy. That came out in the local paper
and I thought "That's my first ad," and I was very proud of
that. I've probably still got it somewhere.

Then I told another lie: I went along to an agency called
Charles Barker Advertising and said I was a typographer; there
was no set salary for the job they were offering but I lied to
them and said I was getting £12 a week with my old job (this
was about 1963–64 or maybe a bit later, 1965–66).

You see before that I'd had other jobs; I worked for Trust
House Forte in a restaurant in Oxford Street from 8 o'clock in
the morning until 6 o'clock at night with half an hour for lunch,
although you couldn't actually leave, you ate the café's food six
days a week – and I was doing that for £6 a week. Overtime was
three-and-sixpence an hour. So £12 a week was good money. I'd
started courting heavily and by Sunday nights (I got paid on
Friday) I was broke; I had about five bob to last me the rest of
the week, about 25 new pence. So yeah, £12 a week was not
bad.

Then when I went to this other place I think I asked for £16
a week as a typographer. I got the job but the Chairman said
to me, "Yes, well, Jim, we want to take you on – but I think
the salary we are prepared to pay is £14 10s per week" and of
course my face lit up and I said "Okay, okay!" and I took it.

I found typography was a piece of cake; I knew a bit about
it from what I'd learned at Art School and the bit I did at the
previous studio agency, but I was certainly no expert and it
took a few weeks to actually get into it but it suddenly clicked
like driving a car or swimming.

Once that happened I was in *every* six months for more
money and made them pay – and that parallels exactly with
publishing. The first deal I did, for *The Rats*, was a real rip-off,
but I didn't mind that, it was just getting my foot on the first
rung. That's the great thing about what we do: there's no set
rates for us. You set your own rates; that's what I always liked
about advertising, that's what I like about publishing.

So then I was at Charles Barker, a great place, a great
agency. What I found there was that the agency was just begin-

ning to change. It was very much a financially based agency, they did all the big banks: Barclays, Midland Bank, NatWest (which at that time wasn't NatWest but Westminster Bank and the National Bank), Lloyds Bank; and all these other City accounts: big money things, but not glamorous advertising.

Most of the people there were very staid. The studio was very old-fashioned, that's the only way I can describe it; great blokes, great people but a little bit behind the times because they'd only done this financial advertising. I found them all a little bit lazy as well. They used to all cluster in one room and have long debates while I was there just to get on with the work. Do you know what a "type mark-up" is? Well, if you have a newspaper ad, you have the Art Director who designs the thing and the Copywriter who writes the copy, and you take their design and make it work: you put the typeface in, you specify the typeface, you work out all the grey bodymatter – all the text – you work out how it's going to fit and you actually do sums to make sure it's going to fit; you pass it on to the printer who works from your specification: so that's what I was doing. The average for type mark-ups in a day was three or four. I used to do about eighteen or nineteen. I found short cuts, different ways of doing them. You still had to work them out in detail, and that took a while, but there were other ways in which you could cheat a little bit, or you could assume that it would fit in that size, you didn't have to work it all out. So I was actually running ahead.

What I started doing then was getting involved in design. I was getting through all this typography and I was actually finding myself with spare time, so I would sneak in to where they kept the pile of job slips (they were a written brief of what the client wanted, what they wanted to advertise) and then I went away and I worked on it. I used to take all the plum ones, the really good ones, sit down, design the ad and hand it in.

Because it was such a nice company they didn't like to say, "Well, you *shouldn't* be doing that, *this* is what you're supposed to be doing", and I got the other work done.

You see, it's that old thing that, to begin with, you've always got to give more than you're being paid for, always. If you want to get ahead you've got to work twice as hard for what you're being paid for, if not three times as hard. I didn't mind because I used to like design and suddenly I was doing a lot more design – and the nice thing is that the clients were liking it and the account handlers were liking it, so they started coming to me direct.

I was becoming quite a good designer, in fact that's when

"With the supernatural, whenever you get bored with what you're writing you can just go way over the top and make something quite outrageous happen. If you're getting bored with what is happening you can be sure that the reader is too, so it's important to do something drastic."

– JAMES HERBERT, from "Herbert's Rats", *Books & Bookmen*, February 1983 the Art School training came into its own. I'd learnt the basics about being in advertising – the paste-ups, the typography, the photography – but all this aesthetic side of design that I'd learnt at Art School started coming out then, years later, when I'd got the groundwork. I did some nice ads.

Then I had the choice of becoming an Art Director or staying a typographer, and this is one of these roads that you always come to in life. I had to decide whether I wanted to stay in this very safe, secure job of a typographer, which was a mechanical job – it still needed a bit of skill and a bit of flair but you could get by. Whereas to be an Art Director you had to come up with ideas all the time, you had to design things, you had to get ideas for photography; it was a bigger thing to take on. So I had to decide whether I wanted the security of this typographer's job, reach a certain level and never go beyond it, or take the next step and become an Art Director. This would be 1965–66.

Of course, really, it was no decision. I decided I wanted to be an Art Director.

I started work as an Art Director and just really fell into it, it's what I should have been all the way along. I worked in a group with a Group Head, me as Art Director and a typographer, and we still had this system where there was almost a typing pool of copywriters.

The Agency was going through changes, and suddenly they wanted to go after more consumer advertising, the real glamorous stuff. We had a really good base – we were even doing Chanel perfumes in those days, Van Heusen shirts as well, so we did have the odd accounts that were very good, but they got this Creative Director in called Dennis McDonnell. This guy was a great talker and he had what I call that common touch, he knew what he was talking about, it wasn't all bullshit – you could connect with it. I really sort of switched on to this man, I could see what he was aiming at, I could see what he wanted to do with the Agency.

The thing you find in advertising is that if you do a big campaign it's actually easier to do than make a four-inch double look good and work; if you've got a crap job to do, it's very difficult to make it not *look* crap. The extension is when you've got a full-page ad to do, it's very easy to make a full-page ad look good. So I could do full-page ads, I could do campaigns and because I was doing a lot of copy headlines as well and coming up with ideas for ads, I don't know, I just built up a good reputation.

My other reputation was for being very (to use an old-fashioned word) *bolshy*. I was a bastard, because it was a game

NEIL GAIMAN

to me – I wasn't into the politics of advertising, but I liked to see it all going on there.

Gaiman: That does seem to be a common thread that has run through your entire career, from Art School to the present day. I'm sure that even now there are people at Hodders who are terrified of you – or at least regard you as one of their bolshiest authors . . .

Herbert: I wouldn't use the word "bolshy" any more but . . . A lot of people say I'm a perfectionist but I'm not really; I know there is no such thing as perfection, but I like to get it as right as possible. We all make mistakes, everybody makes mistakes, so I can always forgive mistakes. What I hate is somebody who won't admit a mistake, that's when I go for them. I did always want the best possible result in the days when I was a typographer to Art Director and then to Group Head, and I got a reputation.

Gaiman: You didn't go out of your way to be nice to people?

Herbert: I never did unless I liked the person. If you like me, it's pretty sure that I like you and that's the way it's always been, but I must admit I did upset people and I used to do it deliberately – it was the old devil in me, because I enjoy life so much, I was out to have a good time and stir things up, get things going.

Gaiman: You were getting restless in advertising. Why do you think you started writing at this time, rather than painting or drawing?

Herbert: The truth was that the art side of me was being fulfilled anyway; I did quite a bit of illustration for the work I was doing, so that side of me was being fulfilled. Even going along to photographic sessions, I used to work well with photographers, they were usually friends anyway and you could say "Let's put that over there and this here and let's have a look through the camera." For some of the campaigns I actually took the shots myself as well, and that's all to do with art, composition and colour. So that was actually being fulfilled.

Also, inside me, I'd come to realise that the writing was there, it had always been there, it just hadn't been unleashed.

Gaiman: So you wrote *The Rats* and sold it to New English Library. What was the reaction in the advertising world?

Herbert: I hadn't said anything to anybody when I was writing the book. I walked in that morning when I'd had the letter from NEL and it was a very small scrap of paper it was written on, saying, "Yes, we like your novel *The Rats* very much, and we'd like to offer you £150 in advance, four and a half per cent royalties." I thought wonderful, this is *wonderful*, I was walking

"I'm not really a nasty person. I don't mind scaring grown-ups with my books. That's my trade. But I don't like scaring kids."

– James Herbert, from "Fear is the Key to Having a Bestseller" by Tom Moore, *Brighton Evening Argus*, May 25, 1987

Selected advertising campaigns art directed by James Herbert

on air. It was one of the most unbelievable experiences of my life. So I went into the office and I said to the copywriters, "Good morning, Hacks." The word got round very very fast in the agency.

The initial reaction was terrific but obviously it didn't go down too well with all these copywriters.

Gaiman: All of whom were writing novels about advertising . . .

Herbert: Exactly, and not just advertising, they were writing historical romances, Godfather-type novels as well. So it was beautiful, and when the book actually came out, I came back from lunch one day and they had these big display windows outside the agency, it was in Farringdon Road, and in one of them there was a huge photograph of me and inside there was a big party waiting for me, so they were really good. They presented me with a rat doll and a bunch of grapes – sour grapes – this was from the copywriters. But it was nice, they made a fuss. And in a way it was good for the agency as well to introduce the Art Director Group Head as a novelist also.

But there was a lot of resentment there and it built up over the next couple of years, a very weird situation. It was almost, "Is this guy getting too big for his boots?" Whereas in the past I'd already *been* a bit too big for my boots and that's the way I actually got on, suddenly I was actually becoming a bit more humble.

In fact you'll find that the more successful you get, you *should* become more humble; it's a very weird thing that when something's happened to you, you feel very, I don't know, as though you can't believe it, it's too much and it shouldn't really be happening to you. That's the truth of it. So rather than being too big for my boots, I was going into reverse. Whereas before I'd done a lot of what I would call false boasting – jokey mock boasting – I found I couldn't do that any more. I couldn't be cocky any more because suddenly it was too real.

Gaiman: Was *The Rats* bringing in money?

Herbert: Yes, it was. But the trouble was, in those days there was a Labour government and the highest tax was eighty-three per cent. So it didn't actually make me rich. The book did extremely well, but financially I didn't do well out of it, and then of course over the next five years I stayed in advertising and got very well paid and did the books and the books got bigger and bigger, but financially, because of the eighty-three per cent, I didn't actually make a fortune.

Now look at it this way: from my background and actually working very hard to get where I was at that time, the year

"I get letters from people saying I should be burned in Hell, that I'm wicked, that I'm Satan's child. Usually those letters are from people who haven't read the books . . ."

– JAMES HERBERT, from "James Herbert: Growing Up in Public" by Neil Gaiman, *Gaslight & Ghosts* (1988)

"If someone actually proved to me that any one of my books had incited someone to do something nasty then I'd perhaps think twice about continuing, but you can't be responsible for everybody in the world. There's got to be a few lunatics about who still do something and then blame it on something or somebody else."

– JAMES HERBERT, from "From Rats to Riches: The Horror Fiction of James Herbert" by Martin Coxhead, *Fangoria*, No. 30, October 1983 that I made £100,000 I had to write out a cheque for the Inland Revenue for £83,000. Imagine how you would feel, imagine how anyone would feel.

Gaiman: I'm surprised you didn't leave the country.

Herbert: Well, that's the inclination, but I did like England – I still like England, that's why I'm still here now.

The only thing I ever did was I went to the Channel Islands for two years, much later on. The main reason was to get away from the telephones and get away from business things and interruptions so I could actually work, on my own, away from the fans. Of course on the Channel Islands the tax advantages are very good, but that wasn't the reason I went. It was just very handy to do that and get a sort of solid base behind me and then come back.

Now I have the opportunity to stay away, I could go and work anywhere but I won't: I agree with paying taxes and I actually do like England and it's good for me. It's like Steve King won't move away from Bangor, Maine, because it's good for him; I wouldn't want to move away from England because it's good for me.

Gaiman: You did *The Rats, The Fog, The Survivor, Fluke* and *The Spear*, while holding down a full-time job . . .

Herbert: At that time I was young, enthusiastic and I was on a high, so it carried me through. But it wasn't fair on the family and also because, as I said, the money was going out of the window to the taxman, it just didn't seem worthwhile. I had to give one up.

It was immediately after that that I gave up the advertising work. The first book I did full-time at home was *Lair*.

Gaiman: I've noticed that if you look at the first five books, then you look at the second, post-advertising, sequence of books, there is a level on which you simply tended to go back and do it better.

Herbert: Oh yeah, very much, it's very much a cycle. You see, I love to do the big blockbuster type, I loved to do *The Fog, Domain, The Dark*: the big ones, that is, all hell breaks loose, murder, mayhem, the whole bit. Then I like the quieter ones. That cycle is a limited cycle. I actually introduced humour with *Fluke* then that came back with *The Magic Cottage* and it's now come back with *Creed*. I introduced the real hard, mean stories with *Sepulchre* particularly, and *The Spear*, but they're to do with thrillers as well, it's another genre introduced into it. You do go round, you don't do it intentionally, it's just the way the mood shifts and you want to go back to do that. The one I'm doing after *Creed*, again is the big blockbuster type, madness and mayhem, which I really enjoy and has lots of vignettes. I haven't done that for a while and I miss it – *Domain* was really the last one and it's something I have to go back to.

Gaiman: For two years you tried to get fired from advertising, and in the end you had to resign.

Herbert: I knew I was going to be a writer, and once I'd fallen into that water and realised I could swim and actually enjoy it, I knew that whatever I did I was going to be a writer. I got so much satisfaction from writing and still do to this day. The thing about the advertising job, I got a lot of satisfaction from that, *but* every job you did, there were always other fingers in the pie: the client, the Creative Director, the copywriter, even the public (because everything was researched) and I realised you never did the pure job. As soon as I started writing I realised that this was the pure job, that nothing interfered with it.

Well, there was no choice. I decided I was going to write but I thought, for me to leave advertising, it's hard. I still enjoyed the work, I still liked the company, the firm I worked for, they were good people, but I thought *well, the thing to do now is to go out outrageously and be fired so that you get paid a lot of money and you don't have to come in and work any more.* My contract was for six months, I couldn't just leave the following week.

I sort of went on a binge – not a booze binge, but a binge of doing exactly what I wanted to do. I put everybody's back up. The only thing I couldn't fall down on was I would still do the work and I would do it professionally because that was part of me, I couldn't not do the job properly. Certain jobs I refused to do. We had a client who wanted a particular shot of a glamorous girl showing her boobs in a low top, real crass stuff, and I refused to do it. Another client wanted something else done and I just told him I wouldn't do it. We had a big deal client who actually rang up the Chairman and told him he didn't want me on the account any more, but nobody would fire me. It went on for two years and at the end I thought *okay you've won, I've got to resign.*

Gaiman: You seem to have mellowed a lot since then.

Herbert: I have mellowed, yeah. You wouldn't believe the person I was in those days. None of us change that much but I don't know, I used to get a great kick out of upsetting people – but for the right reasons, totally for the right reasons.

Gaiman: Looking at the design aspect of the books, the first one that obviously has your hand in it is the hardback of *Moon*, with the repeated images, and the black endpapers . . .

The Rats *establishes Herbert as a writer of the kind of horror fiction that confronts its readers with aspects of reality they might prefer to ignore.*

– RAMSEY CAMPBELL, from *The Penguin Encyclopedia of Horror and the Supernatural* (1986)

Do spiders give you the horrors? . . . What about rats? In James Herbert's novel of the same name, you can feel them crawl all over you . . . and eat you alive.

– STEPHEN KING, from *Danse Macabre* (1981)

Herbert: No, it was before that, *Fluke* was the first paperback cover that I actually designed. They changed it a little bit, spoilt it a little bit. *Survivor,* again they changed that so all these very subtle little things that they changed made it look bad, you know they didn't understand what good, pure design was.

Gaiman: When you went into the re-design, the basic design was often almost exactly the same only better painted. Take the difference between the first version of *Fluke* and the second version of *Fluke* . . .

Herbert: Well, what I did – I think it was after *Lair* – I said, "No more of this, I'm going to actually do all the jackets myself now." I did all the backlist, to get them in some kind of order, so that they looked good together on the book shelf.

Gaiman: So you did the first major re-design?

Herbert: Yeah, I did it to make them all look uniform and I was the first guy in this country to put gold and silver foil together. Before they were just getting into using a bit of foil for the lettering but they could only do one – it was either gold or silver. I said, "No, what we're going to do is we're going to have gold *and* silver," so I think the name was in silver and the title of the book was in gold. I also said, "We are going to have white covers as well," 'cos they'd automatically think that if it's horror it's got to be black – and the rows I had about that – but I said, "No, we are going to have a combination, some are going to be black and some are going to be white," and it just uplifted the genre.

The Art Director at Hodders is a great man and he knows me well by now, and he knows it works – and if it doesn't work he'll tell me. I think he's actually benefited from my point of view as an Art Director. He's told me that a lot of the artists that he's used for the illustrations, they moan when I get the artwork in and I say, "Well, no that's not quite right, *this* is what they should do here." Usually small points, but telling points. He's told me that, yes, they've grumbled but when they've come back they've all said the same thing: "He was right."

So that is another reward I get out of publishing, nothing to do with the telling of stories but again, it's that fulfilment, it's that other side, the art side of things.

I like doing things with books that have not been done before, lots of things, subtle things. The black endpapers and trim on *Moon,* for instance. The average reader is never going to notice, but I will, and in years to come when my grandchildren pick up these hardbacks or the paperbacks and they see the quality and production in them, they'll think, well, that's not bad. It's something you get no credit for, because who the hell is going to know about it?

Gaiman: Which ones are yours?

Herbert: Well, I guess every one from *Shrine* on.

Gaiman: So you did the basic design of the two snakes for *Sepulchre* and for *Haunted* you came up with the idea of the girl coming towards the house . . . ?

Herbert: Oh yeah, I did all that, even the mnemonic for *Haunted* that was used on the T-shirts.

Gaiman: And the watches and pens.

Herbert: Once they had that mnemonic everything else followed.

In the contents pages of *The Magic Cottage*, there's a drawing of flowers and the artist just couldn't get it right, so I drew those flowers myself. For the contents pages and the chapter headings I actually sat down and did a type mark-up for the whole thing. That's how much I was into it.

Gaiman: I'm partly amazed that they let you.

Herbert: It's called clout.

Gaiman: But there's a level on which, even in the friendliest departments, when someone comes in and says "Right. This is exactly how we are doing it . . ."

Herbert: Oh, they all had tantrums. You see, it's only because it's worked; if it didn't work then they could say to me "You're wrong," but time after time it worked.

Gaiman: You obviously don't feel that you wasted or lost any of the skills that you learned in advertising.

Herbert: I don't think you do. I mean I'm not sure that I could ever go back to advertising, I certainly wouldn't ever want to, although I do miss the company, the sociability of advertising and I miss the buzz that goes on.

But no, I think new trends come in. I think that if I'd stuck with it then I'd have been fine, but after all these years, to go back into it, then no, I don't think I could hack it. The same with illustration, because I haven't sat down and drawn or painted for a long, long while. You get rusty, it would take me another couple of years to bring back what I had before.

When I have time, yes, I'd love to do all that but at the moment there's just no time for it.

So I'll stick to the writing, I think, which I'm improving at because I'm practising all the time. You know, you learn your craft.

Truly horrifying first novel about plague of man-eating super-rats spawned in aftermath of atomic test. While the development owes something to The Birds, *the effectiveness of the gruesome set pieces and brilliant though sickening finale are all its own.*

– The Sunday Times, May 19, 1974

BREAKFAST

James Herbert

ELEVEN

THE cold water trickled to a halt and the woman clucked her tongue. She twisted the tap off and placed the meagrely filled kettle on the electric stove. She left it to boil on the stone-cold ring.

Walking through to the hallway, the woman picked up the telephone receiver and flicked open the book lying beside it on the narrow hallstand. She found a number and dialled.

"I've already complained twice," she said into the mouth-piece. "Now the water's gone off completely. Why should I pay my water rates when I can't have bloody water?"

She flushed, angry with herself and the noiseless receiver. "You've made me swear now, that's how angry I am," she said. "Don't give me any more excuses, I want someone round today to sort it out, otherwise I shall have to speak to your supervisor."

Silence.

"What's that you say? You'll have to speak up."

The phone remained dead.

"Yes, well, that's more like it. And I'll have you remember that civility costs nothing. I'll expect your man later this morning, then."

The earpiece could have been a sea shell for all the noise it made.

"Right, thank you, and I hope it isn't necessary to call again."

The woman allowed herself a *humph* of satisfaction as she replaced the receiver.

I'm very grateful to him [James Herbert] because he taught my son Felix to read. Didn't he write a book called The Rats *or something? It's all about necrophilia and Felix couldn't put it down.*

– JILLY COOPER, from "Jilly's Horror at Ghost Writer Who Toppled Her" by Chris Hutchins, *Today*, November 4, 1989

"I don't know what this country's coming to," she said, pulling her unkempt cardigan tight around her as a breeze – a warm breeze – flowed down from the stairway. She went back into the kitchen.

As she rinsed the teapot with water from the cold kettle, the woman complained to her husband seated at the pine kitchen table, newspaper propped up against the empty milk bottle before him. A fly, its body thick and black and as big as a bee, landed on the man's cheek and trekked across the pallid landscape. The man ignored it.

". . . not even as though water's cheap nowadays," his wife droned. "We have to pay rates even when it's off. Should never have been allowed to split from normal rates – it was just their way of bumping up prices. Like everything else, I suppose, money, money, it rules everything. I dread doing the monthly shop. God knows how much everything's gone up since last time. Afraid you'll have to give me more housekeeping soon, Barry. Yes, I know, but I'm sorry. If you want to eat the way you're used to, you'll have to give me more."

She stirred the tea and quickly sucked her finger when cold water splashed and burned it. Putting the lid on the teapot, she took it over to the kitchen table and sat opposite her husband.

"Tina, are you going to eat those cornflakes or just sit and stare at them all day?"

Her daughter did not even shrug.

"You'll be late for playschool again if you don't get a move on. And how many times have I told you Cindy isn't allowed at the table? You spend more time speaking to that doll than you do eating."

She scooped up the dolly that she, herself, had placed in her daughter's lap only minutes before and propped it up on the floor against a table leg. Tina began to slide off her chair.

The mother jumped up and pulled the child erect again, tutting as she did so. Tina's small chin rested against her chest and the woman tried vainly to lift it.

"All right, you go ahead and sulk, see where it gets you."

A small creature with many eyelash legs stirred from its nest in the little girl's ear. It crawled out and scuttled into the dry white hair of the child's scalp.

The woman poured the tea, the water colourless, black specks that were the unbrewed tea leaves collecting in the strainer to form a soggy mould. Silverfish scattered from beneath the milk jug as she lifted it and unsuccessfully tried to pour the clots of sour cream into the cups.

Now, the moment you've all been waiting for: Yuppie Fiction! Going on sale this autumn are the first of what could be a whole new industry: Filofiction. Yes, now you can get a whole book just the right size to fit into that essential item of any Bright Young Thing's wardrobe – and ready punched, at that: Insert a whole book in your Filofax, or just a few chapters to show that you're In with the In Crowd. And there are eight exciting flavours to choose from, all bestsellers of course, and featuring our very own James Herbert amongst them with his first and still mega-selling horror novel The Rats. *At a fiver apiece, how could you afford not to snap up this offer?*

– STEPHEN JONES and JO FLETCHER, from *Science Fiction Chronicle*, Issue 108, September 1988

"Sammy, you stop that chattering and finish your toast. And will you put your school tie on straight, how many more times do I have to tell you? At ten years of age you think you'd be old enough to dress yourself properly."

Her son silently gazed at the green bread beside his bowl of cornflakes, the cereal stirring gently as small creatures fed beneath. He was grinning, a ventriloquist's dummy, cheek muscles tightened by shrinkage. A misty film clouded his eyes, a spoon balanced ungripped in his clawed hand. A length of string around his chest tied him to the chair.

The woman suddenly heaved forward, twisting her chair so that the ejected vomit would not splatter the stale food. She retched, the pain seeming to gut her insides, her stomach jerking in violent spasms as if attempting to evict its own internal organs.

The excruciating pain was in her head too, and for a brief second it forced a flash of lucidity. The moment of boundless thunder, the quietness after. The creeping sickness.

It was gone, the clearness vanquished, muddy clouds spoiling her mind's fleeting perspicuity. She wiped her mouth with the back of her hand and sat upright. The hurt was easing, but she knew it would linger in the background, never far away, waiting to pounce like Inspector Clouseau's Chinese manservant. She almost managed to smile at the memory of old, better times, but the present – her own vision of the present – closed in on her.

She sipped the tasteless tea and, with an impatient hand, flicked at the flies buzzing around Tina's head. Her husband's pupilless stare from the other side of the table irritated her, too, the whites of his eyes showing between half-closed lids a silly affectation he assumed to annoy her. A joke could be taken *too* far.

"What shall we do this morning, everyone?" she asked, forgetting it was both a work and school day. "A walk to the park? The rain's finally stopped, you know. My goodness, I thought it never would, didn't you, Barry? Must do some shopping later, but I think we could manage a little walk first, take advantage of the weather, hmn? What do you say, Sammy? You could take your roller skates. Yes, you too, Tina, I wasn't forgetting you. Perhaps the cinema later. No, don't get excited – I want you to finish your breakfast first."

She leaned across and patted her daughter's little clenched fist.

"It'll be just like old times, won't it?" Her voice became a whisper, and the words were slow. "Just like old times."

Tina slid down in her chair once more and this time dis-appeared beneath the table.

"That's right, dear, you look for Cindy, she can come to the park too. Anything interesting in the news today, Barry? Really, oh good gracious, people *are* funny, aren't they? Makes you wonder what the world's coming to, just what on earth you'll read next. Manners, *Samuel,* hand before mouth."

She scraped away surface mould from a drooping slice of bread and bit into it. "Don't let your tea get cold, pet," she lightly scolded her husband, Barry. "You've got all day to read the newspaper. I think I'll have a lie-down in a little while; I'm not feeling too well today. Think I've got flu coming on."

The woman glanced towards the shattered window, a warm breeze ruffling the thin hair straggling over her forehead. She saw but did not perceive the nuclear-wasted city outside.

Her attention drifted back to her family once more and she watched the black fly, which had fully explored the surface of her husband's face by now, disappearing into the gaping hole of his mouth.

She frowned, and then she sighed. "Oh, Barry," she said, "you're not just going to sit there all day again, are you?"

Tiny, glittering tear beads formed in the corners of each eye, one brimming over leaving a jerky silver trail down to her chin. Her family didn't even notice.

Many people believe that a follow-up to a previous book never creates the same excitement – but here's a sequel that breaks the rule, such is the tension generated by the famous Herbert rats . . . If you thought highly of The Rats, *then rest assured you'll want to hear about* Lair.

– from *Bookshop,* June 14, 1979

BREAKFAST

SEASON OF THE RAT

Adrian Cole

TWELVE

I T happens to all writers.

A great idea for a short story or a novel. You begin to embellish it, maybe make a few notes; you start getting it down on paper. Yes, this is it, you can feel it. This one will grab them by the throat. Then, just when you're ready to hit your agent or publisher with it, you happen to pick up somebody's latest novel, or collection and – *aarrgh*! Your idea, your *pièce de résistance*, your masterpiece, is staring back at you. Someone else has just written it! Almost down to the last detail, as if they've invaded your mind and sucked it out while you weren't awake.

You tell me a writer who hasn't had the experience.

It's happened to me a few times (just like the flu it can get you over and over). However there was one time I remember in particular, and it was a bit uncanny. But we're talking about horror fiction, so you've got to expect these things, right?

I'd not been writing for long, and I'd had a few sword and sorcery novels published, together with two science fiction/horror books. These latter two had a contemporary setting and leaned more heavily towards horror than SF, reflecting my predilection for the former. I had decided to develop this literary bent in my work, and came up with what I thought would make a damn good yarn: I would use as my setting the city of Birmingham (in which I lived at the time) only the place had been evacuated almost totally. Why? I suspect you can figure that one out easily enough. Yup. Rats. Oversize, ultra-nasty and

New English Library report that sales of Lair *by Jim Herbert* are far greater than expected. Four reprints have already been gone through and NEL have printed 465,000 copies to date. Sales of Jim Herbert's other titles are also increasing.

– *Newsagent and Bookshop*, August 2, 1979

ADRIAN COLE

spreading a deadly variation of bubonic plague, Bubonic Plus. This was to be *Season of the Rat*.

I worked in a large library, so I was able to get to work on the research, and learned some fascinating things about the Black Death, warfarin, sewers, rodents and other such delicate matters. The file grew thick. Soon I would be ready to unleash my creation on an unsuspecting audience.

The rest, as they say, is history.

I walked into a bookshop one morning, and came face to face with . . . *THE RATS* by James Herbert. I must have gaped at the huge rat that mocked me from the cover. But I recovered my wits enough to buy a copy, which I promptly stuffed in my pocket, like a little boy caught doing something naughty. If anyone asked, it was for research. And although I read the book and found it wasn't a story of bubonic plague-carrying rats devouring Birmingham's survivors, I recognised enough of my own prospective epic to shelve my idea. Shelve it? No, I buried it.

So you'd be forgiven for expecting me to go on to say how much I *loathe* James Herbert's Rat books, how I never miss an opportunity to hide them in bookshops and how I burn effigies of the man every month when the moon is full. After all, I'm only human – well, partly.

Not so.

When I first read *The Rats*, at breakneck speed, I was immediately struck by the way in which it was written. It was in stark contrast to the sort of horror diet I had been used to at the time. This consisted principally of writers like Lovecraft, Blackwood, the *Weird Tales* school, and Dennis Wheatley (one of the few writers who wrote full-length horror novels). They were all writers that I loved, and I still admire them (although it may surprise you to learn that I have reservations about Wheatley's mania for propaganda).

The Rats jumped the tracks altogether as far as I was concerned. It was a brash, no-holds-barred, sometimes extreme thriller, and James Herbert ripped in to his material with no regard for moral or social sacred cows. He dealt bluntly, crudely with his characters, zeroing in on their prejudices, their seediness, their indifference to human values. Or should I say, the human values I had been used to reading about in horror fiction.

I began to feel that here was an author with little but contempt for his fellow man, venting his spleen on anyone and everyone, meting out suitably sadistic retribution to a society that he saw as essentially rotten to the core. The bastards

Unless you happen to lace your Ovaltine, [Lair] can't be recommended bed-time reading . . . No one can say that James Herbert doesn't write a rattling tale. Tomato kitsch-up it may be, but all those Herbert fans are gonna love it!

– from *Paperback and Hardback Book Buyer*, May 1979

His new "chiller", Lair, falls halfway between his early rapid-fire clauses and his recent descriptive prose – thank goodness! Jim Herbert was in danger of losing his fans as he cast aside the slick, instant style which he handles so well.

– FRD, *Newsagent and Bookshop*, May 3, 1979

deserved all they got! It's certainly how Herbert's critics viewed him, and their abuse was at times hysterical.

But it isn't that simple.

Jim Herbert is now firmly established as Britain's leading contemporary novelist of terror . . . Lair, *sequel to* The Rats, *adequately spoons out fear by the gallon but also has a very definite storyline which Mr Herbert never meanders too far away from – convincing the reader that giant, killer rats could easily take over Epping Forest and threaten to devour the human population of London and more . . .*

– FRD, from *Newsagent & Bookseller*, May 1979

The Rats, to my mind, cannot be dismissed simply as a piece of exploitation. Apart from its radical approach to its subject, it contains scenes of high-octane suspense (that of the children trapped in the rat-besieged school is superbly visually realised) and the terrifying experience of the rat plague is highly plausible. Sure the book is blunt, ugly and brutal, but it draws on a kind of raw creative energy that makes it compelling, undeserving of scorn.

It is a work put into better perspective when read against the wider background of its two sequels, *Lair* and *Domain*, where Herbert's growth as a writer is clearly evident. If he can be accused of a somewhat cynical approach in *The Rats*, it's an attitude I find less apparent in the later volumes. Both are equally, if not more, hard-hitting, aggressive and uncompromising, but the characterisations and dialogue are deeper and more thoughtful, and intensify the suspense.

Put crudely, *The Rats* was written principally from the guts and from the balls, whereas *Lair* and in particular *Domain* are written as much from the heart and the head. Herbert obviously does empathise with his characters, and writes with compassion, but he writes from a very personal viewpoint, openly and instinctively. It is his tremendous energy that communicates itself so dynamically and makes compulsive reading. There's no time to stop and deliberate, to chew over the niceties of style: this is a roller coaster and there are no breaks until you smack up against the wall.

James Herbert is not noted for pulling his punches. No gut-wrenching detail is spared. Domain *is gross. Keep sick-bags handy.*

– *London Alternative Magazine*, August 20, 1985

Lair develops its main protagonists with a realism that Herbert has continued to hone in more recent works (I especially enjoyed *Moon*) although in *Lair* he still has a tendency to depict sex in either an idealised way or chauvinistically, especially from a woman's viewpoint. But as *Lair* draws to its tremendous conclusion, I identified enough with Luke Pender to cringe at the possibility of his suffering a worse fate than Harris in *The Rats*. I just *love* a novel where the hero/heroine is just as likely to get nailed as anyone else, and with the Rat books, you never know who's next. Herbert simply doesn't believe in cushioning any of his characters, major or minor, from the harsh realities of life, one of the strengths of his work. And, unlike many lesser writers, he is not content with merely setting up a procession of grisly deaths just for the hell of it. His use of the vignette

ADRIAN COLE

works to great effect, a device which creates dimension in a natural way without slowing the pace of his narrative – not an easy trick to pull off.

In *Lair*, as in many of Herbert's books, the style and pace is dictated by the action, the terror element. It's as near as you can get to a movie without actually watching one – fast, compact, relentless. The rats are totally credible: I never questioned their development, their mutation, their vampiric tendencies. And it's no accident that Herbert's descriptions of them, particularly *en masse*, parallel humanity, an analogy developed further in *Domain*.

Domain, for my money, is as good a book as Herbert has yet written, a book Stephen King would have been proud of. *The Rats* was an aperitif, *Lair* an entrée, but *Domain* is the twelve-course banquet!

Here Herbert tightens up his style, his characters, his dialogue and launches into a hair-raising nightmare, a vividly realised *tour de force*. As if the mutant rats weren't bad enough, we now have a post-atomic London, brilliantly depicted with all its attendant horrors for the protagonists to deal with, a grim, merciless hell, a physical and spiritual wasteland.

From the outset, as the bombs fall, we are plunged into chaos, an all-too-real one, and through the pages of the novel we witness the rapid disintegration of society as it snarls and claws in its efforts to survive. Man becomes the rat with his back to the wall. And it's the primal urge, the nerve probed as disturbingly as it was in Peckinpah's *Straw Dogs*. Furthermore this is no cynical bloodbath, it is a highly perceptive vision.

Herbert's attitudes and prejudices are still here, but they don't intrude and are absorbed into his characters. They are all the more credible and hence potent because of it. They reflect a very dark side of Man's nature and consequently make very uneasy reading at times. I sensed that the rats-as-Man concept in *The Rats* and *Lair* was a convenient device, gimmick even, whereas in *Domain* Herbert gives far more thought to the analogy. His assault on bureaucracy, on authority comes home far more convincingly in *Domain* (and not merely because Authority has destroyed its world).

David Culver, Dealey and Kate are characters who have evolved from those in the earlier books, and Herbert's sensitive development of Culver's relationship with Kate forms a solid backbone to a book that could so easily have torn loose from its moorings and plunged headlong into self-indulgence. That isn't to say *Domain* is a soft ride – Herbert is an absolute natural

"I got so absorbed in what would happen if the Bomb did drop that the rats are just an added ingredient, to give the book an extra dimension and end the series."

– JAMES HERBERT, from "James Herbert: Growing Up in Public" by Neil Gaiman, *Gaslight & Ghosts* (1988)

The plot [of Domain*] is fast and furious, more horrifying than ever. Herbert certainly has an amazing ability to give the reader the impression that the story he tells could happen. Maybe will happen?*

– DON JACQUES and ALAN FARNELL, from "The Book Column", *Nuneaton Evening Tribune*, August 8, 1985 when it comes to stretching his readers' nerves, and you're never fully prepared for the next injection of undiluted fear. But without that foundation of character, our identification with the wretched survivors would have been watered down, and we would have become mere voyeurs.

Herbert's sense of humour, which threatens to reduce the effect he seeks to create at times (for example, in *Lair*, when he uses it to deride a "flasher" and almost removes what should be our disgust at the monster) is put to far better use in *Domain*, a facet of the book, underplayed this time, which adds a very natural dimension to the characters.

Set against the macrocosm of a ruined world it is the microcosm of the small group of survivors that focuses our suspension of disbelief. Again the use of the vignette to develop the wider background of the setting, and in this case the hopelessness of Man's predicament, is used to powerful effect. There is one particular scene, in which a woman, deranged by the appalling events which have overtaken her everyday world, still pathetically attempts to feed her family, which sits at the kitchen table. But they are all dead. This scene, a short story in itself, captures the enormity of the wider events and brings home their real horror with provocative clarity.

Herbert voices his anger, his disgust even, at Man's excesses, but he is no defeatist, and has, after a downbeat start in *The Rats*, taken a more realistic stand. In *Domain* he also proclaims loudly his faith in Man's driving will to lift himself out of the mire, his humanity. At worst, we may not be much better than the things we despise, but Herbert sees enough in us of value. As readers, the intensity of our desire, our need, to see the survivors through is a testament to the triumph of the book.

The Rats have done for horror what the punks did for rock music at a time when it needed jerking out of its smugness, its comfortable near-torpor. And the rats kicked open doors just as the punks did, doors to rooms that had once been safely locked. The inmates of those rooms may once have been sanitised, distanced from the real world we live in, but not any more. Now these doors open inwards. Horror isn't safe any more. James Herbert, as much as any of his contemporaries, has made sure of that.

I'll leave my prospective rat novel where it is in its dusty file. But I've seen the light. Or should I say, the dark? And I've got this great idea for a horror novel . . .

. . . and this time, *this* time –

HORROR OF THE RATS

John Gilbert

THIRTEEN

I N dark alleys they wait, ready to feed on the flesh of any human who passes by. Whiskers twitch, tails slither on greasy paving stones, furry bodies throb gently in patient anticipation. The Rats have arrived.

Based on horror writer James Herbert's first famous thriller *The Rats* is two games in one. You can have all the excitement of a one to thousands confrontation with the furry creatures in the adventure part of the programme and you can also oversee the operation to bring about their destruction.

The first part of the package to load is the demonstration which is a classic and classy piece of work. Once loaded the screen goes black and after a few moments a pair of tiny red eyes peer out at you.

Suddenly a yellow light illuminates the darkness, showing the arch of a waterlogged cellar and a rat scurrying away back into the darkness. A torch moves across the scene and suddenly you are confronted by a mass of rats, all with glaring red eyes.

The excellent music of the Commodore 64 version then blares out together with a well constructed title screen. The Spectrum version of the game does not have the same sound quality as that of its Commodore counterpart but the graphics are just as good.

Once the demo has finished you can load in the first part of the game – there are three in all. Each part consists of a group of routines selected randomly by the control programme from those on the tape. The problem is that you are not warned that

The whole point of Domain *was London being blown up but the leaders in our society – politicians and the people with influence – they have their underground shelters that they're going to go to once that four-minute warning sounds – they'll be down in the shelters. Us lot – we've had it.*

– JAMES HERBERT, from *Danse Macabre*, No. 8, January 1986

JOHN GILBERT

some routines will not load and you may suspect that a tape loading error has occurred.

The main display once loaded is a map of London on which appears the battalions of rats as they surface from their underground lair and try to escape into the home counties. If they do manage to escape from London you lose the game.

You can send forces to do battle with the hordes of creatures, equipping the police, fire brigade, army and rat catchers with devices such as sonic beams, water cannons and rifles. Both forces and equipment are limited and can be obtained during the part of the game using the icons on menu driven screens.

The position of the rats' lair is different every time you play the game, unless you have saved a particular version of it. They do, however, usually start spawning near the centre of London and spread quickly outwards.

When the siren goes you know that the second type of action within the game, the mini scenario, is about to come into operation. Each mini scenario deals with a minor or major character's experience with the rats.

The scenarios are run in an adventure format but commands are constructed using a cursor which picks out command words from a window on the left of the screen and deposits them on a window at the bottom.

You will often have to sacrifice minor characters but major ones such as rat catcher Harris should avoid the deadly bite of the rats unless either an antidote is available or you want to lose the game.

The programme, which is available from most retail stores, is an excellent first for Hodder & Stoughton. It is, however, unlikely to be the company's last product. There are rumours of a sequel or a game based around one of Stephen King's best-selling novels. Either is awaited with eager anticipation.

This time the conflict between humans and rats, which have become further mutated, takes place in the aftermath of a nuclear strike on London, and the devastated landscape becomes one of the book's main concerns. [Domain] is necessarily one of Herbert's bleakest books, relieved only by irony and the occasional sense of the nightmarishly absurd.

– RAMSEY CAMPBELL, from *The Penguin Encyclopedia of Horror and the Supernatural* (1986)

"I've even made video games of The Rats. *I made them take out a lot of the gore. It's still quite punchy but I didn't think it right to have a game that was so gruesome."*

– JAMES HERBERT, from "Kids Hooked on Horrors of Rats and Fog" by David Spark, *Darlington Evening Despatch*, August 8, 1985

THE FOG

James Herbert

FOURTEEN

THE FOG made me a lot of enemies. Fortunately it also made me a lot of friends.

It was first published in 1975 (written in 1974) when spy stories and historical romances were the vogue. In the United States, William Peter Blatty had made his definitive mark with the movie of *The Exorcist*, and word was going around about an interesting new writer by the name of Stephen King. In England a new kind of horror tale involving mutant rats on the loose in London's East End, a story that held scant regard for conventional moderation in its depiction of violence and the consequences, had created something of a stir. It was a book that (literally, you might say) went straight for the jugular. *The Rats* was my first attempt at a novel. *The Fog* was my second.

For better or worse, they were the initial part in a growing explicitness of narrative, stories that rarely balked at expressing horror's true physical reality. Judging by the genre's swift return to public attention, through both the novel and the screen, that reality had been suppressed far too long (whether or not the sudden healthy release has transmuted in an unhealthy fascination is another matter). Readers or moviegoers no longer wanted to be merely frightened, they wanted to be shocked rigid too.

Yet, for all that, is *The Fog*, a tale of murder, madness and mayhem, as graphically horrific as its longlasting notoriety would suggest? By comparison with today's standards, certainly not. But when it was first published in 1975? Well, even that's debatable. Ramsey Campbell, perhaps one of the most respected authors of the genre, has said in a reappraisal: *"The Fog* contains remarkably few graphic acts of violence, though two are so horrible and painful that they pervade the book. Herbert concentrates rather on painting a landscape of (occasionally comic) nightmare, and most of the human episodes are of terror rather than explicit violence." My point is – and this is an observation, not a defence – that much of the controversial extremism is in the mind of the beholder rather than on the page. I must confess, however, to being pleased with the effectiveness of its images.

Nevertheless, with the new edition, the temptation was to rewrite, to smooth out the rougher edges, perhaps endow some of the characters with a little more depth. After all, a dozen novels on, and by the very nature of practice, I must have picked up a few more skills along the way.

But by so doing, would I detract from the original? To me, *The Fog* provides an honest reflection of the transient mood of the horror genre in the seventies, being in some ways a throwback to the fifties and much earlier, whereby due homage (albeit subconsciously) is paid to Wells, Wyndham and Kneale – *War of the Worlds, Day of the Triffids* and *Quatermass* respectively – while advancing very firmly towards the eighties. And it's sheer energy that carries the story through to the climactic finale; refinement might well sap its strength. I think change would be an unnecessary indulgence on my part.

Besides, I like the beast the way it is.

His images of violence are powerful because they are painful (as in the films of Dario Argento, with whom he also shares a talent for set pieces). The Fog *is also distinguished by its breathless pace, a quality usually inimical to terror, which makes the book something of a tour de force.*

– RAMSEY CAMPBELL, from *The Penguin Encyclopedia of Horror and the Supernatural* (1986)

James Herbert takes the controls (circa 1960s)

THE CURIOUS CASE OF *THE SPEAR*

Jo Fletcher

FIFTEEN

IN 1978, with more than a million copies of his first four novels already sold, James Herbert started to settle more comfortably into his relatively newfound status as one of Britain's continuing bestsellers. His latest horror thriller, *The Spear,* was published in hardcover by New English Library and he sat back to watch the royalties roll in. Instead, this blend of neo-Nazi terrorism and the occult led directly to one of the most traumatic experiences of his life.

James Herbert was accused of infringing the copyright of another author's work and dragged through the British High Court. He saw both his character and his writing publicly assassinated, all within the privileged confines of the Law Courts in the Strand, on the edge of the City of London. After more than a year of harrying and heckling, and a court case that stretched over three months, he was found guilty of infringing copyright and ordered to remove the infringing lines from *The Spear.* They were all contained within five of the seven prologues and comprised just four per cent of the book.

In 1948, at the age of twenty-seven, Trevor Tenant Ravenscroft sought out the Austrian historian Dr Walter Johannes Stein, who had fled to Britain in 1933 and built up a thriving medical practice. Dr Stein's intense opposition to Nazism led him to infiltrate the Nazi secret society known as the Thule Gesellschaft before he made his escape from Germany.

Ravenscroft had discovered the historical works of Dr Stein, in particular *The Ninth Century,* a study of the background to the romances of the Holy Grail, which echoed his own intense

I had not heard of James Herbert until I picked up The Fog. *Now I am sure that James Herbert is a writer who, if he does not burn out invention, will grip a growing readership . . . he is already powerful in a way that suggests he is a compulsive writer.*

– HYWEL WILLIAMS, *Gallery International,* February 1976

interest in the occult and supernatural. Dr Stein claimed to be able to recapture, through meditation, lost moments in history. During their evening meetings in Kensington, West London, where they both lived, Dr Stein related to Ravenscroft the history of the Spear of Destiny, the lance with which a Roman soldier pierced Christ's side when he hung, dead, on the cross at Golgotha.

The Spear of Destiny (also known as the *Heilige Lanze,* or Holy Lance, one of the Habsburg Treasures on display at the Hofburg Museum in Vienna) has apparently been wielded throughout the centuries by men who tried to use its supernatural powers to change the course of history. It was Dr Stein's interest in the Spear which led in 1909 to his friendship with Hitler, who was developing his own obsession with the artefact. (Hitler invaded Austria in 1939 and took possession of the Spear, intending to use its reported powers for his own world domination. It was discovered in an underground chamber in Nuremberg and, after biding a short time in the hands of the US Army's General Patton, it was returned to the Hofburg Museum in 1946.)

In 1957 Dr Stein summoned Ravenscroft and told him that he would have to be the one to tell the world the truth about the Spear. The following day Dr Stein fell ill, dying in hospital soon after. Ravenscroft always believed Dr Stein had an early premonition of his own death and had to discharge his duty to reveal the truth about the Holy Lance before he died.

Ravenscroft started work on his book twelve years later, in 1969, giving up journalism to concentrate on the task. *The Spear of Destiny* finally saw publication by Neville Spearman in 1972, with Corgi paperbacking it in 1974.

Using the idea that the real Holy Lance was actually switched in Nuremberg and a replica returned to Austria, Herbert wove a deft thriller around the private investigator and one-time Mossad agent Steadman and his sudden and unexpected involvement in a plot by neo-Nazis who had revived the Thule Gesellschaft and were planning to take over first England, then the world. Each of the seven sections was headed with a prologue, relating the story of the Spear from the time of the Crucifixion, through to the end of the Second World War.

The Spear took nearly a year to complete and was finally published by New English Library in 1978. Herbert thought nothing more of Ravenscroft or *The Spear of Destiny* until his whole world was thrown into chaos by the arrival, completely out of the blue, of a lawyer's letter.

"I remember the whole thing very clearly, even now, more

For its time, The Fog *was a shockingly graphic and disturbing second novel by a man who was to become Britain's best-selling horror writer. Reissuing the book, when critical acclaim has found James Herbert's following novels of such class as* Fluke *and* Haunted, *is certainly a step backwards in the eyes of those who don't know Herbert's murky past. However, since I re-read* The Fog *myself this year, I can still recommend it as a powerful and chilling novel . . .*

– DAVE HUGHES, from *Skeleton Crew,* Issue III/IV, 1988

Mr Herbert's style, potently direct with few words above two syllables, is what elevates [The Fog *] beyond the level of pulp fiction. Obviously a method which works well, as those million sales prove.*

– REG HUGHES, from "Return of a Horror Bestseller", *Eastern Evening News,* November 10, 1988 than a decade later," he said. "We had just moved down to Sussex – hadn't been there long at all. My wife Eileen's eldest brother had been killed in an accident and we were having a mass said for him at the local church that morning. Through the letter-box came this solicitor's letter saying – and I can remember the words almost exactly – 'The facts that you have used in your book *The Spear* were taken from our client's, Trevor Ravenscroft's book *The Spear of Destiny*. Those facts were gained by him through transcendental meditation; therefore they are unique to him and no other person or author can use those facts. However, if we can agree an appropriate sum, you can use those facts.'

"I just couldn't believe it. I was totally devastated."

Herbert said what appalled him most was that there had never been any intention to ignore Ravenscroft's contributions to *The Spear*: "I acknowledged many books, but especially this one: in the hardback I actually said *The Spear of Destiny* was the inspiration for my book, so I don't think I could have done more."

Ravenscroft's solicitor initially demanded £25,000 for the use of "facts gained by transcendental meditation" and this was turned down out of hand. Five subsequent applications, each time for lesser payments, were also thrown out, until Herbert was finally invited to name his own price for using Ravenscroft's work. He refused point blank to pay a penny.

"It was wrong," Herbert said. "I felt that if I gave in to that sort of thing, then every author in Britain would be in trouble. You *have* to research, and I'd used thirty or forty books, some to do with Hitler and the occult, others about the Nazis, and Ravenscroft's book was just one of a huge number. You have to take on face value certain things and although Ravenscroft dealt with the mystical and the occult, I didn't use that. *I* used dates where Hitler was somewhere at a certain time, things I thought were *factual*.

"It was the most heavily-researched book I'd ever written and it wasn't all from his book, I'd used thirty or forty others, and no one else was suing me! I didn't see that I had any choice but to fight it."

Fired with the courage of his own convictions and with the backing of his publishers New English Library, who were also named as co-defendants, Herbert girded his loins and prepared to fight. An early victory gave him hope when the case was thrown out of court in America: even the world's most litigious nation seemed to think the whole idea a joke. The Wheels of Justice turned a great deal slower in Britain, however, and it wasn't until March 1979 that the case was finally completed in the High Court, presided over by Mr Justice Brightman for the three-month-long duration.

There were fifty alleged instances of copying, one in the jacket copy and the rest in the prologues. Throughout the case, Herbert maintained that he never saw any reason to change the words: "They were saying exactly what needed to be said." He told the court they were included as a form of historical background, to add credence to his fictional story, and although not central to the plot, they formed an important part of the structure of the novel. He said that he believed Ravenscroft intended his book to be read as a factual account of historical events and that he did no more than repeat certain of those facts.

The pent-up bitterness and venom Herbert feels even now about the way the case was handled is revealed whenever he speaks about it. "I don't trust the law any more, so I am careful about what I say," he explained. "We found out a great deal about Ravenscroft but we couldn't use it in court – the more shady we made the guy seem, the more people would say 'What was I doing using these so-called facts when the guy wasn't the genuine article?' Well, I didn't realise – I thought he was a real professor and it was only later I found out how weird he was. My barrister always maintained that bringing Ravenscroft down in court would get us nowhere: 'Jim,' he said, 'you've done a perfectly natural thing, you've done nothing wrong – and that's the way we're going to play it, straight down the line.'

"I quite honestly think that was our mistake, because the things they said about me in court were terrible. They're very silk-tongued, these guys – that's why they've taken the Silk! – and what they say are things like, *I don't wish to be unkind about, er, Herbert, my Lord, the sort of books he writes are airport books, the characters are cardboard cut-out characters.* This went on day after day. One of the remarks – 'and of course, this chap was in advertising' – even that was a black mark against me."

Even more upsetting to Herbert than the implication that his books had no literary merit whatsoever were the not-so-subtle references to his East End birth and upbringing, a part of his life he has never made the slightest effort to hide or deny.

"It was being implied that this was where the wide boys, the spivs, come from. That got me, more than anything, because I've always been straight, always. I've never been devious, never had to be crooked, and that really hurt me.

"Even in my advertising days, and advertising can be a very

corrupt business, even then, when I was in quite a high-powered position, putting work out all over the place, all the times people came to me with bribes, I just wouldn't have it. A couple of bottles of booze at Christmas to say 'thanks for all the work', that was it, all I would ever touch.

"Yet there I was in court, listening to all this, and you can't touch them, you can't sue *them*. It went on day after day and it was soul-destroying. You think surely the judge can see through all this, but my own brief said to me that the law had less to do with right and wrong than with how the barrister puts over a case and how the judge feels that day. I told him it was a terrible indictment on his profession and he had to agree.

"One day we were in court and my QC said to Ravenscroft, 'You are saying terrible things about Mr Herbert, but you don't know him, you've never spoken to him.' And Ravenscroft turned round and said, 'I *do* know him' – and he was thumping the old witness stand in front of him – and he said, 'I have met Herbert, I was there and he was there.' And the QC said, 'I'm sorry, where? Where were you both?' He was kind of bemused. And Ravenscroft said: 'At the Crucifixion! I was on the right-hand side of Christ and Herbert was on the other side.'

"We all looked at each other and thought, 'Oh God, you *can't* possibly be taking this seriously!' But I think the judge had the impression that he was an eccentric – from any other class, Ravenscroft would have been dismissed as a nutcase, but because of his background, he was eccentric, eccentric but harmless, while this other man, this Herbert chap, who'd made a lot of money from rubbishy books on horror and the supernatural and all that, well, it just shouldn't be allowed.

"Anyway, we showed in court that Ravenscroft himself had copied paragraph after paragraph from other historians like Hugh Trevor-Roper – but *he* wasn't the one on trial, *I* was, and although my brief told the court he was just trying to show that it was quite usual for authors to do this (even if Ravenscroft had gone further than most by copying great chunks), in the end it cut no ice.

"They said they wanted to see everything I had on *The Spear*, all my notes. It was like being raped: they could go through my notebooks in court and see where my daughter, who was only about eight at the time, had drawn little pictures or written little notes and poems. All that was being exposed in court, like an invasion of my privacy. But I gave them everything, all above board, because I'd done nothing wrong and I wanted them to see that.

"Then we asked for Ravenscroft's notes, and would you

believe they were all on a little sailing boat that he had which got shipwrecked and everything was so waterlogged it had to be thrown away? He didn't have one scrap.

"This just dragged on, day after day, just wearing you down. My barrister told my publishers, 'Jim is the best witness for his own case that I've *ever* had' – because I didn't have to lie or be devious. But in the end sheer boredom sets in."

Mr Justice Brightman turned book critic in his summing up. Newspapers as diverse as the *Daily Telegraph* and the *Daily Mail* included the memorable sentences: "One must not under-estimate the commercial attraction of the rubbish I have attempted to describe. The book is written with much inventiveness and a racy flow of language and incident, and the numerous scenes of violence exercise a strong appeal to certain readers."

Mr Justice Brightman went on: "The defendant's novels have enjoyed great financial success. Mr Herbert does not think of himself as a serious novelist."

Herbert added: "He said *The Spear* was about espionage and the supernatural and dead people rising from the grave and that sort of rubbish. To pick up a newspaper and see that quoted is terrible, you know?"

In finding Herbert (and NEL) guilty of infringing Ravenscroft's copyright, Mr Justice Brightman said: "I find as fact that in writing five of the prologues to *The Spear* Mr Herbert made use of *The Spear of Destiny animo furandi*, that is to say, with an intention to take from *The Spear of Destiny* for the purpose of saving himself labour. . .

"In doing so he annexed for his own purposes the skill and labour of the plaintiff to an extent which is not permissible under the law of copyright."

But he did add: "There was no cover-up. The author's note printed on the last page of the text draws attention to the fact that [Herbert] had drawn inspiration from the plaintiff's work, which is referred to by both its title and its authorship. I am satisfied that [Herbert] did not intend to injure the plaintiff and did not appreciate that he was doing so."

"So I lost," Herbert said. "I had to take out the so-called 'facts' from my book. I had these sort of prologues in *The Spear* which contained all the historical bits, and for the paperback, we just took those out, as simple as that."

In spite of – or maybe because of – the instant notoriety Herbert achieved by being plastered across the press as a stealer of words, the hardback (which was, of course, withdrawn) did well and the revised paperback, brought out by New

The man who first struck horror in our hearts with books about menacing rats and a fog which drove people insane has done it again . . . The Spear is violent, creepy, and compulsive reading. Certainly a Spear with an edge to it.

– GEORGE THAW, from "New Nasties Will Give You the Creeps!" *Daily Mirror*, October 16, 1978

[The Spear] contains vintage Herbert scenes with a woman crucified in a London street, a man sent mad by an apparition of death, and the threat of a worldwide holocaust. As ever, the violence makes for compulsive reading – these are the sort of books that once picked up cannot be put down until the last page is read.

– *Greater London & Essex Newspapers*, May 9, 1980

*"Had I given in,
then every writer
would be in
jeopardy from
people like him. It's
a long story, but in
the end we went to
court. He thought
he was going to get
a lot of money but,
in the courtroom,
we had his own
publisher on our
side! At the end of
the day he lost out
far more than I
did. He got some
lines taken out but
he spent so much
on legal fees and
that sort of thing."*

– James Herbert,
from "From Rats to
Riches: The Horror
Fiction of James
Herbert" by Martin
Coxhead, *Fangoria*,
No. 30, October
1983

English Library the following year, went straight to the top of the bestseller's lists.

At the end of the case, Jim's publishers gave him a seventeenth-century cartoon showing two farmers, one pulling the horns of a cow, the other the tail – while the barrister is in the middle milking it, and the judge is presiding over the group, laughing.

"For me, that sums it all up," Jim said. "In the end, you have to force yourself to be philosophical about the whole thing, but I still feel that humiliation, that anger, that bitter injustice. I always thought the law was there to protect people like me, but it's not."

The stress of the court case affected Jim's writing tremendously. He was in the middle of *The Dark* and was continuously having to break off to produce statements and reply to Ravenscroft's solicitors.

"*The Dark* was such a dark, moody book, and I think that is because I was going through hell while I was writing it. There just didn't seem to be any light on the horizon, and I think that comes across more than anything."

Herbert made a conscious decision not to proffer comment on the case: not just because he was upset and furious about it, but because the court had made its decision and he felt it better simply to give the facts and leave others to draw their own conclusions.

*A neo-Nazi cult in
Britain . . . A
woman crucified in
a London street,
and Himmler
resurrected . . .
scenes of vintage
Herbert.*

– *Birmingham
Evening Mail*

"I vividly recall a launch party in Manchester a few months after the trial, a really great do with a lot of media people; even my aunts were there," he said. "Then at the end of the party these three guys came up to me and one asked, 'Well, how do you feel about ripping off Ravenscroft?' I said, 'Wait a minute, it wasn't like that' but he didn't want to listen, he wouldn't hear what I had to say. I lost my rag – I won't tell you what I said to the guy, but he was lucky he got out in one piece. I mean he actually did run out of the room after I'd finished with him! I thought then that was it, people would rather believe the bad than the good, and so I've kept very quiet about the whole episode.

"The lesson I learned, though, was that whatever happens in your life, you just have to get on with your own work, and it's that work that actually gets you through.

"You can't ignore the rest, but you can't let it destroy you. I remember going back down to Sussex after the case was over and I'd lost and I felt devastated. The train was between stations, but I was so agitated I just couldn't sit still, you know? "I walked to the train door and I was just standing there when it swung open, it was like an invitation to jump. There was no apparent reason, the door just swung open and it was so weird, like a voice saying 'Go on, jump!' I remember saying to myself, 'You've got to be fucking joking!' It was bizarre, but the whole thing was bizarre, the most weird experience I've ever had in my life. Maybe old Ravenscroft was trying to send me these vibes, because he was into all these strange things!"

The long arm of the Ravenscrofts reached out even further. Some years later Herbert was enjoying a drink in his local in Henfield, the small village in Sussex where he and his family live, when the landlord introduced him to a stranger.

"The publican said, 'Jim, you're into music, aren't you?' and he introduced me to this great big guy, with wild sort of curly hair, who was sitting drinking with a beautiful blonde girl, looking a bit lost down in the country. So I was introduced to him as 'Jim' and he was introduced as 'Raf' and I found out he'd hired a farmhouse as a studio for six months. We got on really well, we had a really good evening – it was a Friday – and when I left I told him I'd be there Sunday lunchtime if he fancied a drink.

"Then I started to get these premonitions, you know, this strange sort of feeling. I knew Ravenscroft's son played the saxophone, but the more I thought about it, the more I knew I was imagining things. I went back to the pub and I said to the landlord, 'Terry, what was Raf's surname?' He said 'Ravenscroft' and I thought oh, no; I just couldn't believe it . . . At that moment the door opened and in came Raf and he was white. I called him over and he said, 'I know what you're going to say: buy me a pint first!'

"I told Raf his father was pretty low in my esteem, and he said: 'Jim, he is in mine: when I was fourteen I punched his front teeth out!'"

In spite of the hostile background, Herbert and Rafael Ravenscroft, the musician responsible for the haunting sax solo on Gerry Rafferty's *Baker Street*, amongst other things, became fast friends, even collaborating on music which was intended for the BBC's now-shelved project for *Haunted*.

"You think that you are doing something which is unique to you and that no one can interfere with. I stood by my reputation and yet the system gets you every time . . . You may have your own private battles which you win but you can't win the war."

– JAMES HERBERT, from "From Rats to Riches: The Horror Fiction of James Herbert" by Martin Coxhead, *Fangoria*, No. 30, October 1983

Author James Herbert has produced a brutal horror story, as he intended from the start.

– from "The Spear", *Manchester Evening News*, September 21, 1978

MAURICE AND MOG

James Herbert

SIXTEEN

"[The Spear] was aimed against the National Front. They were getting a lot of publicity at the time and their ideas and doctrines were just based on evil and hatred.

"After it was published they were out to get me for a while. I got death threats, the lot. They reckoned I'd given all their little secrets away. The whole thing was a really heavy scene and the thing is that now I don't like The Spear *very much. It holds far too many bad memories for me."*

– JAMES HERBERT, from "From Rats to Riches: The Horror Fiction of James Herbert" by Martin Coxhead, *Fangoria,* No. 30, October 1983

THEY had laughed at him, but who had the last laugh now? Who had survived, who had lived in comfort, confining though it might be, while others had died in agony? Who had foreseen the holocaust years before the Middle East situation finally bubbled over to world conflict? Maurice Joseph Kelp, *that's* who.

Maurice J. Kelp, the insurance agent (who knew better about future-risk?).

Maurice Kelp, the divorcee (no one else to worry about).

Maurice, the loner (no company was more enjoyable than his own).

He had dug the hole in his back garden in Peckham five years ago, much to the derision of his neighbours (who was laughing now, eh? Eh?), big enough to accommodate a large-sized shelter (room enough for four actually, but who wanted other bodies fouling his air, thank you very much). Refinements had been saved for and fitted during those five years, the shelter itself, in kit form, costing nearly £3,000. Accessories such as the hand-and-battery-operated filtration unit (£350 second-hand) and the personal radiation measuring meter (£145 plus £21.75 VAT) had swollen the costs, and fitting extras like the fold-away wash basin and the own-flush toilet had not been cheap. Worth it though, worth every penny.

The prefabricated steel sections had been easy to assemble and the concrete filling-in had been simple enough, once he had read the instruction book carefully. Even fitting the filter and exhaust units had not proved too difficult, when he had fully comprehended what he was supposed to be doing, and the shelter duct connections had proved to be no problem at all. He had also purchased a cheap bilge pump, but mercifully had had no reason to use it. Inside he had installed a bunk bed with foam mattress, a table (the bed was his chair) a heater and Grillogaz cooker, butane gas and battery operated lamps, storage racks filled with tinned and jarred food, dried food, powdered milk, sugar, salt – in all, enough to last him two months. He had a radio with spare batteries (although once below he'd only received crackling noises from it), a medical kit, cleaning utensils, an ample supply of books and magazines (no girlie stuff – he didn't approve of that sort of thing), pencils and paper (including a good stock of toilet paper), strong disinfectants, cutlery, crockery, tin opener, bottle opener, saucepans, candles, clothing, bedding, two clocks (the ticking had nearly driven him crackers for the first few days – he didn't even notice it now), a calendar, and a twelve-gallon drum of water (the water never used for washing dishes, cutlery, or drinking, without his Milton and Maw's Simpla sterilising tablets).

And oh yes, one more recent acquisition: A dead cat.

Just how the wretched animal had got into his tightly-sealed shelter he had no way of knowing (the cat wasn't talking) but he guessed it must have crept in there a few days before the bombs had dropped. Rising tension in world affairs had been enough to spur Maurice into FINAL PREPARATIONS stage (as four or five similar crises had since he'd owned the shelter) and the nosy creature must have sniffed its way in as he, Maurice, had scurried back and forth from house to shelter, leaving open the conning tower hatch (the structure was shaped like a submarine with the conning tower entrance at one end rather than in the middle). He hadn't discovered the cat until the morning after the holocaust.

Maurice remembered the doomsday vividly, the nightmare impressed on to the back of his brain like a finely detailed mural. God, how frightened he'd been! But then, how smug afterwards.

The months of digging, assembling, equipping – enduring the taunts of his neighbours! – had paid off. "Maurice's Ark" they had laughingly called it, and now he realised how apt that description was. Except, of course, it hadn't been built for bloody animals.

He sat bolt upright on the bunk bed, nauseated by the foul smell, but desperate to draw in the thinning air. His face was pale in the glare of the gas lamp.

How many would be alive out there? How many neighbours

had died not laughing? Always a loner, would he now be truly alone? Surprisingly, he hoped not.

Maurice could have let some of them in to share his refuge, perhaps just one or two, but the pleasure of closing the hatch in their panic-stricken faces was too good to resist. With the clunking of the rotary locking mechanism and the hatch airtight-sealed against the ring on the outside flange of the conning tower, the rising and falling sirens had become a barely heard wailing, the sound of his neighbours banging on the entrance lid just the muffled tapping of insects. The booming, shaking, of the earth had soon put a stop to that.

Maurice had fallen to the floor clutching the blankets he had brought in with him, sure that the thunderous pressure would split the metal shell wide open. He lost count of how many times the earth had rumbled and, though he could not quite remember, he felt perhaps he had fainted. Hours seemed to have been lost somewhere, for the next thing he remembered was awaking on the bunk bed, terrified by the heavy weight on his chest and the warm, fetid breath on his face.

He had screamed and the weight was suddenly gone, leaving only a sharp pain across one shoulder. It took long, disorientated minutes to scrabble around for a torch, the absolute darkness pressing against him like heavy drapes, only his imagination illuminating the interior and filling it with sharp taloned demons. The searching torch beam discovered nothing, but the saturating lamp light moments later revealed the sole demon. The ginger cat had peered out at him from beneath the bed with suspicious yellow eyes.

Maurice had never liked felines at the best of times, and they, in truth, had never cared much for him. Perhaps now, at the worst of times (for those up there, anyway) he should learn to get along with them.

"Here, moggy," he had half-heartedly coaxed. "Nothing to be afraid of, old son or old girl, whatever you are." It was a few days before he discovered it was "old girl".

The cat refused to budge. It hadn't liked the thundering and trembling of this room and it didn't like the odour of this man. It hissed a warning and the man's sideways head disappeared from view. Only the smell of food a few hours later drew the animal from cover.

"Oh, yes, typical that is," Maurice told it in chastising tones. "Cats and dogs are always around when they can sniff grub."

The cat, who had been trapped in the underground chamber for three days without food or water or even a mouse to nibble

"Unfortunately The Jonah bombed in the States. It didn't sell very well at all. It might have been because it was too British, dealing with the London Drugs Squad. Also possibly the title, which is London slang for a jinx, someone who brings trouble wherever he goes. Maybe they just didn't understand that."

– JAMES HERBERT, from "From Rats to Riches: The Horror Fiction of James Herbert" by Martin Coxhead, *Fangoria*, No. 30, October 1983

James Herbert's seventh and most horrifying novel yet . . . The Dark follows very much the established James Herbert style with the main plot being punctuated by short personality studies linked to the story.

– Greater London & Essex Newspapers, May 9, 1980

at, felt obliged to agree. Nevertheless, she kept at a safe distance from the man.

Maurice, absorbed more by this situation than the one above, tossed a chunk of tinned stewed meat towards the cat, who started back, momentarily alarmed, before pouncing and gobbling.

"Yes, your belly's overcome your fright, hasn't it?" Maurice shook his head, his smile sneering. "Phyllis used to be the same, but with her it was readies," he told the wolfing, disinterested cat, referring to his ex-wife who had left him fifteen years before after only eighteen months of marriage. "Soon as the pound notes were breathing fresh air she was buzzing round like a fly over a turd. Never stayed long once the coffers were empty, I can tell you. Screwed every last penny out of me, the bloody bitch. Got her deserts now, just like the rest of them!" His laugh was forced, for he still did not know how secure he was himself.

Maurice poured half the meat into a saucepan on the gas burner. "Have the rest later tonight," he said, not sure if he was talking to the cat or himself. Next he opened a small can of beans and mixed the contents in with the cooking meat. "Funny how hungry a holocaust can make you." His laughter was still nervous and the cat looked at him quizzically. "All right, I suppose you'll have to be fed. I can't put you out, that's for sure."

Maurice smiled at his own continued humour. So far he was handling the annihilation of the human race pretty well.

"Let's see, we'll have to find you your own dinner bowl. And something for you to do your business in, of course. I can dispose of it easily enough, as long as you keep it in the same place. Haven't I seen you before somewhere? I think you belonged to the coloured lady two doors along. Well, she won't be looking for you any more. It's quite cosy down here, don't you think? I may as well just call you Mog, eh? Looks like we're going to have to put up with each other for a while . . ."

And so, Maurice J. Kelp and Mog had teamed up to wait out the holocaust.

By the end of the first week, the animal had ceased her restless prowling.

By the end of the second week, Maurice had grown quite fond of her.

By the end of the third week, though, the strain had begun to tell. Mog, like Phyllis, found Maurice a little tough to live with. Maybe it was his weak but sick jokes. Maybe it was his constant nagging. It could have been his bad breath. Whatever,

"I got the idea of The Dark *on a publicity tour. I was in a hotel room and I picked up the Gideon Bible. They've got all these references to darkness – 'The darkness befell the land'. And the thought came to me: what if this darkness wasn't some metaphysical symbolism but was an actual physical entity?"*

– JAMES HERBERT, from "The Darker Side of Fiction" by Victor Olliver, *Woman's Journal,* January 1984

The Dark *is packed with sex, violence, death and evil.*

– QUITA MORGAN, *Bristol Evening Post*

the cat spent a lot of time just staring at Maurice and a considerable amount of time avoiding his stifling embrace.

Maurice soon began to resent the avoidance, unable to understand why the cat was so ungrateful. He had fed her, given her a home! Saved her life! Yet she prowled the refuge like some captive creature, shrinking beneath the bunk bed, staring out at him with baleful, distrusting eyes as if . . . as if . . . yes, as if he were going mad. The look was somehow familiar, in some way reminding him of how . . . of how Phyllis used to stare at him. And not only that, the cat was getting sneaky. Maurice had been awakened in the dead of night more than once by the sound of the cat mooching among the food supplies, biting its way into the dried food packets, clawing through the cling-film capped half-full tins of food.

"When I was writing The Dark, *about halfway through I thought, 'Wait a minute, I've been here before – this is* The Fog, *a re-run!' And what I realised was there was so much left over from* The Fog, *so much to explore in that total madness, that I hadn't finished the book. Plus I was making* The Dark *a 'supernatural' book, adding a lot more to it. So I was actually fulfilling the promise of* The Fog.*"*

– JAMES HERBERT, from "Haunted by Rats" by Dave Hughes, *Skeleton Crew* II, 1988

The last time Maurice had really flipped, really lost control. He had kicked the cat and received a four-lane scratch along his shin in return. If his mood had been different, Maurice might have admired the nimble way Mog had dodged the missiles directed at her (a saucepan, canned fruit – the portable own-flush loo).

The cat had never been the same after that. It had crouched in corners, snarling and hissing at him, slinking around the scant furniture, skulking beneath the bunk bed, never using the plastic litter tray that Maurice had so thoughtfully provided, as though it might be trapped in that particular corner and bludgeoned to death. Or worse.

Soon after, while Maurice was sleeping, Mog had gone on to the offensive.

Unlike the first time when he had woken to find the cat squatting on his chest, Maurice awoke to find fierce claws sinking into his face and Mog spitting saliva at him, hissing in a most terrifying manner. With a screech, Maurice had tossed the manic animal away from him, but Mog had immediately returned to the attack, body arched and puffed up by stiffened fur.

A claw had come dangerously close to gouging out one of Maurice's eyes and an earlobe had been bitten before he could force the animal away from him again.

They had faced each other from separate ends of the bed, Maurice cringing on the floor, fingers pressed against his deeply gashed forehead and cheek (he hadn't yet realised part of his ear was missing), the cat perched on the bedclothes, hunch-backed and snarling, eyes gleaming a nasty yellow.

She came for Maurice again, a streaking ginger blur, a fury of fur, all fangs and sharp-pointed nails. He raised the blankets just in time to catch the cat and screeched as the material tore. Maurice ran when he should have used the restraining bedcovers to his advantage; unfortunately, the area for escape was limited. He climbed the small ladder to the conning tower and crouched at the top (the height was not more than eight feet from hatch to floor), legs drawn up and head ducked against the metal lid itself.

Mog followed and claws dug into Maurice's exposed buttocks. He howled.

Maurice fell, not because of the pain, but because something crashed to the ground above them causing a vibration of seismic proportions to stagger the steel panels of the bunker. He fell and the cat, still clutching his rear end, fell with him. It squealed briefly as its back was broken.

Maurice, still thinking that the wriggling animal was on the attack, quickly picked himself up and staggered towards the other end of the bunker, wheezing air as he went. He scooped up the saucepan from the Grillogaz to defend himself with and looked in open-mouthed surprise at the writhing cat. With a whoop of glee, Maurice snatched up the bedcovers and raced back to the helpless creature. He smothered Mog and thrashed her body with the saucepan until the animal no longer moved and tiny squeals no longer came from beneath the blankets. Then he picked up a flat-bottomed cylinder of butane gas, using both hands to lift it, and dropped it on a bump where he imagined Mog's head to be.

Finally he sat on the bed, chest heaving, blood running from his wounds, and giggled at his triumph.

Then he had to live with the decomposing body for another week.

Not even a triple layer of tightly-sealed polythene bags, the insides liberally dosed with disinfectant, could contain the smell, and not even the chemicals inside the Porta Potti toilet could eat away the carcass. In three days the stench was unbearable. Mog had found her own revenge.

And something else was happening to the air inside the shelter. It was definitely becoming harder to breathe and it wasn't only due to the heavy cat odour. The air was definitely becoming thinner by the day, and lately, by the hour.

Maurice had intended to stay inside for at least six weeks, perhaps eight if he could bear it, all-clear sirens or not; now, with no more than four weeks gone, he knew he would have to risk the outside world. Something had clogged the ventilation system. No matter how long he turned the handle of the Microflow Survivaire equipment for, or kept the motor running from the twelve-volt car battery, the air was not replenished. His throat made a thin wheezing noise as he sucked in, and the stink cloyed at his nostrils as if he were immersed in the deepest, foulest sewer. He had to have good, clean air, radiation packed or not; otherwise he would die a different sort of slow death. Asphyxiation accompanied by the mocking smell of the dead cat was no way to go. Besides, some pamphlets said fourteen days was enough for fallout to have dispersed.

Maurice rose from the bed and clutched at the small table, immediately dizzy. The harsh white glare from the butane gas lamp stung his red-rimmed eyes. Afraid to breathe and more afraid not to, he staggered towards the conning tower. It took all his strength to climb the few rungs of the ladder and he rested just beneath the hatch, head swimming, barely inflated lungs protesting. Several moments passed before he was able to raise an arm and jerk open the locking mechanism.

Thank God, he thought. Thank God I'm getting out, away from the evil sodding ginger cat. No matter what it's like out there, no matter who or what else has survived, it would be a blessed relief from this bloody stinking shithouse.

He allowed the hatch to swing down on its hinge. Powdered dust covered his head and shoulders, and when he had blinked away the tiny grains from his eyes, he uttered a weak cry of dismay. He now understood the cause of the crash just a week before: the remains of a nearby building, undoubtedly his own house, had finally collapsed. And the rubble had covered the ground above him, blocking his air supply, obstructing his escape exit.

His fingers tried to dig into the concrete slab, but hardly marked the surface. He pushed, he heaved, but nothing shifted. Maurice almost collapsed down the ladder, barely able to keep his feet at the bottom. He wailed as he stumbled around the bunker looking for implements to cut through the solid wall above, the sound rasping and faint. He used knives, forks, anything with a sharp point to hammer at the concrete, all to no avail, for the concrete was too strong and his efforts too weak.

He finally banged dazedly at the blockage with a bloodied fist.

Maurice fell back into what was now a pit and howled his frustration. Only the howl was more like a wheeze, the kind a cat might make when choking.

The plastic-covered bundle at the far end of the shelter did not move but Maurice, tears forcing rivulets through the dust on his face, was sure he heard a faint, derisory *meow*.

"Never liked cats," he panted. "Never."

"With Shrine I've taken children's poems, but the really nasty ones, and they are all through the book before each chapter . . . I picked out the nastiest I could find, and that was just to say to the people who knock me for violence and horror, look, this has been happening for years. I'm not doing anything worse than what's in these old poems and nursery rhymes. Kids were brought up on these and I'm not doing anything different."

– JAMES HERBERT, from "From Rats to Riches: The Horror Fiction of James Herbert" by Martin Coxhead, *Fangoria*, No. 30, October 1983

Maurice sucked his knuckles, tasting his own blood, and waited in his private, self-built tomb. It was only a short time to wait before shadows crept in on his vision and his lungs became flat and still, but it seemed an eternity to Maurice. A lonely eternity, even though Mog was there to keep him company.

ILLUSTRATIONS BY JAMES HERBERT

Scenes of Petticoat Lane drawn for National Diploma of Design Thesis

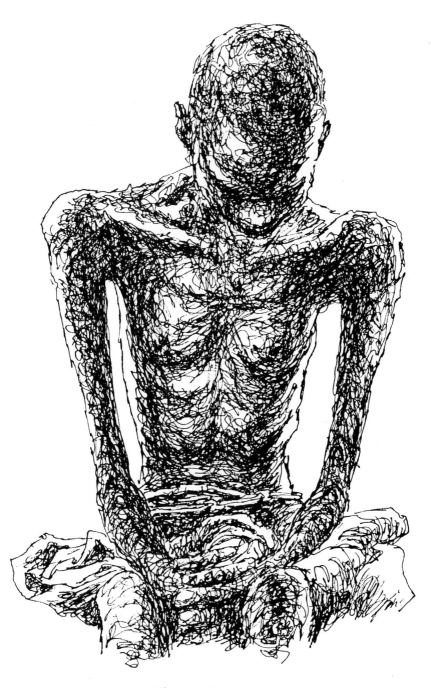

FAMINE

View from study window ~ 24th May 1991

Keith Richard
of The Rolling Stones
1992

Extract from James Herbert's storyboard for his graphic novel, The City, *to be published in 1993*

JAMES HERBERT AND SCIENCE FICTION

Michael A. Morrison

SEVENTEEN

The Technicolor descriptions of the agony and fear brought to a village by an innocent deaf-mute child linger long after the book has been read . . . It would be advisable to get someone to hold your hand while you read this book.

– GILL ELLIS, *Huddersfield Daily Examiner*, February 10, 1983

I N 1818 Mary Shelley inaugurated modern science fiction with a novel of Gothic horror. *Frankenstein* shares with predecessors such as Horace Walpole's *The Castle of Otranto* (1765) the aesthetics of the British Gothic. But its premise is scientific rather than supernatural; to readers in the early nineteenth century, the idea that a sufficiently gifted (albeit neurotic) scientist could use the power of galvanism to imbue a patchwork corpse with life seemed credible, if unlikely.

Later in the nineteenth century, Robert Louis Stevenson contributed to the genre his enormously influential novella *The Strange Case of Dr Jekyll and Mr Hyde* (1886). By combining in a single character the rational scientist, soon to be the protagonist of countless SF stories, and the psychopathic intuitive, soon to be the antagonist of innumerable horror tales, Stevenson created a true archetype of SF-horror: Jekyll/Hyde, the scientist/monster.

Shelley and Stevenson thus begat two of the three major icons of modern horror fiction, identified by Stephen King in *Danse Macabre* (1981) as "the Vampire, the Werewolf, and the Thing Without a Name". Only the vampire sprang from works of pure horror – Bram Stoker's *Dracula* (1897) and its fictional predecessor, John Polidori's *The Vampyre* (1819) – and even that myth received a science fiction gloss in Brian Stableford's alternate history *The Empire of Fear* (1988). The beast-man and the nameless monster first appeared in these progenitorial works of SF-horror.

Now, a century later, the marriage between the modes of

138   MICHAEL A. MORRISON

science fiction and horror is still alive. But its course has ne'er been smooth. A scan of the literary and cinematic landscape since the early nineteenth century reveals precious few works that manage to preserve their identity as science fiction and to engender real fear: a handful of short stories by Fritz Leiber, Richard Matheson, Theodore Sturgeon, Charles Beaumont, and Harlan Ellison; a few novels, from H. G. Wells' *The War of the Worlds* (1898) and *The Island of Dr Moreau* (1896) to more recent works such as *The Clone* (1965) by Theodore Thomas and Kate Wilhelm and *The Puppet Masters* (1951) by Robert A. Heinlein; a scattering of films, such as Ridley Scott's *Alien* (1979) and David Cronenberg's *The Fly* (1986); and, perhaps most successful of all, the Quatermass plays of Nigel Kneale, which are best known in their film versions as *The Quatermass Experiment* (1955), *Quatermass II* (1957), and *Quatermass and the Pit* (1967). But these are exceptions. Typically, the creators of science fiction choose to ignore (or fail to realise) the intrinsically horrific potential of many of their plots and motifs.

Perhaps the failure of most SF-horror tales is not that surprising. As critic Brian Stableford has noted, science fiction incorporates a worldview based on a rational, methodical approach to solving problems and resolving crises – hardly the stuff of horror. To be sure, fear is very much a part of the SF aesthetic, which in some works depicts a cosmos as malign as that of H. P. Lovecraft. But in true SF, fear is subordinate to reason: that's what makes John W. Campbell's 1938 story "Who Goes There?" science fiction and John Carpenter's 1982 film adaptation *The Thing* (itself a remake of a 1951 Howard Hawkes film) horror. Typically, the creators of horror strive not for clarification but for incertitude; not for wonder, but for dread.

James Herbert writes at the far extreme of the SF-horror continuum. Few readers think of his novels as linked to science fiction. But consider what happens in his books: radiation-induced mutants run amok, nuclear holocaust reduces civilisation to a wasteland, ordinary people must come to grips with newly developed or hitherto repressed extra-sensory powers, an accident of nature releases a man-made bacteriological scourge that threatens the world, and a scientist animates evil itself, spawning a formless entity that ravages England. Although these novels don't *read* like science fiction, the paraphernalia of SF clearly play some kind of role in them. Some critics have described (or dismissed) them as pulp thrillers. True, Herbert does write in the pulp tradition; but his novels are more than mere pulp horror stories decked out with pseudo-scientific trappings.

"The village is based on Henfield. And the pub I talk about is the one I use. The churches all exist, in fact, all the locations exist . . . I suppose evil in Sussex is the same as anywhere else. But I think it's true that Sussex was the last pagan place in Britain. They were the last to be converted to Christianity."

– JAMES HERBERT, from "Better the Devil You Know" by Kathryn Bailey, *Brighton Evening Argus*, January 28, 1983

More than any other genre the horror story seems to show up every stylistic blemish and to make creaking plots groan. James Herbert is one writer who can make horror exciting and believable, moving confidently between the everyday world and the unknown as he does in Shrine.

– From "Taste of Horror", *Western Daily Press*, February 4, 1983

Sometimes Herbert tantalises us with a science fictional conceit, then opts for the supernatural. At one point in *Shrine* (1983) he hints that the visions and miraculous cure of eleven-year-old deaf mute Alice Pagett may herald her evolution into a superbeing with psychic powers. In *Lair* (1979), he gives hero Lucas Pender, who must venture into a 6000-acre nature reserve to investigate an outbreak of mutant rats, the profession of entomologist. And in *Sepulchre*, he assigns hero Liam Halloran the job of protecting Felix Kline, who has been adopted as house psychic by the rapacious Magma Corporation because his telepathic talents include the ability to find vast deposits of rare minerals. But Herbert shapes *Shrine* into a novel of possession and metempsychosis, *Lair* into a straightforward man-versus-monster story, and *Sepulchre* into a blend of spy thriller and occult horror story.

So even when Herbert appropriates premises, motifs, and metaphors from science fiction, he uses the aesthetic and narrative strategies of horror fiction to mould these elements into contemporary thrillers. His primary narrative, the skeleton of nearly all these books, tells of a solitary hero who confronts a supernatural/paranormal threat at a moment of crisis or disaster for his community and who, after overcoming personal limitations that usually stem from repressed guilt, uses instinct and intuition to restore that community to a shaky status quo. He fleshes out this frame with scenes of interpersonal confrontations and vivid violence. The latter vignettes are practically trademarks of his fiction – long, lovingly detailed descriptions of mayhem and mutilation that variously evoke terror, horror, or revulsion.

Thematically, too, Herbert's novels reflect views about the physical universe, human community, and human nature that typify modern horror. The universe according to James Herbert is no friend to man; at times nature seems to conspire with human wickedness and the techno-horrors of an abused science to bring down the human species. Like nature, groups – especially organised religion and government – are precarious at best, pernicious at worst. Usually the scientific/military establishment poses as great a threat to his heroes and heroines as do his spectacular supernatural or man-made monsters. But he also questions the value of the communities on behalf of which his heroes act. Typically, these men are isolated from their communities, either by their profession (Liam Halloran in *Sepulchre*), by reputation (James Kelso in *The Jonah*), or by unique psychic abilities (Jon Childers in *Moon*), or all three (David Ash in *Haunted*). Heroes they may be, but like all Herbert's

MICHAEL A. MORRISON

characters, they are essentially human animals, self-victimising and inherently corrupt. Herbert vivifies this conservative, essentially Christian theology, based on original sin and universal guilt, more intensely than any other modern horror writer. These characteristics appear in Herbert's second novel *The Fog*, achieve full flower in one of his best novels *The Dark*, and assume their most extreme form in his most recent work of SF-horror, *Domain*.

The Fog is the very model of a major modern techno-monster. Spawned by ill-conceived bacteriological weapons research and later accidentally released when army weapons tests (of bombs, not bacteria) trigger an earthquake near the village in Wiltshire, the Fog is a "mutated mycoplasma" wrapped in a shroud of poison gas. Like the killer clouds of the SF ecocatastrophes depicted by Philip Wylie in *The End of the Dream* (1972) and John Brunner in *The Sheep Look Up* (1972), it carries symbolic weight and man-made virulence of smog. For one thing, the Fog feasts on carbon dioxide and industrial pollution. For another, Herbert makes explicit his novel's eco-doom theme via an incidental character, a soldier named Ray Evans, who explains that the Fog

> [has] got something to do with the pollution, I reckon. It's like those rivers where they've found thousands of dead fish, all because the bleedin' factories have dumped their rubbish into them. Well, this time somebody's dumped something into the air, y'see, gas or chemicals. I dunno what, but it's got out of hand. Like one of those 'orror films.

Out of hand indeed. The mycoplasma is a cellular parasite that invades the mind where it breaks down healthy brain cells and replaces them with "new, parasitical cells". Immersion in the Fog leads to "complete and utter mental breakdown" manifested as insanity and uncontrolled violence. Many of the Fog's victims ultimately commit suicide; the others are left "vegetable[s], capable of no action at all".

As one would expect in a work of techno-disaster, the Fog is the creation of a mad scientist. But although Prof. Broadmeyer, who fifteen years earlier bred the beast, is hardly the sort of man you or I would put in charge of a mycoplasma, mutated or otherwise, in the understated description of Chief Scientific Adviser Hermann Ryker, he emerges as less evil than maladroit:

Broadmeyer was a brilliant man . . . but he was, what shall we say, a little irresponsible . . . He was careless and allowed himself to be exposed to the mycoplasma. Naturally, he went mad. And in his madness he destroyed all his papers, notes, the work of years, not just on the mutated mycoplasma, but other projects, more admirable conceptions, completely and utterly wasted. He died a lunatic, a victim of his own creation, and with him he took many secrets.

Although hardly flattering, this view of the scientist is considerably more balanced and tolerant than Herbert's portrait of Boris Pryszlak, the depraved power-mad scientist of *The Dark*.

The real villain of *The Fog* is not science but the government, "the great, faceless *they*". As in most of his novels, Herbert here excoriates the banal but baneful ineptitude of the technocratic establishment, as though to suggest that the mere congregation of humans in organisations endowed with political or social power brings out the most foul traits of the species. In its irresponsible decision to create so destructive a weapon, then in the inept decision that leads to its release, the military acts out the self-destructiveness that the victims of the Fog mirror in their individual behaviour.

As it roams first the English countryside, then the streets of London, the Fog sunders the bonds of community. Under its noxious influence, love, friendship, and moral order give way to savagery and "the subconscious will for self-destruction every mind possesses, hidden deep down in the darkest recesses of the brain, but always ready to be brought to the surface". This view of human nature as innately self-destructive prefigures the more extreme vision of later novels such as *Shrine* and *The Dark*.

Herbert leaves ambiguous the precise ontological status of the Fog. At times, it seems almost alive, as when it reappears from underground "as though it had been lying in wait, mustering its forces, waiting for its new ally, the north-east wind". Later Herbert teases us with the fascinating possibility that the mycoplasma may have mutated into an intelligent entity. As protagonist John Holman, made immune through a near-fatal early exposure to the Fog, wanders the Fog-enshrouded streets of London in search of the nucleus of the mycoplasma, he wonders, "Could it possibly be self-motivated? It was an incredible idea and he tried to dismiss it from his mind. It was too fantastic, too much like science fiction." But, like Holman, Herbert dismisses the notion, which soon gets lost amidst

MICHAEL A. MORRISON

the violence and carnage that accompany the Fog's tour of London.

At first glance, *The Dark* seems a mere re-working of materials from *The Fog* – a formless evil entity drifts about England transforming citizens into killing machines. But *The Dark*, which at times echoes the SF-horror plays of Nigel Kneale, is both a more complex merger of SF motifs and the aesthetics of horror and a more extreme rendering of the themes of guilt, human nature, and the abuse of science. Even as horror, *The Dark* is a fascinating hybrid, containing essential elements of the traditions of both nineteenth- and twentieth-century horror fiction: quite traditional in its central good-versus-evil story, which is laden with religious overtones, it also portrays a very modern universe, one inimical (or, at best, indifferent) to man, where uncontrollable anarchic forces threaten a shaky social order whose roots are too rotten to stand up to the onslaught.

The Dark is a novel of dualities. Its primary conflict at the level of character is scientist versus scientist: parapsychologist and psychic investigator Chris Bishop versus power-mad scientist/industrialist Boris Pryszlak. But Herbert structures the novel less around this conflict than around thematic oppositions of good versus evil (light versus dark), the individual versus the establishment, and science versus mysticism (paranormal versus supernatural).

Each of the focal characters of *The Dark* espouses one or the other polarity of one or more of these oppositions. At a library lecture early in the novel, Chris Bishop explains that "parapsychology – the study of paraphysical phenomena – uses technology rather than the more unreliable and, if I may say so, the dubious spiritualist methods. Graph paper will usually tell you more about strange disturbances in a house than self-imposed mental trances." Bishop, an ardent adherent of "practical scientific reasoning", would replace the supernatural with the paranormal, dispense with religion, and secularise the soul. For him mysticism "is just tomorrow's science dreamed today". This tension continues throughout the novel, which at times echoes other thrillers about parapsychology and mysticism, such as Frank DeFelitta's *Golgotha Falls* (1984) and John Farris' *Son of the Endless Night* (1985). But, as usual, Herbert offers a quite original variation on this theme.

Protagonist Bishop belongs to the distinguished fictional fraternity of rationalist ghost hunters that includes John Montague of Shirley Jackson's *The Haunting of Hill House* (1959) and Lionell Barrett of Richard Matheson's *Hell House* (1971). But

[Shrine is] the latest offering from the talented Mr Herbert, whose skill at casually planting ideas into the reader's mind keeps you enthralled from start to finish . . . suddenly all the pieces fall together and the real horror appears, written in a way that will keep you reading until the very last word.

– Peterborough Evening Telegraph, January 28, 1984

Bishop is even less sympathetic than they are to the possibility of the supernatural. His view of ghosts is, to say the least, reductive: "a scientific phenomena," he proposes, "brain waves . . . telepathic images . . . electrical impulses . . ."

Bishop and his mentor Jacob Kulek, a shadowy figure who heads the London-based Research Institute for Parapsychological Study, exemplify one type of scientist in *The Dark*. Opposed to them is Boris Pryszlak, a man so evil that he appears even to the casual observer as "a son of the devil". With Bishop, Pryszlak carries the burden of the science-versus-religion theme. But Bishop, disillusioned by the injustice of his daughter's death and his wife's subsequent descent into madness, has just adopted atheism. Pryszlak was out to do in God:

. . . For him, science was the key to mankind's salvation, not religion. Disease and deprivation were being overcome by technology, not by prayer. Our economic and social advances were achieved by science. The decision to create new life was now our own; even the gender of the newborn would one day be decided by ourselves. Death itself, if not entirely thwarted, could at least be delayed . . . Pryszlak claimed that one day we would even discover scientifically . . . how, in fact, we were not created by a mystical someone, but created ourselves. We would prove by science that there is no God.

Actually, Pryszlak is present in *The Dark* only in spirit, so to speak, since by the time of the novel he has been long dead. But his "ethereal force", not to mention a horde of evil disciples, lives on, continuing his mad quest.

The focus of that quest is Pryszlak's fascination with "the study of energy", but his goal is not knowledge but power – the power of "the evil lurking in every human soul". Pryszlak's view of evil is nothing if not pragmatic:

Pryszlak believed [evil] was a physical energy field within our mind and, just as we were learning to use our psi faculties – energies such as telekinesis, extra-sensory perception, telepathy, telergy – so we could learn to use physically this other power.

In order to gain control of this power, Pryszlak and members of his secret sect killed themselves and in so doing somehow "became" the energy of evil.

The evil that Boris Pryszlak has become is now loose as *The Dark*:

MICHAEL A. MORRISON

[The Dark] was as old as the world itself. It was a power that had existed even before human life, a dark power that man had allied himself with from the beginning. Now it dwelt in man. It had always been there, the darkness where evil lurked, the darkness that bestial things crept in, the darkness waiting for man to give himself up completely to it. And now was the time.

The Dark is a physical force, a formless, predatory shadow that feeds on pain, mutilation, and death. Like the Fog, it dehumanises its victims by transforming them into zombie-like killing machines. Targeting "people who were in some way mentally disturbed, whether they were criminals, insane, or . . . had evil in their minds", the Dark absorbs that evil as a vampire does blood and leaves behind "empty shells" stripped of all motivation except a limp affinity for darkness.

The Dark is a masterful conception: an entity distinctly anterior to man yet constituted solely of evil "derived from man alone". In Herbert's rather Catholic conception, it is man's "moral wickedness" – "the unclean force that was in every man, woman, and child" – externalised as rapacious monster. In the Dark Herbert deftly combines the dual representations of evil that have dominated horror fiction for the past two centuries: the forms King calls "outside evil" (Satan, Dracula, Godzilla) and "inside evil" (Norman Bates, the Werewolf). This dualism is essential to the novel's central conceit: to treat as literal the mythic associations of good with light and evil with darkness. Just as Boris Pryszlak is allied with and becomes darkness, so Jacob Kulek (who dies late in the novel) metamorphoses in the book's climax into the power of Light.

Most horror fiction externalises the archetypal war between good and evil into a conflict between symbolically resonant forces external to the mind. But like such overtly science-fictional works as James Blish's *Black Easter* (1968) and *The Day After Judgment* (1971), *The Dark* dramatises this conflict in the context and language of contemporary science. "Perhaps," Kulek speculates, "the biblical concept of the constant battle between Light and Darkness is a true scientific concept. Whatever energy light-rays contain, be they from the sun or artificial, it may be that they counteract or negate the catalytic qualities of darkness."

The words energy and power recur throughout *The Dark*, becoming its dominant metaphor for evil. This association gains its full force at the climax, as Herbert deftly interweaves the novel's various dualities. By now the best efforts of science,

Shrine, *at 430 pages, is Herbert's longest book to date: sadly the story does not justify such length . . . Herbert's writing has matured greatly since his early gross novels and the description of people flocking to see Alice, to witness a miracle, is vivid and convincing . . .*

– PHILIP COLLINS, from *British Fantasy Newsletter*, Vol. 11, No. 4, April–May 1984

I rate Shrine *Herbert's most accomplished novel to date. The build-up to the horrifying climax is subtle and sophisticated.*

– PETER GROSVENOR, from "Thrills and Chills Galore from Best-Seller Herbert", *Daily Express*, January 29, 1983 individually in the person of Chris Bishop and collectively in a team led by a pompous popinjay named Prof. Marinker, have failed to combat or even contact the Dark. It is left for the mystical intervention of the spirit of Jacob Kulek, reborn as a "blinding white light", to cast out the darkness. In an explanatory afterword Chris Bishop, who has been rendered blind but telepathic by witnessing the confrontation, explains Kulek's transformation:

> Jacob had found himself among an awesome realm of energies, a new dimension that was partly of this world [where] others awaited him. He had become part of them, joined the flow that never ceased growing, moving, yet which, again in our terms, had no reality; and eventually a part of that flow was allowed to return to its beginnings and combat an opposite energy that threatened its embryo. We are that embryo. The Dark is that opposite energy. The Light is the power we will become.

For many readers the name James Herbert brings to mind giant mutant rats. This association is a bit unfair, for it overlooks the range and diversity of his work. Yet of all his novels, *The Rats* (1974), *Lair* (1979) and *Domain* (1985) best show his characteristic blend of SF motifs, pulp plotting, and naturalistic description.

In this century, science fiction stories in which mankind is menaced by enlarged or otherwise mutated creatures date from as early as H. G. Wells' *The Food of the Gods* (1904). This rather limited sub-species of the techno-horror tale attained a kind of zenith in the 1930s, when John Taine, Jack Williamson, Edmund Hamilton, and many another writer filled the pages of the pulps with technologically induced mutant monsters. Nowadays, the strain in SF is dying out – although as recently as 1963 Australian SF writer A. Bertram Chandler unleashed giant rats in his largely (and justly) forgotten *The Hamelin Plague*. Closer to horror fiction is Hugh Sykes Davies' *The Papers of Andrew Melmoth* (1960), which bears a thematic resemblance to Herbert's novels but is far more introspective and subdued.

Remarkably, the mutant rat novel has reappeared in the mainstream. Surely the strangest entries in this odd literary sub-genre are William Kontzwinkle's award-winning 1976 fable *Dr Rat*, in which the title creature, a victim of laboratory experiments, leads a revolt of the animals; and Gunter Grass' 1987 dream fantasy *The Rat*, in which the protagonist, a grey-brown sewer rat, narrates a fervid, polemical tale of the aftermath of

"With Shrine *I went to my local priest for information and I told him, 'Look, I'm going to knock the Catholic Church, but I hope that it will be okay in the end, and I'll say, yes, there is something out there that's good.' But I told the priest, 'I don't know if I can do that. I never know the endings of my books. I'm trying to go somewhere and I don't know if I'll reach it.' And very fairly he said, 'Jim, that's up to you and your conscience.' So the book knocks religion, it knocks commercialism, but at the end there is something good out there."*

– JAMES HERBERT, from "James Herbert: Growing Up in Public" by Neil Gaiman, *Gaslight & Ghosts* (1988)

MICHAEL A. MORRISON

a nuclear holocaust that strips the earth of humankind.

Unlike these books, *The Rats* and *Lair* are essentially well-crafted pulp thrillers. But in tone they recall not so much their literary antecedents as the American giant-critter films of the fifties – those now-beloved live-action cartoons that featured huge rampaging insects, reptiles, crustaceans, etc. More often than not, these films, which were really horror films masquerading as science fiction, blamed the gigantism of their title monster on technology gone berserk. In Jack Arnold's 1955 film *Tarantula*, for example, mad scientist Leo G. Carroll experiments with an "atomically stabilised" artificial nutrient and inadvertently provokes the excessive growth of the eponymous arachnid; and in Bert I. Gordon's far sillier *The Cyclops* (1957) high-level ground radiation somehow spawns a clutch of farcical overgrown animals. Although these films lack the subtext of social criticism that distinguishes Herbert's novels, they have the same wacky energy, straightforward characterisations and glorious effects.

The first two of these qualities, however, are missing from Herbert's third mutant-rat novel. In *Domain* Herbert appropriates one of the most venerable of SF story types, the post-holocaust survival tale. Some time in the near future, fighting in the Middle East and an invasion of Iran by the Soviet Union precipitate The War. One fine June day the bombs fall, reducing London to a ruin of smashed concrete and twisted metal:

> The familiar London landscape, with its tall buildings, both old and new, its skyscraper towers, the ancient church steeples, its old, instantly recognisable landmarks, no longer existed. Many buildings still stood, but not in their entirety . . . Fires raged everywhere . . . The skies overhead were black, a vast turbulent cloud hanging low over the city. A spiralling column, the hated symbol of the holocaust, climbed into the cloud, a white stem full of unnatural forces.

Herbert excels at this kind of description, and *Domain* is filled with vivid evocations of the post-holocaust wasteland.

Bombs and radiation kill almost everyone. Stumbling through the shattered remains of civilisation, a few survivors try to cope with the usual aftereffects of a fictional holocaust: lack of food and medicine, disease, radiation sickness, psychological trauma, fires, collapsing buildings, shock, moral breakdown – and, as if this were not enough, a plague of intelligent giant mutant rats.

Black-furred, ravenous for human flesh and brains, and at

Herbert is one of the few writers who seem unaffected by the general shrinkage in the horror market; this one has an initial print run of 25,000 . . . Hodder's publicity director Tony Hammond says that with Shrine, *Herbert has shifted his emphasis. Although undeniably a horror story, it is also "a novel in its own right. Herbert is developing into more than a horror writer, and we plan to broaden his base and his readership."*

– from "Herbert Holds on with Horror", *Bookseller*, December 18, 1982

Jeffrey Archer and James Herbert (circa 1991)

Denis Healey and James Herbert at a literary lunch (circa 1989)

James Herbert signs a book for actress Rula Lenska (circa 1984)

James Herbert interviewed by Brian Hayes on LBC News Radio (circa 1987)

least as cunning as their prey, the rats are hostile nature incarnate. Yet, like the Fog and the Dark, they owe their existence to the hand of man. It was not natural evolution but peacetime atomic tests off New Guinea that triggered their mutation. And, as the Fog feeds on industrial pollution and the Dark on human evil, so do the rats thrive on radiation that is lethal to humans.

Early in the novel Herbert cleverly inverts the traditional geometric iconography of apocalyptic fiction by providing an apparent refuge from the hell above ground in a bunker below. Steve Culver, who was formerly a helicopter pilot in London on business, and Alex Dealey, formerly a minor minion of Her Majesty's government, retreat to a well-provisioned government deep shelter in the Kingsway Telephone Exchange where they join a handful of other survivors. But in Herbert's world no place is safe, sanctuary is mere façade. Events soon force Culver and the others to abandon their shelter and to return to the devastated ground above, a landscape of immanent, implacable, unpredictable menace. And so begins their picaresque odyssey through hell.

Domain plays out the final conflict between man and beast, the battle for "the chastised planet" that serves as omnipresent symbol of man's iniquity. Indeed, in this novel Herbert's themes of the universal guilt and shared culpability of humankind overwhelm even the degradations of the rats. Unlike the survivors of conventional post-holocaust SF narratives, no one in *Domain* is innocent. Stumbling through rubble littered with decaying corpses, the survivors of the war cannot shake their awareness that the race itself bears responsibility for the destruction of the planet. Steve Culver rages, in terms we've heard before from Herbert, at the holocaust as "the stark face of ultimate evil, the carnage of man's own sickness! The destructive force that was centuries old and inherent in every man, woman, and child!"

Its depressing theme and seemingly endless graphic depictions of brutality and carnage make *Domain* Herbert's bleakest novel. Even in the broader context of post-holocaust fiction, a literature not known for cheerfulness or hope, *Domain* holds primacy of place as the most horrifying, despairing, and oppressive post-holocaust tale in or out of science fiction.

For all James Herbert's use in *The Fog, The Dark, Domain,* and other novels of motifs from SF, it would be a mistake to overstate their importance. Herbert writes on the fringes of the venerable SF-horror tradition, and most of his novels bear at most a peripheral relationship to science fiction. What is most interesting about those novels that do incorporate SF motifs is

As the author of The Rats, The Fog, *and* The Dark, *Herbert can probably be held responsible for launching – however unintentionally – a whole new subgenre, known in the trade as "nasties". These are books in which the emphasis is on graphic violence and vividly described scenes of visceral horror: no subtle chills, gradual suspense, or distantly fluttering ghosts in these books, but rather a full-frontal assault in which rats (or, in the imitations, crabs or cats or swarms of insects) eat people's screaming faces in bleeding Technicolor.*

– LISA TUTTLE, from "Bloody Good Storyteller", *The Twilight Zone Magazine*, Vol. 4 No. 5, November/ December 1984 how he uses the aesthetics and style of horror fiction, largely those of the late pulp era, to create contemporary morality tales about ordinary people brought face to face with vehemently evil forces. Each of these stories contains a central image which seems to focus their power. Whatever the nature of the catastrophe – ecological disaster, nuclear apocalypse, or wickedness freed by science from its habitat in the human mind – the image of hostile nature (or supernature), enlarged by technological misadventures, political irresponsibility and human evil, laying waste to the works of man resonates beyond the covers of Herbert's novels, assuming the power of a modern myth.

THE DARK DOMAIN

John Fraser

EIGHTEEN

ANYONE who has even a passing acquaintance with horror fiction will have heard the name James Herbert. With *The Rats*, his first novel, he established himself as a one-man industry, spawning a whole sub-genre of "nasties" in which numerous lesser writers attempted to out-shock each other with graphic scenes of helpless victims being eaten alive by mutant creatures from rats to killer crabs.

But Herbert has moved on since then. In subsequent novels such as *Fluke, The Magic Cottage*, and *The Spear* he has proved that he can successfully transcend the popular conceptions of the genre to merge the occult with fantasy, the thriller, or mainstream fiction. His twelve books have now sold over 17 million copies; he has probably been more widely imitated than any other writer. Indeed, his status is such that the ultimate accolade for a new writer is to be hailed as "the new James Herbert".

And yet, perhaps because of his mass appeal, he has been largely ignored by the serious press.

When Herbert's latest novel, *Sepulchre*, was published, I took up the courage to meet face to face the man who has terrified more readers than almost any other writer, apart from Stephen King.

I was asked to go to The Ritz, a hotel which everyone has heard of but where few can ever afford to stay. He was late, and as I waited I peered anxiously into the enormous, elegant lounge, wondering who was going to pay for the drinks.

When he entered, I recognised him immediately. James

[Moon] is well written and will appeal to those who enjoy such subjects. Some sections of the book I found entertaining, but some of the narrative is, to me, too descriptive and horrific to bear the label of entertainment.

– H.W., from "Refuge from the Terrors of His Past", *Guernsey Evening Press and Star*, August 31, 1985

Herbert is one of the few horror writers to actually look like a horror writer: a short, stooping figure with long black hair, dressed in a black suit, and with a mischievous glint in his eye.

"You haven't come all the way from Liverpool to see me, have you?"

"Yes," I admitted. And I was glad I had. For Jim spent almost an hour with me, talking with a quiet confidence, as though we'd known each other for years. Sometimes you got the impression he'd said it all before, but no matter. I had got what I wanted: an exclusive interview.

Herbert's thirteenth novel, *Sepulchre*, is an extremely complex blend of horror and thriller fiction which also deals with some pretty serious issues – torture, concentration camps, cannibalism; the book moves relentlessly from one graphic scene to another, with very little light relief. Its hero, Halloran, an ex-SAS man, is assigned to protect Kline, who lives in a house that is hidden away in a small valley and holds a dark secret. Kline has psychic abilities which he applies to detecting new mineral resources for a multinational corporation. Inevitably, there are those out to discover his secret, and Halloran gradually becomes aware of this man's strange and unique capabilities.

"You can read the book on any level you choose," says Herbert. "As an adventure thriller, a horror story, or a morality play." In contrast to most horror novels, the good-versus-evil aspect is not so clear-cut, since its hero, Halloran, has a vicious streak and is used to defeat a greater evil. The reader discovers why Halloran needs to do what he does at the end of the novel. He is redeemed but, ironically, only by doing something wicked.

"For me that was interesting, a challenge not to have good against evil but something less evil against a greater evil. That's why I start the book with the premise that there are no absolutes. No absolute good, no absolute evil."

Even Felix Kline, one of Herbert's best villains, fails because he's not absolutely evil. He grows weary of himself. It's a subtle story that demands the reader's full attention and is perhaps Herbert's bleakest, with some superbly orchestrated scenes, such as the sacrifice of a young kidnap victim, the old house guarded by fearsome jackals, the lodge with its unseen occupant, and many more.

Herbert's previous book, *The Magic Cottage*, was a complete contrast – a haunted house tale told with a refreshing lightness, a subtle exploration of the characters' relationship with each other and with the rambling old cottage they move into.

"I had a sequence at the beginning [of Moon] with a murder and a body being cut up, and I wrote this chapter in detail explaining what arteries had to be cut, what muscles to slice to take certain things out . . . but I didn't like it. It was too specific. And for the first time in my life I rewrote a chapter. It's still horrific, just a bit more vague. And it works, I think, the better for it."

– JAMES HERBERT, from "James Herbert: Growing Up in Public" by Neil Gaiman, *Gaslight & Ghosts* (1988)

The cottage is bought by Mike Stringer and his girlfriend Midge, who want to escape the city life; he's a musician, she's an artist. At first the tranquillity of the cottage and its surrounding woods inspires them. But gradually they come to see the place in a far more sinister light. Cracks in the walls mysteriously repair themselves; bats lurk in the loft; injured animals heal miraculously; and the place has a strange atmosphere that increasingly dominates the narrative. The cottage becomes a focus for psychic energy, which a nearby cult, the Synergists, exploit to the full. Over the last hundred pages or so a psychic battle is waged between the cult's mysterious leader and the occupants of the cottage.

Unlike many horror novels the pace is slow, suspense achieved more through a careful depiction of atmosphere and the characters' experiences. It couldn't be a greater contrast to *Sepulchre*, could it?

"After *Magic Cottage*, which was for me such a light book to do, so nice and warm and romantic, with lots of humour, I needed to do the antithesis – something dark, brooding, and one that made me feel very uneasy. That's me trying to do something different each time. Contrasting the novels actually keeps my own interest, and if I can keep my own interest going, I can keep the readers going too."

But it has had its critics, who unfairly accused him of "going soft". What does he think of his critics?

"Yes, they're right. That is James Herbert gone soft. But so was *Fluke*, which was only my fourth book. And if you read any of my stories, there is a lot of softness there. It isn't anything new, but in *The Magic Cottage* it's overtly so. That's probably why I enjoy those stories more than any other. Anyway, what do they mean, 'James Herbert gone soft'? He's suddenly mellowing with age? I don't know if they're saying it as a criticism, but it doesn't bother me. So what? I don't write books for the mass audience; I'm basically writing for myself and one other reader, whoever that reader is. It's not millions of people, it's the one guy who loves to sit down and read a James Herbert book. I'm doing it for us, not to sell a lot of copies. I always do what I feel I should do at the time. If people want to criticise me for that, that's their problem, not mine."

And criticism is something he *does* receive – as Stephen King remarked, mostly from people who haven't read him. He is used to it, and to being misrepresented, even by King himself, of whom he is a great admirer. King's comment that he is the greatest pulp writer since Robert E. Howard is not something he is proud of.

JOHN FRASER

"We're old buddies, but I don't thank Steve for saying that. The point he was making was that after *The Spear* I was out of that category. (Actually he was wrong, because *Fluke* was a watershed for me.) People are reading Steve's words as gospel. That was a kind of backhanded compliment to me, and one I don't actually appreciate very much, as much as I love Steve and his work, because it's been misinterpreted so much. He was saying, forget about Herbert the pulp writer, he's on another level. But the reader will read that as saying he was a great pulp writer. He wasn't saying that at all. I've had fans writing to me and asking, what does Steve mean by saying I was a great pulp writer? It's had an adverse effect."

James Herbert was born on April 8, 1943 in East London. His parents were street traders with fruit stalls in the area, and he attended a Catholic school near his home. After passing a scholarship, he went to a Catholic grammar school that was run under the strict supervision of priests.

At sixteen he went on to Hornsey College of Art to study graphic design, print, and photography. Afterwards he joined an advertising agency as a paste-up artist.

Two years later he joined a leading London advertising agency as a typographer, and soon worked his way up to become art director. At twenty-eight he decided to write a book. The idea came to him very quickly, and he swiftly sat down and wrote it. *The Rats* became an instant bestseller.

And yet, prior to that, he had read little in the genre, the only author being Dennis Wheatley, who was before his generation. He had read the old horror comics such as *Frankenstein* and *Tales from the Crypt*, and seen some old movies which he shouldn't have been let into, but that was all. *The Rats* is Herbert at his most graphic and violent, but despite its apparent pulp formula, its essential human concern for the plight of individuals demands serious attention. How did the idea first come to mind?

"I saw an old horror movie of *Dracula*, and there was a great scene where a madman comes into the huge hall and says he has had a nightmare in which he saw a thousand rats looking up at him. I thought that's very visual, and then I tied it up with my East End background, and it came from there."

Herbert clearly saw the decay and neglect around him when he lived in a house in the East End that had been under a slum clearance order for fourteen years before finally being pulled down. The rats symbolised urban decay.

But Herbert is disappointed that so many readers failed

Building to a horrific climax, [Moon] is James Herbert's best book yet. But do not read it alone . . . Especially not on a moonlit night.

– GEORGE THAW, from "Murder on His Mind", *Daily Mirror*, August 8, 1985 to recognise the novel's symbolic dimension, believing he had merely left the book open-ended in order to write a sequel. In fact, he had no idea the book would even be published, let alone have a sequel.

The Rats was followed by *Lair* and then *Domain*, which concluded the nightmarish journey through a ravaged city. "The great thing about that trilogy is its wonderful irony. It comes at the end, in *Domain*. The rats were symbolic of the system we all come up against. They were created by governments and their nuclear armaments, actually by an atomic bomb blast in New Guinea. The system can create these things. That's why the hero fought his own battle. We all fight our own battles against the system. We may win, but they are only temporary victories, because the system still goes on, and that's why at the end of the story the rats are still alive. Our hero had killed what he thought was the queen rat, but it still went on. In the sequel, I showed it wasn't just the city, it affects us all. The great irony in *Domain* was where the system destroyed London with nuclear bombs.

"The system had their own underground shelters. My hero got across London to get to one only to find out that the system – that is, the government – had been wiped out by the symbolic system, the rats. They actually wipe out the people who created them. So that was the whole twist of the story."

Once again, Mr Herbert has written a story of tremendous power and utter credibility. The sheer, nauseating horror of the climax will leave you gasping.

– SPR, from "Grip of Fear", *Grimsby Evening Telegraph*, October 8, 1985

After the *Rats* trilogy came several more blockbusters. *The Fog* is justifiably famous for its gripping portrait of an England plagued by a cloud of gas which causes madness. Again there is a vivid depiction of a derelict London and characters struggling in a nightmarish landscape from which there would appear to be little escape.

Fluke, about a man who comes home one night and discovers he is, in fact, a dog, is one of Herbert's favourite books, and is also a great favourite with his readers. It's a gentle, amusing fantasy despite a surprisingly disturbing ending.

In *Shrine* he deals convincingly with Catholicism and the Church's belief in miracles. Alice, a deaf and dumb child, has a vision and can suddenly hear and speak. How she starts to perform other miracles and attracts vast crowds – the sick, the curious, and the businessmen who wish to cash-in on the event – is vividly told and quite believable.

Like most writers, Herbert's ideas can come from anywhere, at the most unexpected moments.

"The idea for *Sepulchre* came from the dictionary. The idea for *The Dark* came from the Bible. The idea for *Shrine* came to me while I was in the religious section of a bookshop. I saw a book about Lourdes. It just leaps into your head. Just that one idea can set up a whole novel. That's why my books have got such short titles, because the title is the idea."

Herbert doesn't read much in the genre, since he has little spare time. When not writing, he spends his time with his family. He regards himself as being a good agent for Stephen King, but refrains from reading other people's work because, "I don't want to be influenced by anyone else. But there are plenty of good writers in the genre. And you wonder why they are not more successful than they are. I try to promote the genre in my own way. I don't go to conventions, though I've agreed to go to the world convention in Brighton, and that's going to be great for me, meeting guys like Ramsey [Campbell] and Clive [Barker]. Living where I live, in Sussex, it's a bit difficult."

He is a great admirer of Campbell, who he admits can explain his motives better than he can himself.

"Ramsey is a great horror aficionado. He talks wonderfully about horror, and when I read anything he writes about the genre it makes such good sense to me. We need people like Ramsey to explain how good the whole genre is. I'm afraid I'm not very good at doing that."

What does Herbert believe about the supernatural? He deals a lot with religion, and is deeply religious, though he dislikes the dogma and the ritual.

"All I do is speculate. The moment you put down hard and fast theories, you've got to be wrong. I don't think we've evolved enough yet to understand what is going on. All I do is set up a premise and speculate on what could happen, such as what would happen if you went out one night and came back as an animal. There's nothing new in it, but people wrote to me after *Fluke* and said, 'It's good to see you believe in reincarnation.' I don't necessarily."

Herbert's approach to writing may seem surprising.

"I get the idea, then I research whatever is involved. As I'm writing, I'll put down one-line ideas – things that could happen – and I'll do that while I'm actually writing as well. I'll have about 130 to 150 one-line ideas, and they point the book in a certain direction. I'll use thirty to fifty of those ideas, and the rest I'll scrap. But I don't plan. The only time I did that was with *The Spear*, because that was such an involved story. But I got so bored by planning that I scrubbed it after chapter six.

James Herbert is to be preserved for posterity. No, not in aspic, nor by some exquisitely painful and sordid embalming method handed down from pre-history, but in paint. He is one of a number of "individuals of our time and age" to be captured on canvas by artist John Bratby. Herbert, himself a former student of Hornsey College of Art, said the end result scared the hell out of him, capturing all his intensity. Eventually the picture will go on display, with Herbert rubbing painted shoulders with such luminaries as Paul McCartney – now there's fame for you!

– STEPHEN JONES and JO FLETCHER, from *Science Fiction Chronicle*, Issue 70, July 1985

I do have a rough idea of where I'm going. Sometimes I have an idea in mind for the ending, which means I have to build towards that, and that can be tricky. Other times, I have no idea how it's going to end. At the beginning of each chapter I try to set down what is going to happen, but I leave it very loose, so that I can let my mind run free. It's very unprofessional. I don't have a card-index of characters. I never read through as I'm writing. Sometimes I have to check what colour eyes the heroine has, but I never read through what I've written. Only because it dissatisfies me too much. What I have learned is to believe in myself while I'm writing. If it feels good, generally it's okay. If I read back, I'm always disappointed. There's no excitement for me. I know what is going to happen, so I try to avoid that. At the end of the story, I have to read back and make corrections. That's purgatory for me."

Surely there are times when he has to change an ending, for example? But no, Herbert insists he changes scenes only rarely. He's only changed an ending once, for *The Dark*, in which darkness becomes a physical entity, the symbolic darkness of the human soul is an inevitable extension of this.

"I took out the last chapter, because the original ending was so high-minded that I lost my central characters. I lost the intimacy. At the end of the book, the dark was taking over. They had all these lights shining on the darkness, but they faded; the dark overwhelmed the light. Then this miraculous light appeared (here's my religion coming in), but in the original I involved the whole world. It was all about England to begin with, and the whole world was being taken over by this darkness, and people on our side of the hemisphere knew they were going to lose when the sun started going down. It goes right back to mythology, when the cavemen got scared and hid in their caves. But here we were, in modern day England, the sun setting and the darkness rising, and everyone knew this side of the globe was finished. The other side was defeated already, and when the sun went down everyone knew their number was up. Suddenly, another sun rose in the east. That was the miracle. It got so pretentious that I thought, no, this is too much. So I changed it for the first time ever."

In each book Herbert has tried to be more ambitious, although he finds each one gets harder to write. As he admits:

"Each book you do gets more and more difficult because you improve (or hope to improve), so your own standards change. You demand more and more of yourself and become more and more dissatisfied with what you do. That's the way to improve. Novels like *The Rats* and *The Fog* were great for

James Herbert is one of Hodder & Stoughton's top authors, and to prove it, he is to be one of the chosen few promoted by Mrs Thatcher's favourite advertising agency Saatchi & Saatchi. Around £350,000 is to be spent on the promotion of Herbert, Jeffrey Archer, James Clavell and others this year.

– STEPHEN JONES and JO FLETCHER, from *Science Fiction Chronicle*, Issue 79, April 1986 their raw energy. That's why I still love them. But it's like punk music. The great thing about punk when it first came out was that it was raw, all rough edges, but the more the musicians played, the better they became. Today, some of those early punks are quite good musicians. The thing you have to avoid losing is that energy. I try to maintain both: energy and better writing. You're striving for something better. The day you don't, your days are numbered, because the public is not stupid, they know if you're just writing the same old thing."

Herbert also plays a large part in actually designing the covers and marketing his own books. He began by designing the paperback for *Fluke*, but when he let the publishers do a few, he was so disappointed that he decided that from *The Jonah* onwards he would do his own. For the hardcover of *Shrine* he designed the jackets, the typeface, the interior, even took the photograph on the cover.

"If I've spent a year writing a book, I like it to look good on the shelf so the reader will want to pick it up, whether he likes James Herbert or not. I thought I'd get value for money that way."

With *The Magic Cottage*, the publishers went to five different printers to get the inside text. The result is a clear but soft typeface which suits the atmosphere of the book. Herbert even took the author photograph himself, as well as writing the TV commercial for the book.

As to future projects, Herbert is uncertain. He jokingly suggests that he may write a historical romance, but then returns to attempt a serious answer to the question.

"The thing about horror is you get such a vast umbrella to work under. Is *Sepulchre* an adventure, a horror story, or a morality play? Is *The Magic Cottage* romance, humour, or horror? There are so many genres under that one vast umbrella of horror, and that satisfies my needs. I guess the way it's going, for most of us, is into psychological horror. Clive, of course, is into fantasy, which is almost another genre. I'm quite happy with what I'm doing, but I guess it's leading somewhere. I'm not sure where yet. Find out when I've written my last work."

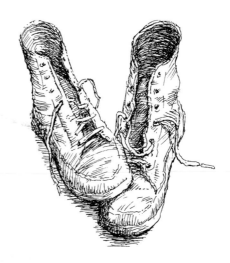

BREAKING THE MOULD

Stephen Laws

NINETEEN

ONE of the most important things about James Herbert's work in my view, is that people who wouldn't normally profess to be fans of "horror", as such, are often regular purchasers of his books . . . and they enjoy them. That points the way to something really important, which I'll come to in a while.

I've been reading Jim's books since he first began writing them. The first, of course, was *The Rats* . . . and there's a sequence in that book which really grabbed me by the throat. I won't recap on the plot, because you've probably read the book, but quite apart from the fact that these rats are big, savage and nasty bastards . . . there's also the added problem that they carry a ghastly disease . . . so that if one of them even gives you a nip with its teeth, you'll catch it and your skin will peel off bit by bit. Given that premise then, there's a particularly effective sequence in the novel where one of the buggers is loose in a school hall, causing panic amidst the kids. Our hero – one of the teachers – manages to grab the rat by the scruff of its neck. It thrashes and twists in his hands, trying to bite. Obviously, he has to do something. If he loses his grip, he'll be bitten . . . and in desperation, the hero ends up drowning it very messily in the school fish tank. It's a bizarre, breathtaking and very *realistic* set-piece which impressed me enormously. It also reminded me that despite the polarisation in horror fiction between "blood, guts and gore" and "psychological terror", despite the fact that at its best it can tell us important things about ourselves, horror fiction can also *thrill*.

STEPHEN LAWS

It reminded me of other moments of electric danger and excitement from books like *I am Legend* and *The Shrinking Man*. Quite apart from the many other dark pleasures in Jim's books, you'll find that "thrill" frequently emerging.

I've got a great passion for certain elements in fiction; one of them is *improvisation in the face of overwhelming peril*. That sounds a mouthful, I know. But for me it all goes back in a filmic sense to Peter Cushing turning the tables on Dracula by fashioning a crucifix from two clashed candlesticks (a trick repeated by actor Francis Matthews with a broken sword). On the fiction front, I often get the same buzz of "Oh My God!" when I read Jim's books. In any event, it was that sequence in *The Rats*, and a subsequent reading of Jim's other books such as *The Fog* which started me off on my own writing career. Which now brings me in a roundabout fashion to the point I was referring to at the beginning . . .

Nowadays, I believe that there's a tendency among critics to categorise horror fiction a little too easily. What does he write? a critic may ask of any writer. Oh well, you know, he's into Splatter . . . or Cyberpunk . . . or Lovecraft . . . or Quiet Horror. There's even been an Anti-Horror lobby, for crying out loud. Hutson, Skipp and Spector, Campbell, Charlie Grant. These names become synonymous with a particular style in the genre . . . and whereas some writers are quite happy with a tag . . . others, myself included, feel that it is much too restrictive. I don't want to be known for one "style" alone. And as I've said on many occasions, I want to be able to write stories or novels with a Quiet Voice or a Loud Voice as the tale demands. It's a difficult battle.

But it's a battle that James Herbert has won. And he has my complete admiration.

Take a look at his books.

Yes, of course he's written what might be called horror novels with a capital H. There are the "Rats" novels, *The Dark, The Fog, The Spear, Moon* . . . each one with a slightly different "voice". But he's also the author of *Fluke* and *The Magic Cottage*, so where do *they* fit in? In style, tone and content, they're completely different. But they're still recognisably the work of James Herbert.

James Herbert has broken the mould.

He writes the books that he *wants* to write, in the particular "Voice" which he has chosen for the tale. He continues to flex his creative muscles within his chosen genre and subsequently leaves critics who try to completely pigeonhole his work a little

Once he's snared us, Herbert engages in some atypical, sophisticated generic play, self-consciously but unobtrusively shaping The Magic Cottage *first into a realistic frame, then into a fairy tale, then into a ghost story, and finally into a horror show. Fortunately, none of these goings-on intrude on the story, which actually manages to generate occasional frissons.*

– MICHAEL A. MORRISON, from *Science Fiction & Fantasy Book Review Annual 1988* (1988)

bamboozled. I believe that it is this very diversity which attracts non-genre fans to his work. I also believe that we'll see further diversity in the future. I, for one, look forward to the next . . . and the next . . . and the next . . .

Simply put, James Herbert is a Storyteller in the true sense of the word.

THICKER OUTLINE AROUND SNAKE FOR EMPHASIS OF IMAGE.

LETRATONE INFILLING OF SCALES ETC TO GIVE METALLIC SHEEN ON PRINTING. (MULTIPLE GELATIN OVERLAYS TO PROVIDE DIFFERING ORIENTATION OF "SHEEN LINES")

THE EIDETIC IMAGE

Michael A. Morrison

TWENTY

YOU'VE seen the film, you've read the book. You know the one – there've been so many: the young couple find the home of their dreams, the wife's ecstatic, the husband's happy but more controlled . . . But *we* know there's something sinister about the place, because we've read the blurb and paid our money. Slowly, THINGS start to happen . . . You know it like you wrote the story yourself.

Well, this is similar. But different. You'll see.

If you like to be frightened, to feel your flesh creep, and if late-night films fascinate, then James Herbert's latest horror, The Magic Cottage, *is something to get a really good grip on.*

– BARBIE BOXALL,
Woman's World, July
1986

This excerpt from the beginning of *The Magic Cottage* neatly summarises the novel's set-up and typifies its engaging, self-aware narrative voice. That voice belongs to Mike Stringer, "sceptic and part-time infidel", who, along with his lover Midge Gudgeon, moves into Gramarye cottage at the beginning of this, the twelfth novel by Britain's bestselling writer of horror fiction. Nestled in the New Forest in Hampshire, Gramarye draws Mike and Midge from the city like a magnet. For Mike, a musician who plays in backup groups, and for Midge, an illustrator who specialises in children's books, Gramarye is a haven, their "first proper home".

Amid the joyful tumult of settling in, Mike and Midge overlook the unreal elements of life in Gramarye – structural defects in the cottage seem to disappear, injuries and wounds heal miraculously overnight, the neighbourhood birds and animals are unnaturally bold. Even a visit from three members of a nearby pseudo-religious cult called the Synergists doesn't spoil their idyll. The Synergists seem friendly enough, and their foun-

MICHAEL A. MORRISON

der and guru, a former toy manufacturer with the unlikely name of Mycroft, appears to Mike disarmingly bland: "This guy was medium height and paunchy, skin smoothly unblemished; almost, but not quite, characterless . . . He could have been anybody's favourite uncle."

But Mycroft is evil, a necromancer with designs on Gramarye, and the cottage is a focal point for ancient, incorporeal forces of which Mike and Midge are wholly unaware. Although they experience moments of subtly altered perception, sensory distortion, and "abrupt and unnatural lucidity", neither realises the extent of Gramarye's influence. But they are unwittingly being drawn into a classic confrontation with evil, a battle for their happiness, their freedom – and for the power of Magic.

This situation is reminiscent of a fairy tale, and Herbert builds his novel around canonical elements: the damsel in distress (Midge), the stalwart hero (Mike), the evil magician (Mycroft), and, of course, the enchanted cottage. And he reinforces this storybook ambience with allusions to witches, spells, pixies and other tropes of the fairy story. But he embeds these accoutrements in a primarily realistic novel set in present-day England, ultimately transmuting his fairy story into something generically quite different.

James Herbert's horror tale, The Magic Cottage, *reworks the formula of disturbing a reassuring and familiar setting (in this case it is an idyllic country retreat for two) with nightmarish occurrences; one to chill you nicely in the deckchair.*

– DB, *Vogue,* July 1986

As Mycroft worms his way into Mike and Midge's lives and the battle lines are drawn, *The Magic Cottage* evolves seamlessly from fairy tale into ghost story – and comes into its own. Herbert eschews the gore and shock tactics of his earlier novels, relying instead on his characters to carry the story. Through Mike's narrative voice, he disarms and distances us with clever allusions to genre conventions, all the while letting the undercurrent of unease that courses through the novel's early chapters surface naturally. And when his beautifully orchestrated crescendo of suspense peaks, the scares have the genuine shivers-down-the-back-of-the-neck quality of the great ghost stories of Shirley Jackson or M. R. James.

The main reason *The Magic Cottage* works so well is that its characters come to life. When Mike has a hallucinatory experience in Gramarye and Midge's unacknowledged anxieties over the unreality of their storybook existence erupt in rage, the scene rings true. And later, when their involvement with the Synergists threatens their relationship, we care for them as we would for a couple of close friends.

During its final chapters, the novel metamorphoses once again, from ghost story to horror show, and Herbert whips up a slam-bang, effects-filled finale that is great fun. But what lingers after the dust has settled and we've put the book aside are our memories of Mike and Midge – and those scares. Moments of genuine *frisson* are rare in the modern horror novel, which suffers from bestseller bloat and a surfeit of violence and gore. The good news is that James Herbert has brought the shivers back to horror fiction.

A BRITISH PHENOMENON

David J. Howe

TWENTY ONE

JAMES HERBERT is undoubtedly a British phenomenon. His success is almost unparalleled in this country and with thirteen best-selling novels to his name already there seems no stopping him. His first novel, *The Rats*, in 1974 was arguably one of the most influential horror novels ever published. With this one book, the horror market was turned on its head as out went the wishy-washy low-key horror fare and in came graphic horror that scraped nerves and caused the readers to shudder with delight at the helter-skelter mayhem that was unleashed on the page. *The Rats* did for literary horror what films like *The Exorcist* and *Halloween* did for the cinema and in the years since there have been many imitators of Herbert's unique style and vision, but none that come as close to the breadth and scope of true horror as Herbert has managed.

Herbert infuses elements of Evil Dead, Amityville *et al in this bricks-and-mortar* Christine *of a story . . .*

– CAROLE LINFIELD, from "The Magic Cottage", *Sounds*, June 7, 1986

James Herbert, or Jim as he prefers to be called, is a modest and self-effacing man. He sees himself very much as foremost an author and the fact that all his books have become bestsellers is a bonus. He is very enthusiastic about writing and all the challenges that this art form presents and really cares about what he does. He has written one book a year since 1974 (with the exception of *Shrine* which seems to have taken two years – there was no new book in 1982) and this relaxed pace allows him the luxury of getting things right: from the ideas, through the writing and ending up with the finished book in the shops. Indeed, his keen business sense and natural flair for what the public want have kept him in the public eye from the very beginning. There would be very few people that did not know there was a new James Herbert book available.

He is often labelled as a writer of "blood and guts" fiction, but nothing could be further from the truth today. That was where he began but since then he has delved into light fantasy (*Fluke*), thrillers (*The Spear, The Jonah, Sepulchre*), ghost stories (*The Survivor, Haunted*) and books that can only be labelled as pure Herbert (*Shrine, Moon, The Magic Cottage*). Indeed, his writing is so diverse that anyone who says they don't like Herbert's books is most likely ignorant of what he has written.

I spoke with Jim as the Hodder & Stoughton publicity machine was just recovering after the promotion of the paperback release of *Sepulchre* and gearing up for the new hardback issue of *Haunted*. In fact the day that the interview was arranged for was the same day that the publishers received the first copies of *Haunted* from the printers and the first time that Jim had seen the finished article. More on this later.

I began, appropriately, with *Haunted* and asked how it came about.

"*Haunted* actually started life as a TV movie, the pilot for a possible series," he explained, "and this is why it is a little shorter than my recent novels. I think it's good for a writer to attempt a shorter book that's tighter in its structure if they're used to writing long blockbusters. *Haunted* is not all madness and mayhem, which, as you know, I like doing, but it's more controlled and much more filmic. It was an interesting challenge – to write a psychological ghost story along the lines of Shirley Jackson's *Haunting of Hill House* or Henry James' *The Turn of the Screw*. Very much that kind of black and white ghost story, and for me, I think it worked. I was also intentionally branching out, trying something new as I don't believe in giving the readers exactly what they want or expect. I want them to wonder what type of book the next one is going to be. I certainly don't want to end up as the literary equivalent of the *Carry On* films!

"I am actually very pleased with *Haunted*. I mean, I've been pleased with all my books so far, except perhaps *Sepulchre*. I admired what I had done with *Sepulchre* because it was another new challenge; to write about evil against greater evil. The hero was quite a bastard because I didn't want any likeable characters in *Sepulchre* at all, mainly because *The Magic Cottage* was so 'soft' in that you really got to know the hero and the heroine. I wanted this to be mean and hard with no sympathy for the main characters. Unfortunately, the end result was that I didn't actually love the book."

"The Magic Cottage *is much softer than my usual stories. There's still horror in there, but the reader is led very gently into it. It's also quite romantic, which I think is why it is so popular with women.*"

– JAMES HERBERT, from "Smiling Face of Horror", *Western Mail*, May 8, 1987

With *Haunted* being the plot of the television pilot, I wondered what had happened to the proposed series.

"The original idea was for it to be a two-hour TV movie, to be shown at Christmas, with a series following on from that. Now I didn't intend to do a series, but Jonathan Powell, the then head of Drama at the BBC, liked it so much that he suggested we make it into a series, thirteen single episodes or something. I was obviously pleased, and although I wouldn't have been able to write every single episode, I agreed to write some story outlines detailing how the series could evolve.

"What the BBC asked me for was a story based on an idea, any idea. So I told them that I was going on holiday and that if I thought of something I'd get back to them. Then while I was on holiday, I woke up early one morning having had a dream, not a nightmare, but a bad dream about ghosts. The transition period between being asleep and waking up was minimal – I just went straight into gear, from being asleep and dreaming to being awake and thinking, and the adrenalin was really flowing. For me, at that time of the morning, that's really unusual. If you want to remember a dream, you've got to think of it instantly when you wake up, and so I scribbled out about five pages of foolscap with the whole plot on, the story just continued from the dream. When I came back from holiday I phoned the BBC and ended up actually acting out the whole story in a restaurant – people thought I was mad – but I really wanted to get over the tension so I was physically grabbing people as I told it. It was one of those ideas that springs upon you and the whole thing just evolved on its own once I started working on it. It became a labour of love and I really enjoyed doing it. I find that's how most stories work.

"When the first draft got to the BBC, the typists were saying that it was great, and the contracts department were saying that it was the best they'd seen and so I figured that it was probably going to be good.

"The next I heard was a phone call about a month or so ago, from the BBC producer who was handling it, Evgeny Gridneff, saying that it was no longer on because his contract had not been renewed. However I haven't yet been formally told by the BBC that they're not doing it. There seems to be a lot of politics involved. The head of drama, Jonathan Powell, was promoted and has now got one of the top jobs in the BBC. The new head, Mark Shivas, came in and he let Gridneff go taking all his projects with him. Which was a great pity."

Having spoken briefly about the development of *Haunted*,

"In Fluke, *Rumbo is Fluke's friend, this dog that gets killed; at the end he arrives back as a squirrel . . . and in* The Magic Cottage *they have this squirrel they decide to call Rumbo. That's the connection between the two. That's me saying 'Life goes on', but I'm not particularly saying that reincarnation is right."*

– JAMES HERBERT, from "Haunted by Rats" by Dave Hughes, *Skeleton Crew* II, 1988

DAVID J. HOWE

I asked how some of Jim's other books were conceived, *Sepulchre*, for instance.

"*Sepulchre* came about while I was writing *The Magic Cottage*. I was looking up a word in the dictionary when I came across the word 'sepulchre', which means 'tomb', and it shot out at me from the page; I thought it was a lovely word. Quite apart from the fact that very few people seem to be able to pronounce it!

"But what an interesting word. I also had an idea about a psychic who finds minerals and oils and gold and so I tied up the sepulchre idea with this. I'd also wanted for years to do a crime story about kidnap and ransom. I'd looked into that area a bit – it's all very hush hush – and so I added this in as well. It's an intricate book because there are these three basic ideas tied into one. I always over-research my books and *Sepulchre* was no exception. I think it was Hemingway who said that you research as much as you can and then discard 98 per cent of it and that's exactly what I do. Of course, bits and pieces still get left in, mainly because they add a bit of authenticity to the story. I researched ancient cultures – the Sumarians; big multinational companies; kidnap and ransom companies; as well as terrorist organisations; the material for the Polish, Arab and American pieces . . . lots of things. This was a great challenge to me as a writer, because with *The Magic Cottage* I only had to sit there and use my imagination, there was hardly any research on that at all. I was going from one extreme to another both in the sense of the research and also in the mood of the books.

"Ideas come from things like that, or they can suddenly spring into my head, just suddenly appear, as if there's some guy up there saying, 'This is your next book.' From there the idea just grows and evolves itself. I research and more things become involved and it becomes a novel. But I start with one single, simple idea. *The Dark* came straight from the Bible, for example. I was staying in a hotel on a publicity tour and they had the usual Bible by the side of the bed. One night I idly flicked through it and read about the great darkness falling over the land, and I thought that that was a brilliant idea. *The Fog* started with a fog, *The Rats* came from rats and I just build from there."

Mention of Jim's first novel took us back to the very start of his writing career. I asked him why he had decided to start writing.

"I started writing simply because it seemed like a good idea at the time. I had reached a point in the advertising business where I was spending more time sitting in meetings and less

At his best Herbert shows a sensitivity to structure, character, and background detail wholly absent from the nasties. And his vigorous, aggressive prose is always stylish and readable. The Magic Cottage *is definitely Herbert at his best.*

– MICHAEL A. MORRISON, from *Science Fiction & Fantasy Book Review Annual 1988* (1988)

With world sales of his books now in excess of 16 million copies, James Herbert is rightly hailed as Britain's answer to Stephen King. To promote his latest hardcover release, The Magic Cottage, *publishers Hodder & Stoughton held an impressive champagne reception for their star author in June. Booksellers from all over the country heard how this was the most successful promotion for Herbert to date, with the NEL paperback of* Moon *currently at number two in the bestseller list, and* The Magic Cottage *zooming up the hardcover charts.*

As if to underline the author's incredible popularity, a few days later London's Forbidden Planet hosted one of their most phenomenal signing sessions ever, when Herbert autographed books non-stop for more than three hours. →

doing what I enjoyed. Physically it was very hard work to write *The Rats* and my wife couldn't understand why I was writing and not relaxing at weekends and in the evenings. There was a driving force in me that I had to do it, and it was tough. But I've always maintained that in order to get anywhere in any job, you've got to give more of yourself than you expect to get back. I've always done that, because that's the way I like to work. If I didn't like writing, I would never have attempted a book; if I hadn't liked art then I would never have gone into advertising. If you love something, then the hard work you put in seems less important. You wear yourself out but it doesn't feel like that at the time.

"With writing particularly, I think you've got to enjoy it to do it because it is very demanding. At the end of each book I'm really drained, physically and emotionally, and I think you've got to really love what you're doing to carry on.

"Sometimes you really hate and detest it. I hate authors who moan and ring up their agents and say they can't work and they've got this block, because I know; you just work through it. It's like doing the four-minute mile; you've got to crash through that pain barrier to make it."

By way of example Jim picked up the new copy of *Haunted* which he had been given when he arrived for the interview. Flicking through it, and admiring the binding, the illustrations on the chapter headings, the black and white frontispiece, and the very effective cover layout and design, he continued, "It is hard and you do hate it at times, but when you've got something like this at the end of it . . . I mean that's the birth of the baby, all the pain has disappeared and there's just a real good feeling."

After so many books, I was impressed that the actual publication still made such an impression on Jim so I asked about the first publication of *The Rats*, how did that feel?

"Well, it was the most wonderful feeling in the world for me. One of those experiences that you get once in a lifetime, perhaps twice. I received a short letter from the publishers saying that they liked my novel *The Rats* and they'd like to offer me so much per cent royalties and an advance of £150. I mean – I would have paid them to publish it! *The Rats* was written more for my own satisfaction than anything, because I wanted to do it, with perhaps a slight thought that it may be published. When it was, I was amazed. My wife kind of expected it – I don't think she realised how difficult it was to get a book published, she took it all in her stride – so I think the most surprised person was myself."

The Rats, of course, was a watershed in horror publishing

DAVID J. HOWE

as it was right at the forefront of the graphic horror novels of the 1970s. As there was nothing like that around, what had made Jim write in that style?

"I'd like to be able to answer that I was really shrewd and saw that there was a big gap in the market; that everything was very tame. But that's not how it happened. When I was writing *The Rats*, I didn't think it was going to be published and so there was nothing holding me back and I wasn't self-conscious about what I was writing. Obviously I've got a very vivid imagination so what was in my mind went down on the page and one thing I remember was thinking that there was something very shocking about being eaten alive by a rat, so why didn't I explain what happened. Why just stop the chapter with 'the rat attacked . . .'? I also thought that it would be really shocking if the hero got mutilated, which is why Harris loses an ear in *The Rats*. It was simply a natural way for me to write and that's how *The Rats* and that style of writing came about.

"With the second book, *The Fog*, I decided to have a real joke on the publishing world and I just went way over the top. I wanted to see how much I could get away with, how far I could go, and a large section of the public tuned in to that.

"I deliberately wanted to shock people and that shouldn't come as a surprise. The person who writes romantic fiction wants to soften the audience, the comedy writer wants to make them laugh. I'm a horror writer – I want to shock the audience, to scare them."

The Rats and *The Fog* have, since their publication, sold over 900,000 copies each, making them the most popular of Jim's books to date. With such a successful formula on his hands, I asked why he had decided to write *Fluke*, a very different sort of novel.

"It was simply what I wanted to do at the time. I've always written exactly what I feel like writing and I wanted to write a story about a dog. My publishers didn't want it at all; after all the success of *The Rats, The Fog* and *The Survivor*, they were amazed that I'd turned in a light fantasy book about a dog. They took me to lunch and asked me to make the dog turn rabid or something, but I told them that they either published it exactly as it was or they didn't publish it at all, as simple as that. I mean I had no risk – I had a good job in advertising, so I couldn't lose whatever they did. In a way they were right in their criticism as *Fluke* did less well than the previous three, although it has now sold over 500,000 copies. However, up until *The Magic Cottage* it was my favourite book, and I'm still very pleased with it."

With most of the long line of customers buying copies of both the new £9.95 hardcover and the £2.95 paperback, it's not surprising that FP's Jon Harrison reported "record takings".

Herbert, although obviously tiring towards the end, still managed to make the effort to talk with each and every customer personally – often remembering their names from previous autograph sessions. Then with a heavy schedule of radio interviews and BBC-TV's Wogan chat show behind him, the personable writer set off on a promotional tour around Britain, which included yet another signing at Birmingham's Andromeda Bookstore.

– Stephen Jones and Jo Fletcher, from *Science Fiction Chronicle*, Issue 83, August 1986

Whilst discussing the success of *The Rats* and *The Fog*, we touched upon a topic that is obviously one which Jim feels very strongly about. This is the labelling of his early books as "nasty".

"That label of 'nasty' really bugs me. It came from the publishers who wanted to find some pigeon-hole into which to put *The Rats*. After they had read it they invented this new category of 'nasty' and then promoted the book as that. As soon as I found out I made them stop, but unfortunately it's a label that has stuck over the years. Yes, there are some very nasty elements in my stories, there are to this day, but they're never quite as bad as people imagine. It was Ramsey Campbell who pointed this out about *The Fog*. There are two very graphic and horrific scenes in that book, which are so powerful that they pervade the whole story and you imagine everything else to be of the same ilk. There are some very graphic scenes in *Sepulchre* but, again, they are not quite as bad as your imagination tells you."

One of the most horrific of Jim's novels is *The Dark*, a terrifying tale of madness and death, how did that one come about?

"*The Dark* was simply an extension of *The Fog*. I'd shocked and horrified the readers with *The Fog* when that was published, but by the time *The Dark* came about, that form of writing was quite acceptable. So with *The Dark* I went for something even stronger; I wanted to see if I could shock the readers again, despite the apparent acceptability of graphic horror at that time. I'd like to think that I managed it."

Moving on to a slightly different subject, I asked Jim why he thought that only certain horror authors, like himself and, of course, Stephen King, are so popular, whereas so many others never get anywhere near the bestseller lists.

"I think the secret of our success is that we're more mainstream in our appeal. I gave a talk and answered questions at the ICA the other week and there was this lady in the audience. She must have been in her late fifties and she said smugly, 'Your audience is just teenagers really, isn't it?' I told her that it wasn't and explained that I knew from experience – from the letters I got and the people I met – that my books were read by eleven-year-old kids to eighty-two-year-old grannies. That's a very broad spectrum, which of course includes the cinema-going audience: the eighteen-to-twenty-fives. She didn't really want to accept this though.

"It's the same old prejudice that I've come up against time and time again. I explained to her that Stephen King and myself

DAVID J. HOWE

would never have consistent bestsellers if we had a limited audience. Horror is a genre, and by definition a genre is a limited audience. Our books go way beyond that. In fact Neil Gaiman summed it up in an article for *Publishing News*, he said that Herbert and King have created their own genre, they are the genre. That's where the majority of other horror writers fail – they don't as yet seem to have broken out."

Despite this mainstream popularity, Jim still feels as though some of the people within the horror genre itself are prejudiced against him and his work, whatever its subject matter.

"The only reason I can think of for this is that I'm not a purist horror writer. I know that whatever I do I'm never going to please them and so I don't try – I just do what I want to do. It is surprising that these horror 'pundits' can say these things about me when I've possibly done more for the horror genre in this country than anyone else. For example, Kim Newman, now there's a guy who totally dismissed *The Exorcist* as a film. How can you take anyone seriously if they do that? He lacks any credibility in my eyes because of that, so naturally he's going to knock whatever I do. There's a few critics around like that, mainly working for the radical press like *Time Out* and *City Limits*. The problem is that if the prejudice towards my work is already there, they're never going to give me a good review. This happens with most horror fiction, not just mine, and if the general public are reading these critical things about horror writers and their books, they're not going to start reading. There's a potential audience being lost there.

"You know, one day, Guy N. Smith, for example, might write a brilliant book. Now I haven't read any of his work so I don't know if he's good, bad or indifferent. I do know that he is categorised, as I was, as an author of 'nasty' books and his output is amazing – he must be the most prolific horror writer in this country. However, because of this apparently huge prejudice against him, nobody's going to take him seriously and they're likely to miss out as a result. I think reviewers have a responsibility to be objective, it's unfortunate that some just can't be."

Jim gave a couple of examples of the sort of thing he is talking about. "I've got two reviews of *The Magic Cottage*. One appeared in the *Washington Post* and was magnificent, possibly the best review I've ever had for any of my books and it was written by a professor of physics at one of the American universities. On the other hand there was a review in one of the American magazines that was a typical 'Let's get Herbert' essay. They related me to Guy N. Smith and Shaun Hutson and

One day last summer horror writer James Herbert liberally sprinkled petrol over his bonfire – then failed to retire after lighting a match.

Within a split second the fumes turned into a flash – "I became a great ball of fire. My eyebrows were burned off. My shirt melted on me. They rushed me to hospital and covered me in a special cream.

"Next day I was totally black. I was in hospital till I shed my old skin and started to grow a new one."

– from "Haunted Tale That Lights Up Your Life", *Daily Express*, August 4, 1988

Also on hand at the Ramsey Campbell signing was James Herbert, who revealed that he had just completed his latest novel: "It's called Sepulchre," *he said, "and I think it's scheduled for July or August publication by Hodder & Stoughton. I am still not sure how I feel about it – it is as dark as I thought it was going to be while I was writing it, and in fact I think there's only one good guy in it . . . and he's not the hero!"*

– STEPHEN JONES and JO FLETCHER, from *Science Fiction Chronicle*, Issue 90, March 1987

all who have claimed that 'nasty' tag today, and said how they couldn't understand *The Magic Cottage*. It was as though the book was *The Rats* or *The Fog*, but it's not, it's a totally different kind of book. It's all a bit mystifying really."

One thing that is notable about Jim's novels is that they are not all "graphic horror". There have been switches in style all along the way and, as Jim pointed out, all his development as a writer is there for the readers to see.

"I haven't got loads of manuscripts in a drawer at home, written when I was thirteen years old. All my development is up front, so to speak. *The Rats* was literally the first book I'd ever written, and after that you can spot for yourself the watershed releases. *Fluke* was one, *The Spear* was another, *Shrine* too, and you can carry on from there."

I was quite surprised that there were no unpublished Herbert stories and asked if he had ever written any short stories.

"I'm asked for short stories all the time, but I like to write the big ones – I like to get totally engrossed in a story. The only short story I have written to date was for Book Aid and I wrote this because of a bit of a *faux-pas* on my part. The organisers had got in touch with me to ask if I could contribute something, and I offered them one of my vignettes from *Domain* because I didn't have any short stories. They were pleased with that so I sent it off to them. Then I remembered that Graham Masterton had been in touch with me for a story for *Scare Care* – another charity project – and I had sent him the same thing! So feeling guilty about this I actually sat down and wrote a short story for Book Aid. It took me a week and although I enjoyed it, it was hard work. So that's my one and only short story to date.

"One of the problems with short stories is that they are not short things to write in terms of the number of hours; they actually take a long time. People like Ramsey Campbell and Clive Barker have the short story down to a fine art, and that tempts me to get more into that area of fiction but I haven't had the time to seriously consider it yet."

Jim was quick to point out that although he has not written many short stories or novellas, not all his books are of mammoth size.

"There's *Haunted*, of course, and the early ones were just of average size. *The Spear* unintentionally turned out to be quite short in paperback. What happened there was that I was sued for breach of copyright. In the original hardback I had used sub-chapters or prologues throughout the book describing the history of Hitler and his fascination for the Spear of Longinus.

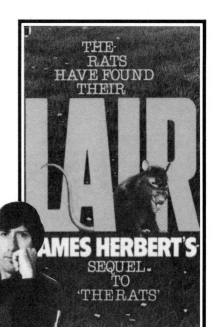

James Herbert delighted the assembled guests at Hodder & Stoughton's recent paperback presentation to the trade when he told the story of how, while on an author tour with Hodders' publicity person Brian Levy, the latter took a laxative in mistake for Valium, keeping both of them more on the run than ever!

– STEPHEN JONES and JO FLETCHER, from *Science Fiction Chronicle*, Issue 92, May 1987

But once it was published I received a writ from this guy who said that the facts that I'd used in my story – I'd used his book for research, along with lots of others and credited them in my book – he gained from transcendental meditation, therefore they were unique to him and nobody else could use them. However if I paid him lots of money I could use them. We spent a year in court, it cost a fortune and in the end I had to take out thirteen lines. Because all these lines were in the prologues, I ended up taking all the prologues out rather than rewrite them all, which was a shame because they were really quite interesting. The original hardback is therefore quite rare if you have one because it contains these 'banned' prologues."

Finally I asked Jim whether he could let us know what the next Herbert bestseller was going to be – apart from *Haunted*, of course.

"At the moment I've got two good ideas for my next novel, and I'm not sure which to do next. One is a big grand-scale James Herbert which I always like to go back to, something akin to *The Fog* or *Domain,* where there's lots happening. The other is a more intimate story, something that won't be written in the first person as such, but in that vein. As I say, I'm not sure which to do and I'm not planning on starting work on the next novel until October."

Whichever idea Jim decides to work on next, I think we can be sure that it will be written with all the skill and emotion that we have come to expect from a Herbert novel. I can't wait.

HERBERT, *HAUNTED*, AND THE INTEGRITY OF BESTSELLERDOM

Stephen Gallagher

TWENTY TWO

C AN one begin with a digression? Because that's the way I have to approach this. Stay with me, and it'll all become clear. I hope.

It was back in the early eighties and I'd been recruited by Mark Gorton, then a researcher on one of those daytime TV talk programmes, to sit in with the studio audience on what was supposed to be a probing discussion but which was really little more than a glorified celebrity interview. The topic was bestsellerdom, the celebrity was Shirley Conran, and the *raison d'être* for the whole thing was that *Lace* had just been published. Remember *Lace*? Maybe there's some deaf mute on a Hebridean island who managed to escape the hype, but most of us weren't so lucky. In a fit of conscientious application, and in the knowledge that there was about a fifty-fifty chance of being called upon to put a point from the floor, I actually got hold of the book and read it.

Now, I realise that this is something of a departure. The world is teeming with people – and until this point I'd been one of them – who are more than happy to condemn or dismiss entire genres of writing without even taking the basic step of picking up an example and sticking their noses between the covers. As someone who'd recently begun to catch up on his horror reading after a youth spent travelling back and forth between the Eng. Lit. and science fiction shelves, I suppose I was sensitive to the basic unfairness of this. So I got hold of the blockbuster in question, and began to read.

And was somewhat dismayed.

Ex-ad man Herbert turned down three campaigns created by agency Saatchi & Saatchi to promote his latest bestseller, Sepulchre: *"They're good people at Saatchi's – and clever," he mused. "I guess I just know too many tricks of the trade."*

– STEPHEN JONES and JO FLETCHER, from *Science Fiction Chronicle,* Issue 96, September 1987

STEPHEN GALLAGHER

I mean, I'd expected all kinds of things – all the usual received ideas about this particular kind of genre – but the one that I wasn't prepared for was ineptitude in the writing. Prose without rhythm, a monotonous narrative voice, not even any switch in tone between narrative and dialogue. Just about the only character that you could feel any sympathy for was the goldfish. For a working writer barely getting his start, it was a particularly disheartening display. I don't object to hype, not at all; but I was dismayed that a book that was having so much invested in it and spent upon it, that through sheer force of money and PR was driving a wedge and making a place for itself in the culture of the time, thereby setting standards for some and targets for others, should have been such a below-par piece of craft.

It was my first conscious exposure to the category-bestseller, by which I mean a book that contains such a clear element of marketing calculation in its planning that this, far more than any storytelling impulse of the author, can be seen to control just about every aspect of the material. There had no doubt been others like it before, and there have certainly been others like it since; but I'd tended to take at face value the old chat-show line of I'm-not-about-literature-I-just-tell-a-good-story, and now it seemed that you could dodge even this most fundamental of hurdles and *still* make a million.

And where does Jim Herbert come into all of this?

Stick with me a little longer.

I left the studio that day with a certain feeling of depression. Not because I hadn't been called upon (I hadn't) and not because a bad book had been unthinkingly puffed (a lone academic, who along with Conran's agent had been brought along to make up the onstage numbers, had given the work something of a rough ride), but because I felt that I'd glimpsed something of the future of British publishing, and I didn't like the look of what I'd seen. Don't get me wrong, I hadn't been living with my head in a bucket until then; but whenever I'd heard all this stuff about brand name-dropping and soft porn and going to the Bahamas to write I'd always tended to think back to Ian Fleming, the first adult popular writer that I read and whose style and approach appear to have been key inspirations to an entire generation of what have come to be called S & F writers (the S stands for shopping. The F stands for . . . wait a minute, are any children likely to be reading this?).

But I'd liked Fleming, and at least he'd been writing from the heart. Such as it was. The author was the author and he was there in the books, his individual personality hidden beneath

The most humorous book I've written is Creed. *Before that it was* The Magic Cottage *and* Fluke, *but you can go as far back as* The Rats *and* The Fog, *there's humour in all of those. The darkest books I've written are* The Dark *and the one with absolutely the least humour, compassion and humanity was* Sepulchre. *The reason for that was because I wrote* The Magic Cottage *– which was a bit soft for me. It's one of my favourites actually, and I enjoyed it so much because there was no overt horror, a lot of humour, and plenty of warmth. Because I did that, I wanted to make the next book the total opposite, the very antithesis of that, which is why* Sepulchre *is such a mean book.*

– JAMES HERBERT at *Fantasycon XIV,* October 7, 1989

the surface like . . . I don't know, like a secret nervous system. I'd sensed nothing like that in the book I'd just read.

And this has a bearing on the one remembered assertion from the studio, coming from the guest author's agent, that stuck in my mind the most.

The preceding question, which had come from the academic, was something like: Don't you think it's a tragic waste, if not a misuse of the form, to spend so much time and effort on a book and yet put nothing of yourself into it?

And the reply was, Well, once Shirley has all the fame and the money that's going to come from this, she'll be freed to write exactly what she wants.

And I came away thinking, *Yeah, that'll be the day.*

James Herbert writes bestsellers.

That's how it's been since *The Rats*, his first; with one book he created virtually singlehanded an entire new subspecies of horror fiction, the "nasty" (as it was quickly called, the term "video nasty" later becoming a direct descendant). Of course, nastiness on the printed page didn't begin in 1974; but in the pulp ghetto where many felt it belonged, it had been a lot easier to ignore. It sure as hell hadn't figured much in the bestseller lists before then; it was almost as if John Belushi had turned up roaring drunk at Compton Mackenzie's funeral.

As an index of value, of course, the term of "nasty" is worthless. What does that make *Titus Andronicus*? A Renaissance nasty? But labels tend to stick, and in a fast-moving world become a substitute for judgement.

I can't say that I was entirely free of this attitude myself when first I picked up *The Fog* and *The Jonah* together. I can't remember the exact circumstances, but I think I was recovering from a dose of the flu and I'd read everything in the house and, besides, it was about time I gave Herbert a try. Not exactly the best frame of mind in which to approach an unfamiliar author, and not one that I feel particularly proud to admit to, either. But bear in mind how my thinking on the whole big-book, bestseller phenomenon had already been shaped, and imagine how I must have felt when I started to read and quickly realised that I was facing another aspect of bestsellerdom altogether.

I touched the man's robe, and, brothers, I was *healed*!

Well, perhaps I exaggerate a little. But I found *The Fog* to be genuinely effective, like a *Quatermass* serial in full colour and 3D, and in the transition from this book to *The Jonah* – across a gap of around six years – could clearly be seen the development of a writer who, having hit big success the first time out,

James Herbert, the British author of some of the most gruesome horror stories ever written, could only shake his head in bewilderment when a young lass accosted him on Monday night and asked him about the pronunciation of the title of his latest novel, Sepulchre.

"We need to know to settle a bet," she told Herbert, who was mingling with the literati at the book's launch at Kinsela's.

"I reckon it's sep-li-cur. My friend says it's sep-olka," she grinned.

"Oh, my God," said the great man. "That sounds like a Polish horror story."

Even after being told, the young woman disappeared into the throng obviously unconvinced.

– from "Author Buries Grave Problem", *Daily Telegraph* (Australia), October 28, 1987

STEPHEN GALLAGHER

hadn't immediately begun to coast on it. Whereas the earlier storytelling had seemed to be largely event-driven in the manner of, say, a Frederick Forsyth novel (Forsyth, a writer whom I otherwise greatly admire, does have this tendency to pack all of his "character stuff" into a few paragraphs and then get it out of the way somewhere around chapter three), the later work showed that Herbert had steadily increased his grip on his craft and begun to take an interest in character and atmosphere beyond the immediate call of duty.

What stayed with me from *The Jonah* was not so much the plotline or its inspiring device, or even any of the set-pieces, but rather the all-pervading atmosphere of the East Anglian coastline and the shabby caravan of the character's inner state. Details in books don't stay with us anyway, that's why we can re-read them after a while; the trick in writing is to use those details to manoeuvre the reader into sharing your outlook for a time so that he or she comes out at the end with a modified worldview which is then taken onward. Some shared outlooks stay with us more than others, some don't connect or stay with us at all; but if the point of stories lay only in their details, then reading would be a temporary and ultimately worthless experience.

What I'm saying is that Herbert passed the test in a way that the "nasty" reputation of his work wouldn't have led me to expect. It was a demonstration that one could achieve and hold on to bestsellerdom and yet still retain one's integrity. The sense of the book's hidden nervous system was clearly there, and not the least effect was that the *schlockmeister* persona that had made such a convenient handle for press coverage now demanded re-examination.

This has been slow coming but it's been happening, helped by classy packaging with no hint of the downmarket to it. Herbert is now bought and read by the kind of people who'll say they never buy or read horror. And, perhaps most encouraging of all, it's been a process in which the writing has led the hype rather than the other way around.

Which brings me to *Haunted*.

The history of this book differs from all of the others in that it was originally intended for the screen, and in so approaching it I was interested to see if any signs of compromise had crept in along the way. Looked at in this manner, *Haunted* becomes something of a test-case; conceived for another medium, will it hang together as a book or will it come over as a piece of quick exploitation, the most convenient way of recycling material that would otherwise have to be written off?

Herbert has discussed the TV origins of the book else-where, so I don't feel that I'm crossing any ethical boundaries by bringing them in here; very briefly, the storyline was originally developed as a TV concept for BBC producer Evgeny Gridneff (*Hold the Back Page, Star Cops*) and was then left without prospect of production on Gridneff's departure. The book was written alongside the script and, ironically, there's now said to be screen interest in the property again.

The first and most important question that has to be answered is, does *Haunted* have the feel of a novelisation? Scripts are scripts, and books are books. One deals in surface reality and the other with the inner lives of characters, and direct transposition is always something of a cheat. A book can't be lifted intact on to the screen, any more than a dog can be turned into a cat by feeding it Whiskas; and a screenplay turned straight into a book doesn't really work either, for the simple reason that screenplay writing is a minimalist art and any extra wordage becomes padding. All necessary insight is supposedly there in the dialogue and the situations – anything added should be superfluous. I know, I've done some of those weird hybrids in my earlier, hungrier days and I reckon that I can sniff one out from a mile away. The job of a noveliser is to tell a 20,000 word story in 50,000 words, treading water like crazy and hop-ing that nobody will spot the deception.

So, is *Haunted* just a novelisation?

The answer in this case is no, happily it isn't . . . for despite the brevity of the scenes and the uncomplicated structure, the sense is that Herbert has returned to his first notions and developed a book from there, rather than taking the easy way out and simply knocking up a facsimile of prose out of script material. It passes the crucial test in that we see the story from the inside, instead of seeing it pass before us. The only significant hangover from the earlier form is one of length; Her-bert himself has wryly pointed out that between the covers lurks a book of big type and thicker-than-usual paper.

And it works pretty well. *Haunted* is the story of David Ash, professional debunker of the supernatural, and his investi-gation of phenomena at a country house named Edbrook; it's traditional ghost story material treated in a modern, twist-in-the-concept manner, made more effective by the casting of its main character as a sceptic. *Haunted* has a freshness about it which has been absent from other recent visits to the genre – I'm thinking particularly of Susan Hill's overpraised *The Woman in Black*, which struck me as all-retread with little in the way

Mr Herbert is showing an alarming tendency to go over the top and into the ludicrous . . . Why does the author of The Survivor *need to resort to cannibalism, sado-masochism and explicit gore? I do not doubt that my criticism will send him crying all the way to the blood bank. In future I will take you home, James, but please spare the coarseness.*

– MICHAEL DOVE, from "Beastly Beat of Old Nick's Heart", *Sunday Express*, July 5, 1987

STEPHEN GALLAGHER

of new rubber at all – and yet there's a sense in which it picks up on some of the time-honoured conventions of the British ghost tale and makes them seem at home in a present-day setting. It's not a ground-breaker of a story in the way that one would expect from, say, Ramsey Campbell working in the same area, but it has an essential success which springs from the way that it combines its weird element with a world that is recognisable and familiar. This is always a potent combination for a popular writer to achieve, a notion that was first brought home to me by the image of H. G. Wells' Martian invaders in their Handling Machines as they cut a swathe of destruction across the London suburbs. All genre writers do this to some degree, of course; but somehow, Herbert has managed to hit upon the note that has made him so successful with a readership beyond the genre.

Given all of this, perhaps one of the strongest impressions that I brought away from the book is what a dumb, dumb decision it was for the BBC to let the property go instead of reassigning it to another producer. The juxtaposition of familiar form and original treatment is exactly the kind of thing that could hook them a mass audience.

Herbert isn't content to use the supernatural or the natural as a source of horror; he tries to use both, and fails seriously in the integration. His good characters all fight well against the encroaching dark, but the muddled view of what that darkness is saps the strength of the book, leaving it unsatisfying at the end, despite some gripping moments along the way.

– TOM WHITMORE, from *Locus*, Issue 330, July 1988

Stephen King, David Tate and James Herbert (circa 1984)

But then, let's face it, as far as Herbert's concerned he's got his mass audience already, and he didn't even have the free publicity of a TV dramatisation or a movie in achieving it (both *The Survivor* and *The Rats* typify the kind of screen adaptation that an author wouldn't much want to be advertised by). The BBC needed him more than he needed them, and they'll probably be the last ones to realise it.

But that's TV thinking for you.

Remembering that day in the studio, something else occurs to me. I already mentioned that the whole slant of the event tended towards being a puff for the book and the author on her publicity tour; only the dissenting voice of the academic, invited along because he'd done a study of a number of bestselling novels, gave the occasion any sense of balance. But if it had been Herbert up there, I can almost guarantee that all of the unstated, underlying assumptions would have been different. The line of questioning would almost certainly have been hostile, however pleasantly put, and he'd automatically have been required to handle the case for his own defence.

He's a horror writer, you see.

And they all just write nasties, don't they?

HAUNTED BY SUCCESS

John Gilbert

TWENTY THREE

BRITISH Master of Horror. British maybe, East End born and bred certainly, but James Herbert hates the MOH tag which even his rapacious critics give him. He's still learning his craft and hardly tapping middle age, although many of his fans have been with him since the days of *The Rats* in the early seventies.

The Rats was the first of the bestselling horror novels to hit Britain. In fact, it beat Stephen King's *Carrie* to the bookshelves by a few months. Since then James Herbert has sold 20 million copies of his books. No doubt you've read at least one critical review of those books. So, you've heard from the critics, now listen to the man . . .

John Gilbert: Why did you choose to start your career in the world of advertising?

James Herbert: I was never a writer to begin with, I was an artist. I was a kid that loved to draw and paint. But also I was good at English, so I guess that storytelling ability was always there, but art was the dominant factor in my life. I knew advertising was a very exciting job, it paid very well, and from my circumstances I was going to get a good job and earn money. I wasn't going to become indulgent and become a fine artist, I just didn't have the luxury of that. Art was my subject and the natural thing for me to do was to go into advertising.

Gilbert: How long did it take you to become an art director?

Herbert: I was one of those lucky guys. I left Art School at twenty, and by the time I was twenty-six I'd become a Group

"I am not usually scared by what I write. But the research I did for Sepulchre *disturbed me considerably."*

– JAMES HERBERT, from "Fear is the Key to Having a Bestseller" by Tom Moore, *Brighton Evening Argus*, May 25, 1987

Head, which is a kind of manager. You're doing creative work but you have a team – copywriter, art director, typographer. I had two around me. Normally to become Group Head in those days you were usually into your mid-thirties, if not forties. I wasn't a whiz kid, but I worked hard and I was good at what I did. It just developed very fast and I found myself in that position.

Gilbert: What made you switch to writing?

Herbert: I was attending more meetings than doing creative work. I still did a lot myself, but that meant working late evenings and weekends because of all these meetings. Eventually I did find that I was getting more and more away from the drawing board, so whatever creative urge was in me wasn't being used up. I needed more challenge. So, I decided to write a book.

This is all post-rationale, you understand. You make excuses or find reasons afterwards. It just seemed to happen with me. Because I was working with copywriters always talking about the great novel they were going to do, I guess that influenced me in some way, I thought yes I'll write a book.

Also, it was very heady days for me because I'd been promoted fairly young, I was making really good money in advertising, enjoying the work, enjoying the people. I seemed to be unable to do anything that was wrong. Everything was good for me. It sounds a bit . . . I don't know . . . I guess I sound as if I'm boasting, but this is just the way it was. Everything I touched seemed to come good and it filled me with a kind of confidence, although I've always been able to step back and look at myself and have a chuckle and that's stopped me getting very arrogant.

I just kind of assumed I could write a book. That was the weird thing, I had that confidence to do it. But I never imagined it would be published. I hoped it would be, but I never really thought it was going to happen. I needed to tell a story and so I did. I sat down and wrote the story at evenings and weekends and it just happened. I filled a gap in the publishing market.

It's some kind of synchronicity of timing that you can be there at exactly the right moment, there is a hole in the market, people suddenly tune in to what you've done. It's not me tuning in to the public taste, it was the public taste – or lack of taste you'd probably say with *The Rats* – that tuned in to me. It's called breaks, isn't it? A good break.

Gilbert: Stephen King came in shortly after *The Rats* . . .

Herbert: Yeah, Steve came very shortly after, with the same

"I think [Sepulchre] is the most intricate and sinister book I have ever written. It is not graphic in detail, but there are episodes in it that make even me shudder. And I wrote one part that was so horrible I couldn't keep it in."

– JAMES HERBERT, from "Smiling Face of Horror", *Western Mail*, May 8, 1987

Like [Dennis] Wheatley's novels of black magic, Sepulchre *is compulsively readable. I read it at one sitting . . . a relief from the seemingly unending re-vamps of Universal horror movie plots.*

– KEITH CURTIS, from *Terror Australis*, Number 1, Autumn 1988 publisher, and that's how Steve and I became good friends. We were both beginning together, he wrote *Carrie* and me previously with *The Rats*. We became good buddies then. He came over here, we did an after-dinner session together, and I reckon I was always Steve's PR man over here.

I get very embarrassed with interviews. I listen to myself and think "well, I'm going over the top and making myself sound too good", and what I used to do in the old days, I'd always divert it to Steve and say: "Yes, I do this, but have you read Stephen King, this guy is fantastic", and not too many people had heard of him in those days.

Gilbert: Did you choose horror, or did horror choose you?

Herbert: Horror really did choose me. I thought of this subject of the rats because of my upbringing. Also I was influenced by the *Dracula* film, the old Bela Lugosi film with the vision of a thousand rats staring up at this madman Renfield. For me as an art director that was very visual.

I think, because I was an art director, I've always written visually, people can see the pictures as I write. So, I tied the two up; but I never intended to be a horror writer. I'd never intended to be a writer. But once I'd done *The Rats* it turned out to be a horror story. It wasn't a conscious effort to make it a horror story. And it was a different kind of horror story. It was graphic, said a lot more than most horror stories said before that and I realised "I like this".

I'd always been interested in the supernatural and the paranormal and horror, I'd always liked horror. I was not a fanatic about it but I'd always liked it, and it seemed to fit me like a glove. And then when the next one turned out to be horror, *The Fog*, I thought "well, that's obviously what I am. I'm a horror writer".

Gilbert: After *The Fog*, unlike other writers, you switched away from the single-threat novel to broader-based novels. Were you worried about being typecast?

Herbert: Not at all. I've never been that self-conscious of what I do. I'd explored the territory of mass violence with *The Rats* and *The Fog*, then I wanted to do something to do with the supernatural and more of an intimate story, hence *The Survivor*. That was horror but on a different level. I've always done this, always gone on to different levels.

If you look at my past five books, they could almost be by five different authors. You could go to *Domain, Moon, Magic Cottage, Sepulchre* and *Haunted*; they're all different in their own way. *Magic Cottage* is a far different tone of voice than any of the others, apart from *Fluke*. So, I've always tried to do something different each time to sustain my own interest, to keep me going. And if I'm interested I can usually be sure that the reader would be interested.

Gilbert: Did you always intend *The Rats* to be a trilogy?

Herbert: No, far from it. People have said to me time and time again that I was really smart to leave *The Rats* open-ended so I could do a sequel, but I didn't even know *The Rats* would be published, let alone have a sequel.

Very basically, *The Rats* really was symbolic of the system that we're all up against, that does us down, every day we have our own short empiric victories against that system, but it still trundles on. That's why the rats continued after the hero, our Everyman, had won his own battle. The system still trundled on.

Years later there was a huge demand for that sequel, but I didn't want to do it. Then I was so drained after writing *The Spear* that I wanted something a bit easier. I didn't need to research *The Rats*. And so *Lair*: I'd moved out into the suburbs. I'd lived near Epping Forest before – when I got married I moved to Epping Forest, Buckhurst Hill – then I moved to Woodford, but still within the region of the forest. And so I was able to stroll over to the forest and get all my locations, details. They weren't going to let me in the forest. I contacted the warden and said "I'm going to write a book about Epping Forest. I should warn you, though, it's going to be a horror story", and he said, "We really don't like this sort of thing, we get too much bad publicity . . ." because all the villains in the East End dump bodies out there.

He said "You should write your book, without going to their [the forest's research] establishment, without seeing their facts and figures. Submit it to us and we'll tell you what is right and what is wrong". I said, "no way". That's why in *Lair* the warden is not a very sympathetic character. I think he may even get gobbled up by the rats.

For me, then, having made that statement that the rats existed in the poor part of London, they bred on that poverty as symbolic of the system, I was saying that it's not just that part of London that's involved, it's everybody, and I moved the rats out to suburbia.

So that was the point of the second book, and *Domain*, well that was the whole irony of the trilogy. *Domain* justifies the other two. I don't think any one stands up on its own, but when you put the three together you understand what the whole series was about. It was me saying that we have this system. These rats which were symbolic of the system were created

Sepulchre is a hard-hitting and intense novel . . . it's a thriller which holds its own with the likes of MacLean and Ludlum . . . combining unique and outstanding characterisation, a driving storyline and originality with rare skill.

– DAVE HUGHES, *Skeleton Crew* II, 1988

James Herbert once again proved to be Britain's bestselling genre author with the year's 7th bestselling hardcover fiction title, Sepulchre, *and the number 3 paperback,* The Magic Cottage.

– STEPHEN JONES, from *Science Fiction Chronicle*, Issue 102, March 1988 by the very establishment that created nuclear arms, and these mutant rats were bred from that. This system happened to be the government of the day.

I'm not anti-right, I'm not anti-left, but it is a fact that whatever government's in power have their own shelters. They're all safe when the bomb goes off. They've got their shelters under the Thames Embankment. I thought I might get served a D-notice on *Domain*. I gave away a lot of secrets, I know where most of these places are, but nobody seems to have picked it up, which is disappointing in a way.

But they had their little base where they were going to be safe, all the élite of our society, and yet when our hero, our Mr Everyman – I used to like my heroes to represent me, you, the woman reader, whoever's reading that book; that's why in the past I've rarely described a hero, because I wanted the person reading the book to put themselves in the hero's place – when Mr Everyman got across to this underground shelter and the establishment had been wiped out by a symbolic system, they'd been torn to pieces by the rats themselves. That was the whole irony, the system being eaten by its own creation.

There's another piece in there that not many people seem to have noticed. Culver, our hero, he found the mother rat and it had just given birth and the embryo, foetuses, resembled the human embryo. That was just one of my little twists, I said "well maybe we didn't evolve from the ape, maybe we evolved from the rats and that's why they were so like us". That's why they were mutating more to what we've become.

Gilbert: Does horror hold more value than just entertainment?

Herbert: It has to, but I think that any piece of good writing does have more than its obvious face value. Again, we can get very pompous about this, and I notice the whole horror genre does tend to get this way. We can get very pretentious. So, I've always held back from that.

But I do have to make the point that, yes, on one level it is entertainment, on another level I try to make lots of points about the human condition, society today, often a lot of politics, all sorts of things. There's also quite a bit of humour in my stories, apart from *Sepulchre*, which is about the meanest book I've done.

There are different levels, and you hope the reader is going to catch them. But if they don't it doesn't matter. They've paid their money and they take whatever they want from these stories. It's just satisfying for me as a writer to put these things in, these great ironies. All my books are full of irony. It's satisfying for me to do that, whether it's noticed or not, that

Britain's bestselling horror writer James Herbert has finally decided to get himself a literary agent. He has always argued that "No one else can do a deal as well as I can", and with sales of his books approaching 17 million, who can argue with that?

However, with the pressure of a yearly novel to be sold and promoted around the world and two movie projects on the go, he has chosen Bruce Hunter at David Higham to represent him: "I needed an English champion to say, 'This is James Herbert and this is what he does,'" revealed the author.

– STEPHEN JONES and JO FLETCHER, from *Science Fiction Chronicle*, Issue 96, September 1987 doesn't matter. I think most of the reasonable critics see that in the stories, the others just don't want to see it.

Gilbert: Some critics seem to start sharpening their knives even before your new book appears. How do you feel about their comments?

Herbert: I've always had that. I'm okay with the national press. On the whole, for every bad review I've had I can show you six or seven good ones. So they kind of accept me for what I am, and a lot of them don't even like horror, but they can accept what I do. Even my worst critics in the national press say that I'm a good writer, I tell good stories. But, it's those within the horror genre, they're the guys that don't like me. They hate my success. One of the several things they don't like about me is that I'm not a purist as regards horror; I'll make political statements, I'll write about terrorist activities, I'll write adventure novels.

I don't often go into the fantasy of horror. I bring it in but I like to take the reader along with me and keep it very real until I decide I'm going to go over the top, and that invites them to take the mental leap with me. I'm resented because of that.

Gilbert: How do you view the films of *The Rats* and *Survivor*?

Herbert: I try not to view them. They had nothing to do with me. They just happen to be adapted from my stories.

Gilbert: Loosely . . .

Herbert: Yeah, very loosely. The film-makers just took them away and filmed them. *Survivor*, I thought I had more say in what went on because I was involved with the production company and saw the first script, but then they sold it to another company who then sold it to another company. So I got lost on the way.

I couldn't believe it. I saw *The Survivor* when I was in Australia on tour and they put it on at this huge cinema in the afternoon. I fell asleep halfway through. I couldn't understand the story. So, yes, it's made me very cautious of films.

Gilbert: Would you want to produce or direct?

Herbert: No, I wouldn't want to do either of those things because they're too time-consuming, too fraught with other people's opinions, that's why I've always refused to do scripts. Writing books is very pure. It comes from you and there's very little change and I like it. But with scripts there's too many other fingers in the pie, although I've done one for *Haunted*.

But now I'm thinking I'd quite like to get heavily involved. This is the thing I admire about Clive Barker, that we can all moan about the film industry over here and that nothing is happening with our books, and yet Clive comes along and he

The mega-personality of the summer has to be our own James Herbert, the subject of a £40,000 Saatchi & Saatchi promotion for his new novel, Haunted, *out in hardcover from Hodder & Stoughton, and the mass-market New English Library paperback of last year's bestseller,* Sepulchre. *The massive media blitz started with a special eight-page supplement in the UK book trade newspaper* Publishing News; *despite being dated April 1st(!), it included an interview by Neil Gaiman (who is rumoured to be collaborating on a new* photographic *book with Herbert) and raves from almost everyone at Hodder who has ever been connected with Jim! Still, with his track record (more than 20 million copies of his books sold worldwide) one can hardly blame their euphoria.*

– STEPHEN JONES and JO FLETCHER, from *Science Fiction Chronicle*, Issue 105, June 1988

Eileen Herbert

Kerry Herbert

Emma Herbert

Casey Herbert

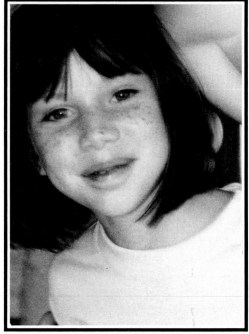

JOHN GILBERT

just does it, he makes it himself. It's great. Maybe later I'll get involved. I always think of Steve [King] though, when he directed his first film. He'd always resisted anything like that. He'd always also said that if he did direct his books for a movie, it would be the most scary horror film yet and unfortunately . . . I haven't seen *Maximum Overdrive*, but has anybody . . . ?

Gilbert: What about the film version of *Shrine*?

Herbert: Yes, funny story about *Shrine*. This has been in, not production even, but trying to get the finances together for a couple of years now. The guy who's writing the screenplay was a legend in his own lifetime, called Jesse Lasky. He's about eighty-two. He wrote *The Ten Commandments* and *Samson and Delilah* – see, there's this religious content. He was writing the script for *Shrine*. Trouble is, he died a couple of weeks ago.

[Short pause for commiserations and hysteria . . .]

Herbert: It's still being written and I don't know, we'll just keep our fingers crossed. The producer is David Wickes, who's making the *Jack the Ripper* film with Michael Caine. But again, it's a matter of getting the finance together.

Magic Cottage; there may be a good film of that. The guy who's doing that wrote *The Fly* and the director wants me to be involved. The other one is *Fluke*, which an Italian is doing. It's going to be made, they say, in Philadelphia.

Gilbert: Which of your books would *you* like to see as a film?

Herbert: *The Fog*. I'd like personally to remake *The Survivor*. I do like that story so much that I think such an opportunity was missed there. *Magic Cottage*, I'd like to see filmed, but then all of them I'd like to see filmed, let's face it.

Gilbert: What's the story on the TV version of *Haunted*?

Herbert: That was an ongoing situation that I had very high hopes of and the BBC persuaded me to do it. I didn't want to do it. They were going to make a two-hour TV movie, to be shown on the screen in the States and on television here at Christmas. There was a great buzz about it. Then, unfortunately, politics got involved. I didn't even get a letter from the BBC, all I got was this phone call from this obviously very disgruntled producer saying "Jim, we're not doing it".

I think it's a missed opportunity for the BBC and it's something the public would want, a good ghost story, not overtly horrific, just a nice psychological ghost story. There's a lot of subtleties in there, but there's a lot of subtleties in all my books. Some of them, the horror pervades everything else, so you lose sight of the twists.

Gilbert: There seems to be some sort of plan within the styles

Hodder & Stoughton decided to mark the paperback launch of James Herbert's Haunted *on August 3 with a stylish champagne reception at the Grand Hotel in Brighton. Just back from a recent PR trip to Dublin, Britain's bestselling horror author described how a bookstore window display, which included life-size cut-outs of Batman on one side and himself on the other, resulted in one young fan commenting, "I didn't know you were Bruce Wayne!"*

– STEPHEN JONES and JO FLETCHER, from *Science Fiction Chronicle*, Issue 121, October 1989

Herbert is one of England's bestselling novelists [and] one of the best horror/ suspense novelists around. Haunted *is just the latest reason why . . . Riveting, nonstop reading.* Haunted *is one of Herbert's best!*

– STEPHEN KING

of your books which throws the reader off the scent of what you're going to write next. Is there a plan?

Herbert: That's exactly right. It's just the way I go on. It's not self-conscious of me doing that, but I don't want the reader to know what's coming next. It's not like the *Carry On*, it's not *Carry On Horror*, you know, *Carry On Herbert*. For me to sustain my own interests I've got to try something a little bit new each time.

Sepulchre is the very antithesis of *Magic Cottage*; it's because having done *Magic Cottage*, having enjoyed it because there's a lot of warmth in there – a lot of humour – the horror is gradual. With *Sepulchre* I needed to go to the other extreme, really hard, quite horrific and again not as graphic as some people might suppose. There's no warmth in that book at all. The hero, I mean this guy is a wicked man, and he has to be that way to do what he does at the end of the story. The challenge was to use this lesser evil.

The other statement I made was that there are no absolutes, no absolute good, no absolute evil and that is one of the reasons that Kline, this archvillain, fails at the end. He's not absolutely evil.

The last few pages of the book are almost a soliloquy of Kline lying there limbless with this mental conversation with his deity, the Devil, saying "have I been too weak?" He couldn't be ultimately evil, he's let his master down, because it was hard work being evil. It's hard work being a saint so it stands to reason that it's going to be hard work being evil. Nobody's absolutely evil, nobody's absolutely good.

Gilbert: Do people often see you as responsible for putting violence and horror into young minds?

Herbert: What I'm doing is not really new, it's of this era. Anything less would be bland. I don't do what certain books do nowadays, certain video nasties. I hate video nasties, I find them distasteful, but mostly I find them very boring. I write for my generation and generations after. I couldn't have done what I did ten years before [*The Rats*] because nobody was ready for it. In every one of my stories there's a strong moral tale. So these kids are reading these stories, and yes, they're getting their rocks off reading about this very scary stuff, but probably, subliminally, maybe overtly, they're taking a message from those stories and they're saying good should win throughout.

The cowboy doesn't wear the white hats any more, that's too unsubtle. For our day and age there's gotta be a little bit more to it. Nobody's perfect.

SELLING A BESTSELLER

Nick Sayers
Ian Hughes
David Singer
Tony Hammond

HAUNTING POINT-OF-SALE MATERIAL

TWENTY FOUR

Nick Sayers, Senior Editor, on James Herbert,
the ultimate professional

IN many ways, James Herbert is the epitome of the modern novelist – interested and involved in every stage of his books from the typeface to the jacket (in fact, his input into the design of his books is unique as Ian Hughes, Hodder & Stoughton's Art Director, will tell you), from the copy-editing to the promotion plans and beyond. But in others he is enjoyably old-fashioned! He thinks about every word before putting pen to paper – he writes each novel longhand before it is word-processed and bound for spectacular presentation to his publishers – and he truly enjoys the craft of storytelling, of turning his ideas into a novel that really works.

The psychological thriller requires a refined sense of timing perhaps more than most forms and I find that Jim's feeling for rhythm and pace, of how much to put in and how much to leave out, is quite uncanny. This is due, I'm sure, not only to his prodigious natural talent but also to sheer hard work and the fact that he has remained in touch with, but never a slave to, the people who buy his books.

I have worked with Jim on two books now, *Sepulchre* and *Haunted,* and naturally we debate points when it comes to the editing, but it's never a case of my wanting fundamental changes to the structure – it's simply too well thought-out for that to happen.

One intervening chapter [of Haunted] – describing Ash and a colleague's visit to the seance of a supposedly charlatan clairvoyant – is so telling and even moving that I became annoyed with Herbert for wasting his serious talents on such a miserable if lucrative genre as horror fiction.

– SEAN THOMAS, from "Wasting His Talents", *Literary Review*, October 1988

He has his stylistic characteristics, a recognisable personality on the page which his vast readership loves, but at the same time, he has a great ability to make each book different, and I think this is another key to his success that I never want to meddle with.

Jim is writing with supreme confidence at this stage of his phenomenal bestselling career. In *Haunted*, he has simply met a genre-topic head on and turned it into something uniquely his own. It's as if he has dared himself to find some new life in the haunted house mystery and won the bet resoundingly.

From my point of view – and any editor's for that matter – there is nothing more enjoyable than working with an author who you know deserves to be a bestseller, on a book that you know will be.

Ian Hughes, Art Director, on the designing of James Herbert's covers

Because of his experience as an art director and then Group Head in the advertising business, James Herbert has more involvement and influence with his cover and jacket designs than any other author on the Hodder list. He is quite simply summed up in three words – the total professional.

Jim produced roughs for both *Sepulchre* in paperback and *Haunted* in hardcover which he then passed on to me to produce the finished illustrations and artwork.

Haunted will look very special. Several artists have been used to get to the final artwork stage as there are many elements which make up the jacket:

(1) A special mnemonic has been designed which will then also be used on the paperback.
(2) A front cover illustration in full colour has also been produced using the mnemonic as reference.
(3) The back jacket illustration is a black and white line engraving based on the front cover illustration.
(4) Special illustrated border design around the back jacket illustration.
(5) Hand drawn lettering on the front.
(6) Hand drawn border design around the front jacket.

As each element of the jacket comes in, it is copied and sent to the author for approval. Jim has a great talent in spotting what is necessary to turn an already great painting into an even better one. We warn each artist to expect a correction even though they believe they have created "their finest hour" already! And I have yet to meet one who has worked on any of Jim's books

James Herbert's Haunted *is a ghost story in the classic Anglo-British tradition. It's much more in the stamp of Henry James'* The Turn of the Screw *than it is in the Stephen King mode into which much of Herbert's work generally falls . . . Herbert keeps his prose moody and the mood tormented in this one.* Haunted *is an effective and disturbing novel . . .*

– EDWARD BRYANT, from *Locus*, Issue 346, November 1989

Haunted *is a genuinely frightening book – one of those where the reader is drawn to the very edge of terror, and then dragged unceremoniously and quite mercilessly further . . . !*

– DAVE HUGHES, *Skeleton Crew* II, 1988

NICK SAYERS/IAN HUGHES

who hasn't agreed at the end of the day that the corrections we have made have benefited the final covers.

The cover for the paperback edition of *Sepulchre* is a derivative from the hardcover jacket, but using a full-colour illustration. The lettering was again hand-drawn along the specifications given by the author. We actually produced a separate full-colour version of the type in air-brushed lettering, but this was thought less striking than the foiled version. We tried white backgrounds and black backgrounds with various colour foils on each before we settled on the present cover. It is very powerful, the lettering bold yet classy, and the illustration is technically brilliant. We have also used a tip-in page as on Jim's previous books. Once again this has a very fine illustration on it and the blurb will appear on this tip-in. I think that this combination of both the cover and tip-in will produce one of the best paperback covers of 1988.

Finally, and this is a *very* important point indeed, the cover and jacket are only a part of the total finished James Herbert package. Jim also designs the prelims, contents list, chapter headings and page layouts for his books. The results are a totally integrated and superbly designed series of titles that show the way for other publishers to follow. And *Haunted* will be the best yet!

David Singer, Commercial Director, on the marketing of James Herbert in paperback

Indisputably, James Herbert is now one of the biggest selling paperback authors. *The Sunday Times* bestsellers of 1987 saw *The Magic Cottage* in the number three slot, whilst the *Guardian* Top 100 of 1987 shows *The Magic Cottage* as the sixth biggest selling UK paperback of the year.

Amongst these statistics there is one particularly significant fact and that is the phenomenal rate of sale following publication, well in excess of 100,000 copies being sold within a few months of publication on top of an already massive subscription.

There are of course myriad reasons why this should be, ranging from, first and foremost, the sheer quality of any James Herbert novel. The projection of Jim himself within the media, the ever-increasing audience in hardcover and the subsequent broadening of his market and of course the enormous commitment which Hodder & Stoughton have to the author.

Specifically, marketing has a major pivotal role to play and to this end we, in paperbacks, whilst being more than satisfied with previous campaigns, are determined that each should be

The ending [of Haunted] is undoubtedly over-blown: untold numbers of corpses rise from the grave, as in Michael Jackson's Thriller, *faces turn and are seen to be half-rotted away, maggots crawl obediently through eye-sockets with such gay abandon one wonders if the effect is meant to be comic.*

– SEAN THOMAS, from "Wasting His Talents", *Literary Review*, October 1988

Herbert's deftly written narrative is supremely subtle, so much so that the awful suggestions that lurk between the sentences stealthily creep up on you unawares until a sudden noise affirms that the chill has truly set into your bones. The terrifying images at the end of the book are particularly difficult to shake off.

– from "Haunting Thriller", *Barnes, Mortlake & Sheen Times*, August 4, 1989 better than the last. The campaign for *Sepulchre* will without doubt be the best ever.

The marketing thrust of course stems from the cover design and we are privileged in being able to have a very close involvement with Jim from the outset. Not only do we have an exceptionally talented author but with his long experience of the advertising industry, an extremely gifted designer/ideas man to boot.

Since the publication of *Moon* in the summer of 1986, each new Herbert paperback has had a highly distinctive look, emphasised of course by a double cover or "tip-in", which not only makes for a wonderful package, but also adds to the cherishment of the books.

The previous two titles, *Moon* and *The Magic Cottage*, and the forthcoming *Sepulchre*, have similarities other than tip-ins, namely that *a*) the author's name and title of the book feature prominently and *b*) the image used, whilst not necessarily dominating, is extremely striking and powerful.

This then is the basic theme continued through the point-of-sale with the addition of the use of photographs of Jim himself. There is a full range of *Sepulchre* POS, including a box tower unit, 36 copy dumpbin, with cut-out headboard, shelf strip, box book and two posters, making up a comprehensive display package for the trade to use, capitalising on the massive business which the publication of a new James Herbert paperback has become.

Slipstreaming all this will of course be a major Saatchi & Saatchi advertising campaign, the third Herbert promotion they have handled for us. We have all now come to expect very special things from the world's Number One advertising agency, and *Sepulchre* promises to be the best yet. At the time of writing the exact plans had not been finalised, Saatchi being in the midst of concluding some specific market research for this title. However it is intended that the campaign be a double media event, utilising both radio and press. We have specifically targeted with a brief to reach a minimum of 4 million listeners who will hear the commercial at least four times. Meantime the press campaign will naturally be targeted at a different audience to the radio, and of course that for *Haunted*. It will run in the *Mail on Sunday*, the *Sun* and *The Sunday Times*, reaching the full cross-section of James Herbert's audience. As a final point I should also mention that unlike our hardcover colleagues and indeed perhaps most other book advertising campaigns, the paperback ads will not appear on either book pages or, in the case of *The Sunday Times*, the Book Supplement, primarily

DAVID SINGER

because we have evidence that in this market the ads are more likely to be seen and responded to in the general context of the overall newspaper.

The final element of course in any marketing campaign is the PR side and as my colleague Tony Hammond mentions in the article on *Haunted*, Jim is a wonderfully promotable author, much loved and in demand both by the media and the trade. You can be certain that Anna Bence-Trower, our Publicity Manager, will be putting together a schedule which brings to the attention of the public the news that James Herbert has his latest book, *Sepulchre*, out in paperback.

In conclusion it is, I hope, evident that a tremendous amount of hard work goes into each James Herbert campaign. I am very fortunate in being able to head an extremely talented team, made up principally of Dennis Le Baigue, our Marketing Manager, who incidentally has years of experience to call upon at the sharp end of selling Jim's books; Robert Bacon, our Sales Promotions Manager, who can rightly be proud of the many promotions he has handled over the years, and of course Anna Bence-Trower, our Publicity Manager, with all the skills of diplomacy and persuasion that this demanding role needs. Add to this the talent of our Art Director, Ian Hughes, and the input of Jim himself and it becomes apparent why, in this fickle business of ours, few things are more certain than that a new James Herbert will be an instant Number One bestseller and, just as important, is so, with sales figures that justify in every way the genuine tag of bestseller, both on publication and for the many months following.

This August saw Hodder giving a big push to James Herbert's latest horror hit, Haunted. *Despite not feeling too well, the popular author travelled the length of the country, meeting fans, being interviewed by radio, television and the press. He even turned up on the BBC-TV* Breakfast Time *show giving his opinions of the day's events! The exhausting tour finished in grand style in London where Jim had a phenomenally successful lunchtime signing in his native East End, followed by a two-hour session at Forbidden Planet, where nearly 200 copies of the hardcover were sold!*

– STEPHEN JONES and JO FLETCHER, from *Science Fiction Chronicle*, Issue 110, November 1988

I was first deputed to work with James Herbert on the hardcover launch of *Shrine*. I had already heard a lot about Jim and his extraordinary success story and the fact that we had both shared a past in the advertising industry (although I was a mere humble copywriter and Jim became a Group Head of a leading agency) made me warm to the idea of working with him immediately.

The word *fun* is one which one doesn't hear too much about these days, but it is a word that constantly springs to mind when working with a complete professional like Jim. Not only do I appreciate all the help and time he puts into getting the promotional package right – both the point-of-sale, the sell-in material and the advertising – but he also tells such a good story!

One of the items I produced for the hardcover campaigns of *Shrine, The Magic Cottage* and *Sepulchre* was what we call at Hodders a double-sided poster, one side utilising the cover artwork of the book and a selling headline and the other Jim's own remarkable life story. Each of the hardcover editions has been sent out to reviewers together with the posters and the media's response to Jim's own life story has been absolutely staggering!

He has appeared on BBC-TV's *Wogan* twice already and I don't think I will be upsetting them unduly if I can reveal that they would love him to make it a hat-trick in the not so very distant future! He has appeared on a whole host of shows such as BBC Radio 2's *John Dunn* and *Gloria Hunniford* programmes (not to mention *Round Midnight*), BBC Radio 4's *Bookshelf* and *Start the Week*, BBC-TV's *Breakfast Time*, the list is as long as your arm! But I think that which gave me the greatest kick of all (I can't speak for Jim!) was when he became one of Michael Parkinson's castaways on *Desert Island Discs*. And he has already been featured in *The Sunday Times Colour Magazine*'s "A Day In the Life of" and *You* magazine among others. The point is that he really does have something to say and he can always be relied upon to leaven it with a good portion of good humour. And yes, he is home-grown, a BRITISH success story, a man who has made his own way and carved out a unique place for himself in the pantheon of bestselling writers.

Putting together the promotional package for *Haunted* has been a particularly rewarding experience. Jim's hardcover success has mirrored his paperback success and every new novel gives me the opportunity to work with Jim, Ian Hughes, Hodder's Art Director, and now Saatchi & Saatchi to come up with a campaign that will do all of us justice.

Jim has a huge international following, people who will queue round the block whenever he does a signing session, people of all ages and from all backgrounds. They are not just buyers of James Herbert novels, they are his FANS. The challenge that Jim has given us with *Haunted* is that he has produced a contemporary ghost story written in the classic tradition of Henry James, Algernon Blackwood and Mary Shelley. We want to be able to reach those hardback fiction buyers who may not have bought a James Herbert novel before, but who will enjoy a superbly crafted ghost story.

Jim sat in on the briefing meeting with Saatchi & Saatchi (who have worked on both *The Magic Cottage* and *Sepulchre* campaigns) and they went away with a very clear idea of what we expected from them. The result is that we will be running a series of high-impact 15cm x three column advertisements in *The Sunday Times* Books Supplement, the *Observer*, the *Daily Telegraph*, the *Guardian*, the *Independent* and *The Times*. This campaign will reach 12,000,000 ABC1 readers and will run on the books pages of all the newspapers.

This extremely powerful consumer advertising campaign will be backed up by windows and in-store displays featuring both 3D "Big Books" and full-colour double-sided posters so that no customer on entering his or her local bookshop will be unaware that there is a very special new James Herbert novel out in hardcover. The POS will utilise the very fine cover artwork and will carry two messages: *To be haunted is to glimpse a truth that might best be hidden* and *A contemporary ghost story in the classic tradition*. And it is no blow to my pride that Jim had a lot to do with both of them!

And if I can make one final point, it is that James Herbert also greatly appeals to a female readership – and this is underlined by the exciting news that *Woman* Magazine will be undertaking a major 4-part serialisation of *Haunted* starting on July 30.

He really is an author who gives his publishers everything – and we try to respond in kind.

James Herbert, Britain's top horror writer, is celebrating his incursion into his twenty-first foreign country: he has just sold rights to Haunted *in* Mexico. *He revealed: "I always get a buzz when I sell into a new market. I got a real kick out of Argentina and getting into some of the Eastern Bloc countries like Czechoslovakia gave me a thrill. I love seeing all those foreign editions of my books – the Japanese ones are particularly wonderful. This is my first deal with Mexico and I'm delighted. If it goes well, there's plenty of backlist for them to pick up."*

– STEPHEN JONES and JO FLETCHER, from *Science Fiction Chronicle*, Issue 123, December 1989

IN THE HALL OF THE MONSTER KING: MUSIC AND THE MAESTRO OF HORROR

Edwin Pouncey

TWENTY FIVE

FIND out everything you possibly can about James Herbert and music . . . So ran my editorial instruction for my contribution to this book on James Herbert. The task was certainly not as easy as it first sounded. Although numerous (mostly hard rock) musicians claim that Herbert's stories have had a massive influence on their lyrics and ideas, any reference to music in general remains elusive in the pages of his novels. Unlike Stephen King, who delights in making rock music references throughout his books, Herbert's work is bare of such added detail; whatever music James Herbert likes is presumably playing in his head rather than on the printed page.

Seated on the sofa in James Herbert's spacious and luxuriously furnished London flat supplies no clues to his musical tastes either. While he busies himself in the kitchen preparing coffee I cast a critical eye around the room, hoping to find a record collection, a bookshelf or, perhaps, a signed photo or poster from some admiring rock star. Alas, nothing catches my eye. The answers to my questions are not about to be found by detective work, only hard questioning will reveal just how important music is to the dark world of James Herbert.

James Herbert's musical interests began as a young rebel during the fifties when rock 'n' roll reached out and touched his innocent soul. "Years ago it was the old rock 'n' roll, I mean the original rock 'n' roll from Bill Haley, who I didn't like very much. I just liked this new sound that was coming in at the time. I was a very small kid but I had two older brothers who would buy the records and listen to this music. We had an old

Dansette record player and I just loved it. I got hooked on Buddy Holly but then I started taking an interest in all forms of music."

Today James Herbert admits to liking light classical music and classic rock 'n' roll; opera he detests, even though he had to research Wagner's *The Legend Of Parsifal* for his book *The Spear*. Neither is he particularly impressed by hard rock or Heavy Metal . . . "I've got some rock tapes in the car but when I'm driving I'd rather listen to classics than rock 'n' roll. I haven't retrogressed to Heavy Metal, I can take it or leave it; some I like but most I leave alone. I don't like much that's in the hit parade but I still, to this day, watch *Top of the Pops* and I guess I've been doing that for some thirty years."

Is this out of habit or is he genuinely interested in what's going on?

"It's not just habit," he insists, "it's interest. I do like to hear new music and, of course, I've got daughters so they like to watch it as well. The terrible thing though is that it's all so much the same now. There seems to be only three categories: Heavy Metal, Rap – which I hate – and the Kylie Minogue crowd."

What about artists such as Phil Collins and their ilk?

"They're quality . . . I'll have to be careful what I say here because I've met Phil Collins, but I find them a bit tedious now. There's nothing new that's really exciting any more, is there?"

But is that because middle age has set in and your musical tastes have become jaded?

"That's the question you always ask yourself if you've got any sense, but I don't think it's that simple. I believe that the raw tone rock used to have doesn't seem to be there any more. Years ago the tunes they got out of using a series of simple chords was incredible. What we're missing now, if I can use a very old-fashioned word, is melody. I remember my first job in advertising where there was this old art director who was my boss. I used to sing in a band now and again and he used to say to me, 'What do you do, Jim . . . Are you lead melody?' [*laughs*] I thought that was great, but I'm hoping today that I'm not sounding like that guy."

Is there anything around at the moment though, that you admire in some way?

"I actually like bands like Bros. I think they're criticised and mocked because of their teen appeal but I think there's a little bit more there than people give them credit for."

How about musical trends in general? Was there ever any

James Herbert goes to very few conventions of any sort. In fact, he said, he was a little worried about this one. Would he be surrounded by weirdos? Perhaps lunatic weirdos? Would the convention members be like some of the people who write him fan mail, such as the one who sleeps with his twelve pet rats who have names like "Marmaduke" and "Fluffy"? Or would they be like the reader who wrote to inform him that she loved his books and considered him one of her three best friends in all the world (the other two were the Marquis de Sade and Charles Manson)?

– JANE JEWELL, from "1988 World Fantasy Awards Banquet", *Locus*, Issue 335, December 1988 uniform you adopted to reflect the musical tastes of your teen-age years?

"My eldest brother was a Teddy Boy, my middle brother was a Mod, and I think I was a combination of Mod and Indi-vidualist."

Individualist?

The high-spot of Saturday was Douglas E. Winter interviewing (I nearly said cross-examining) GoH James Herbert, who, amongst other things, admitted he used to read parts from novels he was working on to his kids as bed-time stories. I wonder what he got them for pets?

– MIKE CHINN, from "The 1988 World Fantasy Convention", *Science Fiction Chronicle*, Issue 112, January 1989

"It's funny, everybody seems to have forgotten that term. If you didn't want to be a Mod you called yourself an Individual-ist. You wore the bum-freezer jacket but you were smarter than a Mod, you had a bit more flair. Individualists wore the long, high collars and the three button jackets. You'd be the first to wear the cuban heels and your hair wasn't quite as short as a Mod's. That was the real trend in those days, it was cooler to be an Individualist rather than a Mod. I must have been a mixture of all those things: Teddy Boy, Mod, Individualist and Hippy, I was a real mish-mash of styles. In those days I didn't have any money to buy clothes, you bought a jacket and wore it for the rest of the year."

It seems to me that the only thing you missed out on was being a Punk! What did you think about the Punk Rock move-ment of the late seventies? I guess a lot of the early Punk Rockers were avid readers of your books!

"The good thing about Punk Rock was that its raw energy carried it through, it was so gutsy and real. That soon became a pretence and a lot of the Punk musicians found that they were learning their craft, they were actually learning how to play their guitars properly and because of that some of the raw energy started to disappear. I actually liken myself to a Punk Rocker. When I started off with *The Rats* and *The Fog* it was sheer energy that carried the stories through. They were a little bit raw, they weren't badly written or anything but there was a mass of energy that carried them through. The more I wrote, the more I learned the craft of writing, so the trick for me was to write better stories but hang on to that energy. What I tend to do nowadays, because I'm aware of that, is to write a book that's sheer style and another which is real mayhem and mad-ness, one that is full of sheer energy but hopefully better written than the ones I did years ago."

The early musical career of James Herbert burst into creative bloom while he was at Hornsey College of Art, studying Graphic Design for his eventual move to advertising. Jim remembers those early attempts with affection, smiling broadly at the mem-ories my probing has reawakened.

"I used to sing all the time," he laughs. "I don't sing now

EDWIN POUNCEY

though because my voice has gone. I was always singing, always rock 'n' rolling . . . at Art School every other person plays a guitar. I bought a guitar for ten bob [50 pence] and I had great coaching there from all the other students who could play. I also used to get up at the art college dance and sing a few numbers. That was good, I was always into that and I guess I could have had the choice to carry on with music or go into advertising [*laughs*]. I did used to enjoy singing in the band though, I used to drive them crazy at the art school because while we were sitting there painting I'd be singing away. One week I was up on stage at the art college singing a bit of Chuck Berry and Ricky Nelson, and a week later a new band on the scene came to Hornsey College of Art and they were pretty good . . . They were the Rolling Stones!"

What was your impression of the early Stones?

"I thought they were great musicians but actually I preferred the Beatles . . . The Stones were exciting though. I didn't think Jagger could sing, and I still don't, but he did have something that carried him through. It was more 'in' to like the Stones than the Beatles and that's probably why I went more for the Beatles. I hate being 'in'."

Did you, or do you now, write your own songs?

"I bought myself a Bechstein grand piano, just one of the few indulgences I've treated myself to, and that's great to bash around on. I can't really play, but again it's all chord stuff. I've always played to accompany myself singing, unfortunately I did that a bit too often so now I'm a chord man rather than just playing single notes. I guess I'd make a reasonable rhythm guitarist in a band, but nothing more than that and it would take me a few weeks to get back into it. If I have a party I'll get the guitar out and have a good old session but that's as far as it goes really . . . I just don't have the time."

I've heard a rumour though that you have a recording studio set up in your home, is this true or false?

"No, it's not true at all [*laughs*]. I do have this great music room though, it's a beautiful room with a wooden floor and the acoustics there are terrific. All my guitars, microphones, amplifiers and keyboards are up there and I hope eventually to turn it into a studio but not at the moment. I really would like to do some proper recording with an 8-track or something, but really for my own pleasure more than anything."

While the recorded songbook of James Herbert remains, for the time being, a dream, Jim reveals plans for a musical project that looks set to become a reality.

"Last year we did the theme music for *Haunted*; we

To celebrate the millionth sale of horror writer James Herbert's yarn The Fog, publishers Hodder & Stoughton came up with the uncomplicated idea of installing a smoke machine at a party in their Bedford Square headquarters yesterday.

Hodders' director, Michael Attenborough, was thrilled with the contraption and James Herbert and his wife Eileen also smiled indulgently at it – until the fine mist became a choking smog and tears ran helplessly down the faces of the distinguished guests.

A gasping Attenborough ordered the windows to be opened while his employees wrestled with the diabolic machine.

Herbert remarked afterwards: "God knows what they'll do when I sell a million copies of The Rats."

– from "Londoner's Diary", Evening Standard, May 11, 1989

believed it was going to be filmed for the BBC but it all fell through unfortunately. I was working with a guy called Raf Ravenscroft who is a brilliant musician, he can do anything from pop to classic and he did some terrific stuff for the *Haunted* project. The book has been optioned for film now after the BBC didn't use it so I'd hopefully like to see that music used.

"What we're working on now is an album of all the book titles. One side would be *The Rats* trilogy – almost like Jeff Lynne's *War of the Worlds* or even Mike Oldfield's *Tubular Bells* – and the other side would be themes based on the other book titles. The composer that we've got doing that is Rick Wakeman.

"It's going to give him so much scope; from themes like *The Fog* where the mood is so bizarre with murder, madness and mayhem, to something like *Fluke* which is a nice, soft story about a dog, to *The Magic Cottage* which is very whimsical, a light romantic fantasy, to a thing like *The Dark* which is probably one of the most sinister books I've ever written. He's got so much scope here as a composer to just sit down and enjoy himself. That's what we're working on and we've got three record companies interested."

Do you have an idea in your head as to what your story themes should sound like as pieces of music?

"I always have, it's because I've always liked music. As I'm writing I'm almost writing my own theme music. That's where it came out when we were writing the music for *Haunted* – it was easy for me to tell Raf exactly what I had in mind and he stuck pretty much to that . . . even to the sound effects. As I'm writing a scene for one of my stories I can almost hear the music. I never have music playing when I'm writing, ever. Ramsey Campbell listens to the classics while he writes but I can't do that, I've got to have total silence. I think to myself sometimes that I could sit down and write this music myself but I'm a great believer in, if somebody can do it better than you then forget your own ego and let them do it."

What would your reaction be if this proposed album of yours was reviewed unfavourably in the music press?

"Well, it wouldn't be entirely my responsibility alone, would it? You could blame somebody else [*laughs*], that's the nice thing about that . . . and the movies. When I get *NME* and *Sounds* and see some of the reviews they write about the albums that come out I think, how do these people read this? I couldn't take that; it seems to me that the music business is a lot of mean-minded little people who have set up this pose. If anything's established then they've got to bring it down because

EDWIN POUNCEY

it's no longer 'in', it's no longer trendy to like it . . . I've seen some terrible things said in these papers.

"With the album, as far as I'm concerned, I can easily walk away from that because it won't be entirely my responsibility – who knows, I might think it's bad myself. The only thing I would hate is if somebody claimed that I was just trying to make some money out of it, it just isn't like that. It's not an indulgence, it's something I'm passionately interested in. To tie the two things together, the writing and the music, would be like an ambition fulfilled.

"The great thing for me at the moment is that I've got control of the art side of things which includes the book jacket designs and the insides of the books – I choose the text. I care *that* much, I even choose the paper for the book. Bringing together the art side and the writing side is great, it's very fulfilling and I think if I can do the same with the music side then I'll be a very happy man.

"Whatever happens to the record is not going to change my lifestyle at all, it's not a financial proposition, it's just an ambition, something that I think would be both good and entertaining. It's not just for me, it's for the people who enjoy my books and for anyone else who likes music – it's another outlet for me. Financial gain hardly comes into it."

Horror and rock music have always been a pretty lethal brew of styles; from Bobby Boris Pickett and the Crypt Kickers and Screaming Lord Sutch, right through to the onstage execution performance pieces of Alice Cooper and Heavy Metal's devil of a racket. Throughout rock's history horror has played a major part, the rebellious bogeyman that is forever thumbing its crooked nose at a so-called decent society while dragging its children into the pit of "corruption". In the nineties "decency" has fought back hard with such teen idols as Kylie Minogue, Jason Donovan and New Kids on the Block, but just what does James Herbert think of how horror has been treated by rock musicians?

"To me that's funny horror, it's not real horror at all. I find it strange that when music is associated with horror then it always seems to be Heavy Metal! When Stephen King did *Maximum Overdrive*, the thing that really killed that film for me was the music. You had AC/DC playing and it totally swamped the movie – I don't understand why Steve went for Heavy Metal in that. You think about *The Exorcist*, that had Mike Oldfield's *Tubular Bells* and that worked. But Alice Cooper and Ozzy Osbourne . . . that's not horror, it's pantomime. Even *The Rocky*

Talking of the inimitable Mr Herbert, hot on the heels of his "extremely substantial" deal with Hodder & Stoughton for his next two novels, he rushed off to take part in a rather unusual and distinctly dangerous fund-raising effort on behalf of Music Therapy.

After asking permission of Hodders' Michael Attenborough – since Creed, *the first of the two volumes, is only half completed – Herbert donned seatbelt and took off in a customised black "Ratmobile", heavily plastered with adverts for* Haunted. *The venue was Wimbledon Stadium in West London; the event was banger racing!* →

Unfortunately the author found himself out of the rat-race in pretty short order when another competitor crashed in front of him and, while executing a nifty manoeuvre around the stricken car, he himself was bashed. Publicist Tony Mulliken, standing on the sidelines with Herbert's wife Eileen and various concerned Hodder personalities, said: "I knew Jim would be furious at being out of the race . . . in fact, I thought all the steam was coming from him!"

– STEPHEN JONES
and JO FLETCHER,
from *Science Fiction Chronicle*, Issue 117, June 1989

Horror Show is pantomime – it's not really horror at all – it's camp horror."

So do you feel that music should be subliminally added to horror subjects, a *feeling* rather than a pounding of the eardrums?

"If you want my view of one of the best pieces of horror music ever written then it's "In the Hall of the Mountain King" from the *Peer Gynt* suite by Grieg. That's so mysterious and creepy, but it also moves along which is why it became a rock record as well some years ago. Music for horror doesn't have to be subliminal."

HALLOWE'EN'S CHILD

James Herbert

TWENTY SIX

James Herbert, always interested in his readers' tastes, took a straw poll when he appeared as a guest of the Arts Society at Christ Church College, Oxford . . . 95 per cent of his audience read horror – and 85 per cent watched the turgid British TV soap East Enders*!*

– STEPHEN JONES and JO FLETCHER, from *Science Fiction Chronicle*, Issue 117, June 1989

IF I hadn't been in such a rush it probably wouldn't have happened.

And if I hadn't been so tired.

Maybe if I hadn't been so scared.

Yes, that above all. So scared for Anne. Our first baby meant seven months (once we knew for sure) of scaryness for both of us. Eleven years of hoping – the last few of those we spent in despair – then those torturous/ecstatic months after we were informed that, yes, something was there and all we now had to do was be patient. Twenty weeks into Anne's pregnancy and the amniocentesis results told us to expect a girl. Everything appeared to be fine, but we took no chances, none at all. Anne had already given up her secretarial job the moment we knew the egg really had embraced the seed, but now she went into underdrive – that is, she cut out all unnecessary effort. Totally. She invalidised herself. You see, Anne was thirty-eight, an uneasy time for some women, and even worse for those who've never given birth before. "Barren" is an appropriate word – "desolate" might be even better. I'm not sure that men, even the most sensitive, truly appreciate the condition. Those of us who have been as desperate for offspring as our wives or lovers might catch a glimmer, but there's no way we can experience the real trauma. Anne explained that to me.

The labour pains started around eight o'clock on a Sunday evening. We were prepared; we'd been prepared the whole of that month of October. Anne was perfectly calm and I did my best to appear that way too (she offered no criticism of my two

JAMES HERBERT

abortive attempts at ringing the doctor – my index finger was wayward). When I got through, Dr Golding asked me the usual questions (usual for *him*, that is; it was all new to me) about time lapses between pains, where the actual pain was coming from, Anne's general condition, etc. He was kind, as if he cared as much about me as he did my wife. But then, I was the one paying for his services for, selfishly, although perhaps under-standably given the circumstances, I'd decided our baby would be born privately rather than nationally, if you get my meaning. Besides, the National Health Service had enough to cope with, so if I could ease their burden in some small way by taking my custom elsewhere, well, that was fine by me and I'm sure by them also.

The doctor informed me he would alert the hospital but that it was too early for panic stations just yet. I was to ring him again when the contraction pains regularised.

That happened around midnight, maybe just a little after. This time Dr Golding told me to get moving.

It was about twelve miles to the hospital, a long drive through country lanes and villages, but Anne, unlike me, was serene throughout the journey. Uncomfortable true, but every time I glanced her way, she was smiling (I tried *not* to look at her during the spasms). The hospital itself was small and cosy, a country establishment that had a few private rooms for those who were willing and able to pay. The night sister herself took charge, leaving me alone while they got Anne settled in. When I next saw my wife she was sitting up in bed looking plump and content, although her smile was a little strained by now.

I stayed for an hour before they told me to go home and get some sleep. Nothing was going to happen for a while and when they were sure things were about to break – literally – they would phone Dr Golding first and then me.

Fine, I said. But it wasn't. I was scared. It was our first time and I for one had all the pessimism that comes with maturity. I agreed to leave though; Sister gave me the impression that choice was not really involved.

Nothing at all happened that day. I rang the office and let them know my week's leave had just begun. My business part-ner informed me of his favourite brand of cigar. I moped around the house for most of the morning, watching the telephone, hoovering, watching the telephone, loading the washing machine, watching the telephone, dusting and . . . you know what.

I went back to the hospital twice, once in the afternoon and then again in the early evening. Anne was still the blissful

I've only ever written one short story, called "Hallowe'en's Child". I love writing short stories and if you notice in the earlier books there are many vignettes within the main plot: I'd take a break and go somewhere else and introduce new characters and write about what happens to them. It's a way of explaining the overall effect of the horror that's happened – you bring it down to intimate terms with other characters, and they're short stories in themselves. In fact, two from Domain *have appeared as short stories. But "Hallowe'en's Child" is the only one that I actually sat down to write, and I did that for charity originally. I really did enjoy it and I regret that I don't have time to do more because of the demand for short stories – every other week I'm asked to contribute to an anthology and I'd love to do it, but I just don't have the time. One day . . .*

– JAMES HERBERT, at *Fantasycon XIV*, October 7, 1989

Buddha, the swelling she cradled in her arms showing no imminent signs of collapse. Dr Golding looked in on my second visit and uttered reassuring words. However, just before he ducked out the door he mentioned something about "inducement" if nothing had happened by tomorrow. It was Anne who patted *my* hand and told me not to worry.

Proving that there is little justice in the literary world, English horror author James Herbert has received an advance of £1 million – twice the sum fugitive member of the literati Salman Rushdie got for putting himself under threat of death writing The Satanic Verses.

– Ross Benson, from "The Diary", *Daily Express,* March 1, 1989

I returned home and cooked a meal, leaving most of it uneaten on the plate. I was over-anxious, to be sure, but after waiting eleven years for this event, who could blame me? The phone call came at quarter to ten that night.

Things were beginning to move, Dr Golding informed me. My daughter had suddenly become curious about the outside world. If I got to the hospital soon enough, I'd be there to greet her when she arrived.

The night was chilly, but I didn't bother with an overcoat. I grabbed my jacket, scooped up the car keys, and was inside the car without taking a breath.

It wouldn't start. The bugger wouldn't bloody start.

I smacked the wheel, but that had no effect. I stomped the accelerator, and the engine rasped drily.

Then I swore at my own stupidity. The night *was* chilly. The car needed some choke.

It roared fruitily enough when I corrected my mistake. I had to brake hard as another vehicle rushed past my drive.

Take it easy, I scolded. Getting myself killed wouldn't have pleased anybody, least of all me. I eased the car out gently and gathered speed once I was on the highway. A truck coming towards me flashed its beams and I quickly switched on my own headlights.

As I left the quiet streets of the town and headed across country, I saw there was a low-lying mist rolling over the fields. The moon was bright though, its cold glow bringing a spookiness to the landscape.

I passed through a village and my mouth dropped open. Soon, despite my anxiety over Anne and the baby, I was grinning.

They were cute, these little kids togged up in their witches' and monster outfits, several bearing homemade lanterns and broomsticks. I could hear their giggling and excited chatter as they "trick or treated" their way along the high street and tried to scare the hell out of each other.

October 31st. My daughter was going to be born on Hallows' Eve. Hallowe'en. I was neither pleased nor dismayed at the idea. I just wanted her there, safe and sound.

A kid jumped to the kerbside and leered crazily at me as

JAMES HERBERT

I passed, his green face lit by a flashlight beneath his chin. My mind was too preoccupied to retaliate with a leer of my own.

My foot stamped on the brake pedal as the headlights picked out more of the stunted ghouls on the crossing ahead. The car rocked and the kids laughed. They crowded around the side window and tapped on the glass. "Trick or Treat, Trick or Treat," they demanded.

Tempted to drive on, I nevertheless dug into a pocket for loose change; maybe the fact that two of the masqueraders had remained on the crossing and were leaning on my car bonnet, luminous plastic fangs caught by the moonlight, had something to do with my decision. Better to pay up rather than waste time arguing my case. Winding down the window I dropped coins into the greedy hands that thrust in. One of them smacked the bodywork as I drove on.

Out into the cold night again, the mist enveloping the car as though it had been waiting for me to leave the village refuge. I shivered, reached forward, turned up the heater. Still a way to go yet. Hold on, Anne, don't start without me.

Now I saw the lights of a hamlet ahead, just a street with a few houses on either side and nothing else. I didn't slow the car; in fact, I increased speed, for the mist had little substance beneath the sodium lights. Just beyond the last houses masked faces turned to watch my approach. A witch in cape and pointed hat waved a broomstick at me. I sped on, waving in response to their banshee wails.

Darkness dropped heavily once again, the car's headlights bouncing back at me from the rolling grey blanket (which seemed even thicker now). I slowed down, dipped the beams. Again I slapped the steering wheel in frustration.

Dear God, let it lift. Please let me get to Anne.

And you know, the mist actually seemed to lift; or at least, a hole in the whiteness opened up before me. Taking full advantage, I accelerated; unfortunately, the relief was only temporary. The swirling clouds came back at me with a vengeance.

I braked, tightening my grip on the wheel, keeping the vehicle in a straight line. I heard the thump – *felt* it – and shouted something, Lord knows what.

Rubber scraped tarmac as the car screeched to a halt. I sat frozen, the engine stalled; a sickness swelled inside me.

I'd hit something. No, the thump had a softness to it. I'd hit *someone*. For the second time that night, this time with a cold dread dragging at me, I beseeched God. Let it be an animal, I said. Please, an animal. But I'd seen a small black bundle hurl

Years of scribbling about giant rats, killer frogs and other evil entities have served horror writer James Herbert well: his publisher, Hodder & Stoughton, has just awarded him a £2 million advance – Britain's highest ever – for the UK rights to his next two books. "They haven't seen the books yet, but I suppose they trust me by now," Herbert observes modestly. "Perhaps I've become the acceptable face of British horror. They're even inviting me to Foyle's literary lunches."

– from "Luncheon Voucher", *Daily Telegraph*, August 7, 1989 over the side of the bonnet an instant after the impact. Its apparent size suggested I'd hit a child.

I think I was mumbling a prayer as I lurched from the car.

There wasn't too much to see out there, although the mist didn't seem quite as dense in the open. Only in the lightbeams was there real substance; beyond them the low fog was more tenuous, less compact. I searched around the car, stumbling over the grass verge on the left, moving in a crouched position, fearful of what I might find.

I called out, but there was no reply. And there was nothing lying close to the vehicle. For one wild – almost feverish – moment, I considered jumping back into the car and driving on. There was nobody there, I told myself. I hadn't run into anything; the haste, the anxiety, had got the better of me. Maybe a bird, a large crow perhaps, had flown up in front of me. I returned to the car.

But a sudden rush of guilt (and reality) prevented me from climbing in.

And a faint scratchy moan caused me to look back along the road.

I moaned myself. The mist had drifted enough for me to glimpse a dark shape crawling along the roadside.

My steps were slow at first, as though apprehensive of what they would lead me to; compassion however soon hurried me forward. As I approached the moving figure, my worst fears were realised: I *had* hit a child.

He or she appeared to be clothed in a long black cloak or gown – not the first such costume I'd seen that night. Except that whereas most of those other children had elected for pointed hats, this one had favoured a cowl, one that covered his or her head completely. Why was the kid out here alone? What the hell were the parents thinking of to allow their child to be unaccompanied at this late hour? These were minor considerations on my part, probably no more than a feeble attempt to shift the blame for the accident from myself.

I reached the crawling figure and bent low to touch its shoulder, the tenderness and pity I felt all but consuming. I became weak; my outstretched hand trembled.

The shoulder beneath the black cape felt fragile, somehow brittle, as if the bones were like those of a small bird.

"You'll be all right," I said softly and with no confidence in my heart. "I'll get you to a hospital, you'll be fine."

I knelt, reaching round to turn the child over, my face close to the hood.

Something sharp raked across my eyes. The figure had

The second annual Gold Ink Awards for best produced printing, sponsored by Publishing Technology Magazine, *included two horror novels among many categories. The Gold Award for paperback cover went to James Herbert's* Sepulchre, *published by Jove Books. The cover included foil stamping, die-cutting and embossing; the print run was 560,000.*

– from *Science Fiction Chronicle,* Issue 125, February 1990

JAMES HERBERT

twisted suddenly, lashing out in panic (I thought then) or in pain. Blinded for the moment, I sensed the child scrambling away; its cries were sharp, little sounds, that were not unlike the yelps of a wounded animal.

"Stop!" I called. "I want to help you."

All I heard was a scurrying.

The sting left my eyes, although a wetness still blurred my vision. I managed to discern a dark shape shuffling away from me though, heading back towards the car.

"Stop! I'm not going to hurt you," I shouted and took off after the cloaked figure. He or she leaned against the bodywork for support, staggering onwards, one leg dragging behind. With surprising speed, considering the injuries the child must have sustained, it was beyond the car and moving into the beams of the headlights. I gave chase, afraid for the poor little wretch, afraid that it might come to more harm because of its hysteria.

I quickly caught up and yelled, "Wait!" A tiny scream that was curious in its fierceness was the reply.

I snatched at the cloak, grasped cloth and held firm. But fear or confusion had lent the child unreasonable strength, for it was I who tumbled on to my knees in the roadway. As I fell, my other hand clutched the figure so that it was forced down with me. The child squirmed in my grip as we rolled over the hard surface and I had to hold fast to prevent damage to either of us. I could scarcely credit the energy of the tiny brute (I admit it – I was getting somewhat exasperated by now).

"Be still," I ordered, feeling inadequate, frustrated and impatient – all those things.

And then I turned the child over to face me.

It was a few seconds before I staggered away to fall heavily on to my elbow. A few seconds of staring into the most grotesque, the most evil, face I'd ever seen in my life.

The cowl had dropped away as she – yes, it was a woman, at least I *think* it was a woman – raised her head from the road to stare with filmy yellow eyes into mine, her ravaged and rotting countenance caught up in the full glare of my car's headlights. But it wasn't just the shock of seeing the sharp, hawked nose, swollen near its tip with a huge hardened wart from which a single white hair sprouted, the cheeks with hollows so deep they seemed like holes, the thick grey eyebrows that joined across her wrinkled forehead, the cruel, lipless mouth from which a black tongue protruded, that made me throw myself away.

Oh no, it was when that pointed black tongue slicked from

Demons today are a shoddy lot . . .

– James Herbert, Creed

There are two equal and opposite errors into which our race can fall about the devils. One is to disbelieve in their existence. The other is to believe . . .

– C. S. Lewis, The Screwtape Letters

sight and she spat a missile of green slime into my face, screeching, as she did so, that did that.

Shocked, bubbly liquid dripping from my chin, I stared across the tarred surface at her. She sat up, thin grey strands of hair stiff against her shoulders. Her dwarfish legs were splayed, the long gown she wore beneath the cloak risen above bony knees, high boots laced around her ankles.

Something moving beneath the hem of her skirt captured my attention. It slid from cover as if uncurling. A grey-pink tip appeared. It slithered further into view, growing thicker. It was ringed with horny and hairy scales.

She watched my astonished face and then she laughed, a high squawky sound, a witch's – yes, a *witch's* – cackle (at least, how I'd always *imagined* a witch's laughter to be – and this was Hallowe'en, after all).

Probably, if I hadn't already been in such an extreme state of tension, I might have behaved more calmly. As it was, that scaly tail weaving between her legs tipped the balance between rational reaction and blind panic. Her gnarled and ravaged features, the scratchy, high-pitched laughter, the sheer aura of *malevolence* around her, didn't help; but no, it was definitely that horny swaying thing that sent me tearing back to the car.

I'd left the door open and I bundled in, the cackling chasing through the mist after me. I flicked the ignition and moaned at the engine's grinding. It fired on the third attempt.

The road ahead, or what I could see of it, was now deserted. I pushed down on the accelerator and tyres spun on the damp road before gripping. The car shot forward.

And suddenly she, it, the *thing*, was on the bonnet, peering through the windscreen at me. The grotesque creature mouthed something, something that I didn't hear but which *looked* foul. She grinned toothlessly, that black tongue flicking out to lick the glass. My brain told me this was all impossible; my emotions were not prepared to listen.

Then she began to scratch the windscreen with clawed fingers, her long, curling nails screeching against the glass. The scratchmarks she left were clearly visible.

Those wicked, filmy eyes glared into mine, and they mocked me, they challenged me, they dared me to *dis*believe this was happening. Her laughter penetrated the screen; and so, too, did those taloned fingernails that she swept down again and again into the grooves already made.

I think I screamed. Certainly the car's brakes did as I jammed my foot on the pedal.

The midget monster disappeared from view, propelled by

the abrupt halt. Immediately, in a reflex action, I stepped on the accelerator again. The brief bump I felt was sickening: I was *sure* I heard the crunching of crushed bones.

My inclination was to drive on, to leave the nightmare behind. But basically, and as far as any of us are, I'm a normal human being: I have a conscience. I also possess – at least I did then – some soundness of mind. I'd hurt someone, someone unlike you or me, but a person, dwarfish and deformed though she was (my mind was already refusing to acknowledge what I'd seen with my own eyes – the tail, the black tongue, the fingernails tearing through glass). I stopped the car.

Once outside I shivered, the night air having grown even more chilled. Or perhaps something else was chilling my bones; maybe it was the prospect of what I would now find lying in the road. My footsteps dragged but I knew I could not just leave her there, no matter how fearful I was.

The low mist had thinned considerably, possibly due to the rush of air the speeding car had created. The body was easy to find. It lay in the road, unmoving, one part – the chest – strangely deflated. A further coldness ran through me when I realised that it was my car's tyres that had flattened her little body like that.

There was no need to look closer to conclude she was dead; yet closer I did look. Her eyes were half-open, just a crescent of watery yellowness showing on either side of her hooked nose. This time I really had killed her.

But as I watched, her eyelids slid fully open, an almost languid movement, and her pupils seemed to float to the surface from deep within the eyeballs themselves.

Her voice was no more than a peculiar croaking:

Hallow's Eve, Hallow's Eve
Beware hobgoblins on Hallow's Eve.

Those taloned claws grabbed my clothing and pulled me down on to her. We rolled and rolled in the road, this way and that, with me yelling and her screeching, and when I felt those fingernails digging into my chest, reaching for my heart, I knew I was in mortal danger (and knew, had I had any doubts, that this was no dream).

Despite the terrible injury, the thing was strong; but I was bigger and more afraid. I managed to rise over her, my hands clasped tight around her scrawny neck. I could feel bones breaking beneath my fingers.

She smiled blackly up at me.

Creed *is not a comedy and yet it made me laugh. It is not an obvious horror story, yet it has sequences of relentless terror. It is not a ghost story, although the supernatural seems to intrude at several points . . . I liked* Creed *a lot. Guaranteed to confuse and frustrate the "literary" critics, it is almost unclassifiable yet sleekly brilliant. Bizarre, original and wholly entertaining.*

– DAVID HOWE,
Starburst No. 145,
September 1990

"Can't kill me, can't kill me," she chanted.

Her pointed tongue shot from her toothless mouth like a long, striking snake. She scratched (the tongue was *rough*) the tip of my nose.

"Beware hobgoblins," she warned when the tongue slithered back.

My only excuse is that total, mind-shocking hysteria took over. I cracked her head against the shiny surface of the road. And then again. Then again. More, until a thick gooey liquid spread from the back of her skull on to the tarred surface. Her eyes blinked.

"Can't kill me," she taunted.

The last crack had a mushy softness to it, like delicate porcelain filled with sugar shattering inwards.

With a rasping sigh, she finally lay still. Then she said: *"We don't die."*

Enraged, and mindless, I screamed.

I scooped up the limp form, my intention, I think, to lay it on the grass verge, or perhaps even in the back seat of the car; but I became overwhelmingly repulsed by what I held in my arms when I heard her say: *"You'll be sorry. You and the baby."*

I threw the little monster over the hedge beyond the verge and was startled to hear a splash. There must have been a water-filled ditch or a pond on the other side. I listened to the gurgling that came through the leafy hedge, not letting my breath go until the bubbly sound had ceased. Dread upon dread. She, it – the *thing* – had said *"the baby"*. What the hell had she meant? I actually clutched my hands to my chest, so powerfully portentous was the sensation that struck me.

I fled the scene (of the crime, I suppose it's not unreasonable to add) and scrambled back into my car. What had she meant? Dear God, what had she meant? Surely . . . I blanked the terrifying thoughts from my mind. I had to get to the hospital, that was the important thing. I could bring the police back here later, tell them the whole story, how it wasn't my fault. Tell them the *whole* story? I gazed at the long scars in the glass before me. Tell them about that? About the creature's black tongue. About how she'd fought even though her chest had been completely crushed? About the horned tail hanging between her legs? Tell them about that? They'd think I was insane, even when they examined the body. *If* they ever found the body. Why did I need to show them where it was? Nobody had witnessed the accident. In all likelihood, it would take ages for the corpse to be discovered, so who could connect it with me? The holes etched in the glass – *should* anyone enquire – might

Herbert has certainly packed in such a concentration of horror that there are times when you begin to wonder whether he's playing it for laughs.

– VAL HENNESSY, from "A Creed That's Beyond Belief", *Daily Mail*, July 26, 1990

JAMES HERBERT

possibly have been caused by a tree branch. That was more feasible than clawed fingers, at any rate.

The car was already in motion as all these thoughts tumbled through my head. I drove crazily, and it was only because I soon approached the town that I didn't have another accident. The lights shone ahead and I increased speed, desperate to get to Anne and my unborn/born(?) child.

By the time I reached the hospital, the long cracks in the windscreen had healed over; by the time I drew the car to a halt near the maternity unit, the marks had disappeared altogether. I spared myself no time to wonder.

Anne's private room was empty. I hurried through the main ward, searching for a nurse, a doctor, anyone who could give me a hint as to my wife's whereabouts. Those women still awake in the ward, some of them suckling newborn infants, looked up, startled at my unkempt appearance (I'd been rolling around in the road, remember; I suppose I was looking pretty wild-eyed too). A nurse came striding towards me.

Fortunately she recognised me. "Your wife went up to the delivery room twenty minutes ago," she said, her voice low. "Now calm yourself, everything's fine."

I brushed by her, heading for the stairs beyond the far doors. I climbed them two at a time, my chest hurting from the exertion, my hand clammy damp as it slid along the stair rail. The waiting room was empty, the door to the delivery room closed. Resisting the urge to rush through, I rapped on the wood.

Someone on the other side murmured something, then I heard approaching footsteps.

"Just in time," the midwife said as she peered out at me. "Come inside and hold your wife's hand. My goodness, I think she might need to comfort you."

Dr Golding smiled at me, then frowned. "Sit yourself down," he said, indicating a chair beside the high bed. He returned his attention to my recumbent wife.

Anne looked drained, but she managed a smile. She clasped my hand and I winced when she squeezed hard as a spasm hit her. Her eyes had a dreamy look that even the pain could not cut through.

"Wonderful," I heard the doctor say. "That's wonderful. Your daughter's well on her way. One last push, I'm sure that'll do the trick. You're doing marvellously."

"You'll be sorry. You and the baby."

The voice was in my mind, not in the room.

Anne gasped, but it was not from childbirth pains; she

swung her face towards me questioningly and I realised it was *I* who had clutched *her* hand too tightly.

"*. . . You and the baby . . .*"

A voice as shrivelled as the creature who had uttered the words.

"Excellent," said the doctor.

It couldn't have happened, I told myself. Stress, exhaustion, the culmination of months of anxiety, praying that finally a child would be ours, that nothing would go wrong, nothing would spoil our ultimate dream . . . I'd imagined everything that had happened during the rushed journey to hospital. My mental state had induced an hallucination. That had to be the answer. Hadn't the car's windscreen been unmarked by the time I'd arrived at the maternity unit? Reason encouraged the explanation.

And the ugly, guttural voice in my head at last withered away.

"Welcome," said Dr Golding.

For my daughter had slid smoothly and effortlessly, it seemed, after so many hours of labour, from her mother's body into the ready hands of the doctor.

The room dipped and banked around me; my head felt feather-light.

"Good God, catch him," I heard someone say as if from a great distance.

Firm hands gripped my waist and I blinked my eyes to find the midwife's face staring down at me.

"It's not the first time the proud father has fainted on us," Dr Golding said cheerily. "You take yourself outside for a moment or two while we tidy things up in here. Stick your head between your knees, you'll soon feel better."

Anne nodded at me and I could see just how depleted was her strength in the wanness of her smile.

"The baby . . . ?" I said.

"A perfect little girl," the midwife said as she whisked the pink, glistening bundle away to the scales.

I rose, just a bit unsteady, and bent to kiss Anne's lips. "You're both perfect," I whispered to her.

I went to the door and turned to catch sight of my child swaddled in white in the arms of the midwife before I stepped outside. With relief I sank into a stiff-backed chair in the waiting room. Thank God, I said silently to myself. Thank God . . .

But I heard a muffled shout from back there in the delivery room. I was frozen, body and senses, as I listened: "It's imposs-ible." It was the doctor's voice. "There can't be another –"

Herbert has an uncanny knack of constructing a story and narrating it in such a style that you are drawn into it – whether you like it or not. In his latest novel there is the added bonus of some well-timed humour, although it's of the blackest variety.

– from "Herbert Tells of Grave Danger", *Hartlepool Mail*, July 28, 1990

JAMES HERBERT

The woman's shriek drove me to my feet. The delivery room door opened before I could reach it. The midwife's face appeared whiter than the uniform she wore. A hand shot to her mouth as her chest seemed to heave. Bending forward, she pushed past me.

I prevented the door from swinging closed with a raised arm. I entered the room.

Anne, our baby held tight to her breasts, was staring from the bed to the doctor, a look of abject horror frozen on her face.

Dr Golding had his back to me. He, too, was strangely immobile. And he, too, held something in his arms.

I knew it was another baby, my daughter's twin.

I heard a tiny, scratchy cry.

And as I watched, a small, scaly tail curled up around the doctor's elbow.

SWAMP THING

James Herbert

TWENTY SEVEN

ME, I was reared on comic books. Before the age of ten I'd had the rare privilege in England of reading all those early DC and ECs: *Tales from the Crypt, Frankenstein, Batman, Superman*, et al. American comics. Full colour! How I got hold of such a rare commodity at that time isn't relevant here (and I'm not sure I want to tell), but suffice to say, the art of comics was my joy in those most formative of formative years.

Naturally enough, I grew out of them. The plots had become repetitive and ridiculous, the characters cardboard, the intent too solid, without subtlety. Of course, *they* hadn't degenerated; my mind was just looking towards the challenge of the more perceptive *un*illustrated word. As I said, natural enough. Comic books had become too juvenile, too stagnant. I was lost to them – or vice versa; however you see it.

Until recently, that is. The name Alan Moore was coming up in conversation quite a lot. A writer of distinction, it was said. Then someone gave me a few copies of *THE SAGA OF THE SWAMP THING*. "See if you like 'em."

Like them? Indeed I did. Here was someone who was finally leading the comic book towards its true potential with insightful scripts and excellent art direction, pushing through those hazed peripheries of the imagination with stories that were not just literate, but – and I don't use the word lightly – inspired. Let's say I was somewhat impressed.

THE SWAMP THING is no quick, satisfying read. No, it's much more than that. The stories give cause for thought and then further, deeper thought long after you've laid them aside. Now that's some achievement in this field. This is no *Incredible Hulk* or *The Heap* (remember *The Heap*?). The Swamp Thing isn't a man transformed, but a dying man's consciousness, his psyche, *absorbed* through circumstances by the environment of his death. Now that's heavy stuff, but when you take the mental leap it makes perfect and fascinating sense. And once you decide to be swept along by Alan Moore's fertile imagination (helped along by some excellently succinct prose), then there's no turning back. You're hooked. Me, I'm glad to be back on that hook.

"Yeah, I used to read them when I was a kid. My brother used to get them – those good, American comics. The American kind were all in colour – the ones we had over here were just black and white. I used to love all those old Frankensteins and Tales from the Crypt.*"*

– JAMES HERBERT, from "Bloody Good Storyteller" by Lisa Tuttle, *The Twilight Zone Magazine*, Vol. 4, No. 5, November/December 1984

THE DEVIL YOU KNOW

John Gilbert

TWENTY EIGHT

A T first, I felt like Wormwood, that trainee demon, invited at last to meet Screwtape – the senior devil who has done so much for Hell – on his own territory.

"I wrote it for laughs. It's a modern day equivalent to an Abbott and Costello Meet the Mummy *type movie, slapstick with lots of laughs but genuinely scary bits."*

– JAMES HERBERT, from "Why I Enjoy Living in Fear" by Vanora Leigh, *Brighton Evening Argus*, August 11, 1990

The parallel between that fictional encounter and my meeting with Britain's bestselling horror novelist is certainly there. At the sensitive age of twelve, I picked up my first contemporary horror novel: *The Rats* by James Herbert. From there to Jim's rare offer to spend a day with him at his home on the Sussex Downs just outside Brighton was like having your heart thrust into your mouth, and then being invited to chew.

The Herbert residence is set in heaven, amongst the hillocks and narrow roadways of the Sussex countryside. It's a peaceful haven for any author, though Jim had to move into a cottage near his home to complete his new novel, *Creed*.

Not that the book has suffered. It's ostensibly a thriller about Joseph Creed, a paparazzo photographer who witnesses the desecration of a famous movie star's grave just after she's been buried. His life is one hectic photo shoot, and he does not believe it could become more complicated. But soon he's on the run from a creature that looks suspiciously like Nosferatu and he becomes embroiled in the greatest international conspiracy since The Fall – and we're not talking Wall Street here.

The life of Joseph Creed, whose sole function is to produce embarrassing bromides of celebs in awkward situations, provides enough potential for a stick-wielding thriller, but James Herbert is quick to point out that there are other possibilities which make the book different from the fourteen others he's written. "It's more humorous than usual. There's always a lot of humour in the books, but this time I've done almost the modern equivalent of *Abbott and Costello Meet Frankenstein*. I wanted to see if it could be done in a modern way."

The name of the book, *Creed*, is also part of that humour. "You think, 'It's Herbert', so it's horror or supernatural, or both. *Creed* sounds very portentous, very religious, but it's the name of the hero, Joe Creed. And I can't really call him a hero.

"We have two clichéd heroes now. The old hero was the enigmatic character who always won through – very brave, very courageous – and I've used that character myself. Then I went for the anti-hero – the world weary cynic, but again someone who was very warm and courageous – which again became very popular. *That* has now become a cliché.

"This time I wanted a different kind of 'hero', that was neither a hero nor an anti-hero. The guy is just a shit. When this man is scared, he faints. If he's up against a terrible situation, he runs away. He's a real sleaze. That's why I chose the paparazzi for his profession.

"The great challenge for me was to get you to like him. You shouldn't, because he reacts badly in any situation. The challenge was to get the reader to have some empathy with the guy so that at the end you may just warm to him."

James Herbert always enjoys the writing process, but the research for *Creed* provided some unusual, if hair-raising, bonuses. "I went out with the paparazzi. I contacted the king of paparazzi in England, Richard Young, and he's great. In fact, he was a bit of a disappointment because I expected someone like the character I had in mind; a real sleaze, because paparazzi are real thieves. They steal moments of people's lives, moments that people don't want stolen. They take candid shots of celebrities, and they take the worst possible shots they can get. Richard Young is a perfect gentleman. He's rough and tough, but he's really great. He introduced me to other paparazzi, who more closely live up to the image.

"So I went around with Richard. We went to openings, book launches, star parties, the clubs, restaurants, particularly Langan's. We actually chased Jack Nicholson down the road. All the stuff I've used in the book, I've named names. That's the tone of the book.

"Now what the hell's that got to do with horror, you may ask? I wanted to do something about the fallen angels of Europe, the demons, the devils. My theme for the book was that it's bloody hard work being evil, and if you've been evil for centuries

The juicy bits in Herbert's fiction are always interrupted by lengths of interminable plot-line. These serve two purposes: they delay, but also whip up a frenzied expectation for the gore that is the book's raison d'être. It is a method shared with the writers of pornography, which perhaps explains the ease with which Herbert slips in the odd bit of soft-porn.

– TOM SHONE, from "Sitting in Front of a Video Nasty", *Sunday Correspondent*, July 29, 1990 and centuries, you must be a little bit tacky around the edges.

"These demons, they're pissed off because suddenly the public has these new hero/villains in the form of Freddy Krueger and Michael Myers. So the real devils, they're not getting any publicity any more – Freddy Krueger's getting it all. Plus the fact that they're losing their powers: one, because they're weary with all the evil over the centuries, and two, because if people are using that kind of evil as entertainment with the movies and the videos that they see, it's all become a bit of a joke. Because they're not believing in these devils any more, these devils are losing their powers. Our hero finds them in an old folks home.

"So that was the basic theme of the book, then I was trying to get this different kind of hero. I thought, 'what sort of profession employs these sorts of people?' Now there is journalism, of course, and another appendage of journalism is the photographers, and the lowest form of photographer is the paparazzo.

"It fitted in so neatly with the kind of guy I wanted, and it was fun for me to explore, to research. I could see plenty of funny situations developing just from the guy's background."

Not your normal kind of horror novel, but the man whose novel *The Rats* appeared in Britain three months before Stephen King's *Carrie* feels that the horror genre has gone through a myriad of phases, and is a little too po-faced. "We are, as writers, taking the horror genre a little bit too seriously. When we do convention panels, we're talking too much about the metaphor and the sub-text, and it's getting a bit too precious. I want to pop that balloon and say: 'It's not.' It's all getting too pompous."

He does, however, point out that there are several types of reader, each getting something different from horror. "Some just like the thrill, the horror, and of my early books they like the blood and gore. Then there's the other reader who's a bit more serious, takes the message behind the books, and sees what the writer is putting in. There are a lot of subliminal messages, points that you hope to make, but they're not necessary for the reader.

"In *Creed*, I've burst a few balloons about the mythology of horror. I've said where we get Frankenstein from and Dracula, but humorously."

Slapstick has often been associated with horror. The many, OTT routines in the *A Nightmare On Elm Street* and *Friday The 13th* films use gore to get a laugh, and even Freddy Krueger's fast one-liners come from the George Burns school

JOHN GILBERT

of groans. But Jim thinks that even the grossest of situations can be elevated with a more subtle humour. "I thought there was quite a bit of subtle humour in *Magic Cottage*, but there's more subtle humour in books like *The Fog* and *Domain*, because you don't really know it's there until you read back. Because they're very fast paced, violent books, you tend to miss anything that's subtle in there. But, I promise you, it is there if you care to look."

That mixture of horror and humour has not only made James Herbert Britain's most popular horror impresario, but has also sold his books in twenty-two countries. "I'm pleased to be in the vanguard of breaking down these barriers. The last book I signed over was for Poland, and that's smashing. You almost give it away, they can't afford to pay a lot of money, but it's such a delight to be able to say, 'Well, now we can get horror into a country like that – they can read it.'

"There are places like Argentina, Brazil . . . Not big markets for horror, but they're suddenly taking an interest. It's like being in that position where you're able to break down doors. It's like how I was fourteen years ago in England when horror wasn't a going concern. The only horror writer we had in those days was Dennis Wheatley, and he wasn't writing any more."

Until recently, James Herbert has been reticent to appear in public, other than at signings – and even now he's careful about the invitations he accepts. The 1988 World Fantasy Convention in London changed all that, and now you'll often find him in the middle of a scrum at a fair number of fan gatherings. He is a great ambassador for horror and has been invited to talk to many learned groups, including a record two appearances at the Oxford Union with surprising reactions from audiences and professorial critics.

Some of these audiences are "very snooty about horror; in fact, you'll find in America that they're much more geared to it. I've had my best reviews from professors of literature in America. But here, a couple of my books are on reading lists, but there is that strain of thinking that it's very non-adult. The only thing is that you're getting the younger lecturers, the younger professors that have been brought up on a diet of movies and horror stories. The attitude is changing. It's mainly the normal schools that hate it; they really detest it. But then they hate Enid Blyton as well, which is why I make a great point of telling them that I have always read Enid Blyton to my kids. Anything to get up their noses."

Jim has also proven his worth to the literary establishment,

Unlike some best-selling authors and unlike the characters in Creed, *Herbert's powers are still waxing, the quality of writing is improving, albeit from an initially workmanlike base, and his sales are rising . . . As buckets-of-blood novelists seek new levels of gore and perversion to attain the ever-elusive high, Herbert maintains a standard of morality and taste . . . He is one of the few writers taking forward the tradition of the great supernatural storytellers – and being innovative.*

– PETER JAMES, from "New Readers Start Here", *Evening Standard*, August 9, 1990 which has always been more than ready to condemn horror and its practitioners. "Last year I was invited as the guest of honour at a Foyle's literary lunch. They give you all the bumf on these events. I looked down the list, and the last horror writer ever to be invited to one of those functions was Dennis Wheatley, and that was about thirty or forty years ago. So I thought, 'Well, again, it's breaking down the barriers.'"

Surmounting barriers may go some way towards achieving an acceptance of horror amongst the literati but there appears to be very little in the way of new writing talent at the moment, and – if we're being honest – there does not seem to be a contemporary author of the stature of King, Herbert or Campbell. But Jim is cautiously optimistic. "People just turn up. It's like Clive [Barker]. Suddenly Clive was there. You need fresh blood all the time.

"About five years ago, I thought the horror industry was dying. I thought it had been done to death with videos, the trashy books, the copyists. And then it revived, it became good again. I think it's about to go into that dip again, but you never know."

Horror is likely to survive any such dip in popularity because it is sufficiently flexible to take on board contemporary political, social and religious debates. James Herbert's own novels provide a case in point. *Sepulchre* looks at terrorism, *Shrine* looks at religion, and *The Rats* can be equated with the all-pervasive political systems that control human lives.

Herbert has some very clear-cut views on all these subjects, particularly politics, although he vehemently denies the many suggestions in the popular press that he is left wing or right wing just because his books portray such characters. "I believe in strength, in fighting anything that is wrong. Now, that doesn't make me right wing. I believe there comes a point where you would have to use violence against anything that is wrong. I don't believe in terrorism, nobody has the right to terrorise anyone, but there comes a point where you may have to fight.

"I would do anything to protect my daughters. If anyone broke into this house, they might get in but they'd never get out. So there comes that point, and in *Sepulchre*, yes, you're talking about organisations that are composed of ex-military men. So in that sense it makes it right wing, but that doesn't mean to say I am. I'm *writing* about those people.

"You have to put yourself in another position, see it through somebody else's eyes. If I write about homosexuals, it doesn't mean I'm a homosexual or that I'm going to be. You can be

Hoorah for Ratty. With Creed *James Herbert has attempted something different . . . Herbert obviously has a soft spot for his anti-hero, despicable though he is, and has turned out a rousing demonstration that Beelzebub is no match for your average scum-of-the-earth Fleet Street lensman, all done in broad comic style.*

– ANNE BILLSON, *Time Out*, August 8–15, 1990

JOHN GILBERT

accused of all sorts of things, merely because you voice the opinion of the person in the book.

"I like things to be right, which again is why I avoid a lot of publicity. There's a certain amount that you have to do, but they can get so many things wrong about you. I remember for years I read things like I always wore black – I have one black suit, a dinner suit – and that kind of thing rankles. But that's what you can expect from the press. They want their image of you."

The public image could not be more different from the private Jim Herbert. He is most definitely a family man, with wife Eileen and three children – the eldest of whom is at university, the second is jittery but confident about her recently finished school exams, and the youngest proved to me there and then that she could outrace even the PR men in Jim's indoor swimming pool.

James Herbert loves writing, but in the end everything he does is for his family. "Whatever I've done I've had to do off my own bat. With my background, I knew nobody, I had no connections, no help from anybody, and I'm very proud of that. But now I'm there I want to do the best for my kids.

"I don't believe in what Jeffrey Archer once said – that he's not going to leave a penny to his children. I find it *incredible*. Kids, that's what you're working for, so they will get every penny I can give them.

"They're hardworking. It's always been a big thing in my family that we've always worked hard. I've got two older brothers. One is a Lloyd's broker – he's very successful – and my eldest brother has got a stall in the market, and he's successful in his own way.

"If you enjoy what you do, it doesn't seem like hard work, because you enjoy it, you just want to go on."

Then is retirement not for him? If he was given the choice of working and losing five years off his life, or living to the ripe old age of ninety, what decision would he make? "Oh, the work. To me there is no choice. I don't particularly want to live to ninety, I don't want to be falling to pieces. I'd rather lose five or even ten years working – and enjoying myself."

A streamlined racehorse of a book, pulsing with energy, Creed *will delight Herbert fans, and surely astonish them.*

– JOHN GILBERT, from "Photo Recall", *Fear* No. 21, September 1990

THE DEVIL YOU KNOW

CREED: THE ADVERTISEMENT

David J. Howe

TWENTY NINE

THE place: Old Barnes Cemetery, South London. The scene: a crumbling, brooding pile of weed-infested gravestones. Sightless angels maintain a silent vigil, the names of the late departed mingle with grass, gorse and brambles and deep in the centre, a small group of people prepare for a photo-session . . .

Hodder & Stoughton have asked the advertising agency Alliance International to come up with a cinema campaign to promote the new James Herbert hardback, *Creed*. A creative team is assembled, comprising Copywriter Hilary Senior, Art Director Gavin Scott and Producer Lyn Glyde. In overall control is Accounts Director Theo Lawton: "What we were aiming for was to take the profile that James Herbert has already got, and maximise it by using a similarly high-profile medium. With this particular commercial for this particular book, the moving image seemed to be an important aspect and so the use of cinema naturally evolved."

Creed is about a paparazzo photographer who catches something peculiar on film and is subsequently plagued by bizarre and inexplicable occurrences. The concept of still photographs seemed promising and the Art Director and Copywriter started working on the storyboards. Gavin Scott: "We got a rough idea of how *Creed* was structured and what it was about and we came up with two strong ideas. What we would normally do would be to present just one idea to the client and adapt it according to their comments. On this one, however, we were in two minds as to which was the best, as were Hodder &

"I will draw a veil over what I say about Sarah Ferguson (The Duchess of York), but I think you will enjoy it. My hero is based on Mickey Rourke. I have written any number of well-known people into my book. It is now being carefully read by libel lawyers."

– JAMES HERBERT, from "Birthday Boy's Novel Characters", *Sunday Express,* April 8, 1990

DAVID J. HOWE

Stoughton, and even James Herbert liked them both. So what we did was to bring the production company on board to look at the ideas and develop further the concept."

The first storyboard presented by Gavin and Hilary shows a photographer looking through a selection of candid shots of people with their hands over their faces, coming out of night-clubs and taxis and so forth. "Some people get very upset when they are caught by a paparazzo photographer . . ." says the voice-over. We then see a photograph of a Nosferatu-like character, crouched by a grave with his hand up over his face, ". . . very upset indeed!" completes the voice as the charac-ter's hand reaches out of the photograph for the photographer.

The second shows a photograph slowly developing in a tray in a darkroom. We slowly zoom in on the photograph as it develops. "In the dark world of the paparazzo photographer . . . there was an unexpected development . . ." growls the narrator as the photograph develops into the character by the grave again. We move right into his staring eyes and mix to white, out of which the final caption – the book title – emerges.

The production company chosen by Agency Producer Lyn Glyde is Helen Langridge Associates and the Directors are Adam Cameron and Simon Cole: "We went away with the two concepts and tried to work out the best way of achieving what was required. Basically we mixed the two ideas together. We liked the idea of the paparazzo photographer and also the developing tray and so we decided to set the whole thing inside a darkroom to give a claustrophobic feel, and also to have the classic horror shock at the end."

Once the concept had been agreed, a team was built up around what was required. Any Effects, a special effects com-pany, constructed the developing tray out of which the hand would emerge, make-up artist Jeanette Rivera provided the ghostly white appearance of the hand and face of the character by the graveside, played by actor Bob Flag (perhaps better known as the face of Big Brother from the film *Nineteen Eighty-Four*).

The black and white photographs of Nosferatu by the grave are taken at the aforementioned cemetery. Bob Flag looks superb in his dirty raincoat and bleached, washed out make-up. His right hand is embellished with evil-looking pointed nails. Darkness rapidly falls as the photographs are taken and an hour later, the photographer (Joe Burns, who also plays the pho-tographer in the commercial) has finished. The crew pack their bags and head off for Stringfellows Nightclub in London to obtain the other required photographs of the would-be celebrities (in

Herbert even manages to shock our hero with a predatory toilet bowl and the book's climax is like a scene from Masque of the Red Death. *Splendid stuff.*

– from "Creed of Horror", *Yorkshire Evening Post,* August 4, 1990 fact hired actors playing paparazzi victims) with their hands and hats covering their faces.

A week later and the crew assembles once more in a small film studio in North London to film the commercial itself. The studio set up is very simple: a camera looks down upon a developing table littered with the tools of a photographer's trade. The commercial will last approximately fifteen seconds and is being made in three sections. The first is a high establishing shot of the table as the photographer develops the first of his paparazzo shots. The second section is a closer shot of the developing tray as another photograph is developed. Finally, we close in on the tray as the final photograph – of our friend by the grave – is developed. The position of the developed photograph is marked, the developer is replaced with water, the photograph is replaced with a specially doctored version (minus the hand across the face) and the photographic hand becomes the real hand of Bob Flag, lying underneath the table, covered in towels, ready to come alive and grab the unsuspecting photographer.

Once these shots have been successfully covered, some additional footage is taken from the side showing the hand shooting out of the tray and grasping the photographer's face and wrist. Other cutaway shots include a clock on the wall and the photographer slipping the photographs into and out of the developing solution.

With all the footage in the can, the entire commercial is edited together, a voice-over provided (by *Edge of Darkness* actor Bob Peck), sound effects added and then the completed commercial is presented to the clients (Hodder & Stoughton) and James Herbert. It is a great success and favourable comments abound. James Herbert: "I think within the restriction of a twenty-second commercial it's come off remarkably well. It has impact!"

After some final polishing and minor re-editing (because an extra five seconds screen-time has been granted) it is ready for cinemas across the country.

The *Creed* commercial ran in approximately 400 cinemas nationwide, according to availability, with the films *Total Recall, Days of Thunder, Gremlins 2* and *Die Hard 2* during the weeks August 3–10, August 17–24, and August 31–September 7, 1990.

Following the success of the hardback campaign, Hodder & Stoughton decided to re-use the commercial as part of the paperback promotion for *Creed* in July 1991. To do this, the

DAVID J. HOWE

final image of the commercial was re-shot, changing the words to refer to the paperback rather than the hardcover.

The advertisement was then copied on to VHS videos and distributed, in attractive packaging, to major booksellers and reviewers across the country. For the paperback launch the advert was also aired on television, with prime-time slots on ITV stations during the first week of the book's release (July 1). A further five-week run in around 350 cinemas nationwide was also planned.

Creed *is often reminiscent of Stephen King's* The Shining *or Ira Levine's* Rosemary's Baby, *but that's not to suggest Herbert's writing is imitative. His supernatural characters are better defined than Levine's. His terror is not nearly as visceral as King's; it has a mordant, loopy edge to it.* Creed *may be a nightmare, but it's a darkly witty nightmare.*

– ALLAN HUSTACK, *Montreal Gazette,* June 29, 1991

Client: Hodder & Stoughton
Agency: Alliance International

CREED COMMERCIAL

For Alliance International:
Account Director THEO LAWTON
Produced by LYN GLYDE
Art Director GAVIN SCOTT
Copywriter HILARY SENIOR

FOR HELEN LANGRIDGE ASSOCIATES:
PRODUCED BY MATTHEW JONES
Directed by ADAM CAMERON *and* SIMON COLE
Lighting Cameraman MIC MORRIS
SPECIAL EFFECTS TOM HARRIS *(Any Effects)*

Photographer .... JOE BURNS
Nosferatu.. BOB FLAG
Male paparazzo victim.................................... TIM BERRINGTON
Female paparazzo victim .... KAY HAMILTON

Locations:
Still shoot: Barnes Cemetery, London SW3
20.00hrs June 28, 1990
Stringfellows Nightclub 23.00hrs June 28, 1990
Studio: Chamberlain Studios, London N1 July 5, 1990

The rats strike in Deadly Eyes *(1983)*

BIG CLIMAXES AND MOVIE BULLSHIT

Stefan Jaworzyn

THIRTY

"**T**HE *main* reason a lot of my books haven't been filmed is that in England you just don't have a film industry. My stories always have a big climax. Although they're very visual, they require a lot of money to film them – they're not small-scale. They're difficult to film. Some of the supernatural books have endings which are so profound it's not possible to do them cinematically . . ."

"One film that really made an impression on me was Psycho. *I've seen the shower scene about eight times and it gets better each time. But even Hitchcock's films seem tame by today's standards."*

– JAMES HERBERT, from "Chill the Spine" by Christine Day, *19*, November 1985

The dearth of film adaptations of James Herbert's novels must come as a surprise to those familiar with his work, and adherents of the two which have been adapted (*The Survivor* (1980) and *The Rats* (1982)) are as silent as the grave. Hapless victims of these two celluloid atrocities might well ponder what had become of the adaptations of Herbert's novels, but few will have had as much time for reflection and regret as their author . . . Until now Herbert has experienced a series of missed opportunities, disappointments and disasters, though with four projects currently under development both he and his fans might finally be treated to films they can watch without sinking deeper into their seats while considering lying in a busy road as a more pleasant option.

The Survivor remains one of the Great Meaningless Horror Films. While running a mere 82 minutes, it still proves virtually impossible to watch in one sitting and actually concentrate on the "plot", which creeps incomprehensibly along at a snail's pace and has succeeded in baffling its own author! Somnambulant acting, sluggish direction and editing apparently achieved by hurling cannisters of film into the air and re-assembling them

STEFAN JAWORZYN

at random, all contribute to a tremendously wasted opportunity, a classic of cinematic gibberish.

"To condense a book into one and a half hours of screen time is difficult and you know there have to be changes, so some of it you can understand. Making my seventy-year-old male spiritualist into Jenny Agutter I thought was a bit extreme, but I didn't actually object to that *too* much . . .

"It started like this: A film company contacted my agent and we went to see them. They were very nice people, but *totally* full of bullshit . . . They bought the option, then we had another meeting with them. They said 'Paul [*Newman!*] is very interested and he's said he'd love to do the movie but it all depends on Larry [*Olivier!!*] . . . Now Larry says he's interested but his commitments for the next two years are a bit much – if he can get over them he'll do the movie, and if he doesn't do the movie then Paul will do it.' Of course you don't really know about these things – this was my first brush with Hollywood, via Dean Street . . . and they said, 'Do *you* have any ideas about who you'd like for the main character?' So I said, Clint Eastwood, because of the enigmatic characters he played at that time, and they said 'Great!' and made notes . . . I heard nothing for months, just the occasional bit of news – they'd worked out how to crash the jumbo jet, and so on. They did a screenplay which wasn't bad, though it wasn't good either. A guy called David Ambrose did it, who's done some good stuff in the past, but unfortunately this was one of his misses.

"The next I heard it had been sold to another company – lock, stock and barrel. What they did was to put a package together and sold it, and that company then sold it to another. By that time I had lost sight of it completely. David Hemmings, the director, was part of the third company. He decided he was going to make it in Australia and Robert Powell was to be the star – for Paul Newman read Robert Powell – I didn't mind Powell, he's a good actor and he does have that enigmatic quality to him.

"I wrote them a letter before they started shooting saying if they wanted my advice or there was anything I could help them clear up then I'd be happy to help. Nothing. Not even an acknowledgement or a 'thank you' note. I saw the film in Australia when I was on tour. It was just outside Adelaide, where they'd shot it, in a huge cinema in the middle of a really hot, sunny afternoon. In this big cinema there's just me, my publisher and my Australian agent. They showed the film on this big screen. I fell asleep halfway through – I didn't understand the story! It was just dreadful, *terrible*. It lost sight of the aims

". . . The Exorcist *was always one of my favourites.* The Innocents, *the old Jack Clayton movie and another called* The Haunting. *Those two really worked because they relied on the unseen. They weren't explicit and they were all the more effective for that. All you heard was the hammering on the door of the bad spirit. Your mind did the rest.* Alien *was great, I could watch that time and time again.*"

– JAMES HERBERT, from "Gnawing at the Movie Screen" by Martin Coxhead, *Fangoria*, No. 32, January 1984

"The Exorcist *was one of the fore-runners of the real blood, gore and vomit, but it's nothing compared with the films and books around today. You wonder where it's going to end. How far can you go?*"

– JAMES HERBERT, from "Chill the Spine" by Christine Day, *19*, November 1985 of my story to begin with. For a horror movie it just didn't scare, and they'd cut out most of the best moments so it didn't make any sense.

"There was dear old Joseph Cotten appearing for about two minutes as a priest – he had nothing to do with it! He disappears about a quarter of the way into it and you wonder, what happened? Did he realise he was in a stinker and try to get out? There were two good sequences – the first of the crash itself, the second where Powell is in the factory near the end and he's turning the lights on as he walks down its length and is illuminated by the pools of light. But I wrote the book and I still don't understand it! It was badly put together, the dialogue was stilted, the direction was awful . . . I still think it's an intriguing story with something to be made of it, but they just go away and do their own thing . . ."

The film crept out without theatrical release in both Britain and the USA, going to cable TV in the latter and the BBC and video in the former. It still infrequently manifests itself on the insomniac's slot on television, where its effect is comparable to a fistful of Valium . . .

The Rats fared only slightly better. Produced by exploitation merchants Golden Harvest, it contains a laughable pot-pourri of trashy exploitation elements (stupid teenagers, a token sex scene, horrible rock music and some quaint giant rat/Muppet heads chomping on chunks of human flesh, not to mention a pack of friendly dogs doubling for the eponymous rodents in shots which should have fans of the fifties schlock classic *The Killer Shrews* smiling nostalgically) but still fell well short of the mark. Grainy film stock makes the film look cheap and sweaty, while the drab cinematography and lifeless direction combine with inept acting to produce an embarrassing débâcle with precious few (unintentional) moments of amusement.

"Not only did I have no input into the film's production," says Herbert, "but I had nothing to do with the selling of it either. It was my first book, and the people who sold the movie rights were my own publishers, New English Library, who actually took 40 per cent of it as well – which was a bit naughty as I knew nothing about it. They sold it to a company called Golden Harvest, who specialised in kung-fu films – I did make one stipulation, that it must *not* be a kung-fu film . . . that was years before it was actually made. They finally dummied up Toronto to look like New York, and they dummied up Muppets and Dachshund dogs to look like rats. They looked pretty good from a distance until they started begging and barking . . . The Muppet close-ups didn't look *too* bad but the movie itself was a

"I wasn't too crazy about ET. *Perhaps I'm just cynical. I saw it with my wife and two kids and they were sitting beside me sobbing away and wailing and howling. It didn't move me like that at all. I do tend to be hypercritical.* Raiders of the Lost Ark, *however, I love."*

– JAMES HERBERT, from "Gnawing at the Movie Screen" by Martin Coxhead, *Fangoria*, No. 32, January 1984

When the pilot, played by a ghostly pale Powell, emerges unscathed from the wreck, echoes of the supernatural begin to reverberate through the picture, imbuing it with a disturbing sense of eeriness that could erupt into terror at any moment.

– from *The Aurum Film Encyclopedia Volume 3: Horror* (1986)

STEFAN JAWORZYN

"When I first heard that David Hemmings was going to direct it I wrote to him wishing him good luck with the film and if there was anything to do with the plot that I could help on, explaining little details and such, just let me know. He never ever replied. So I've kinda disowned the whole thing."

– JAMES HERBERT, from "Gnawing at the Movie Screen" by Martin Coxhead, *Fangoria*, No. 32, January 1984

total disaster. I saw a preview in London and there was nothing to say, the damage was done. It was just based very loosely on my story.

"It went out in the US as *Deadly Eyes*. New American Library, my US publisher, didn't even tell me about bringing out the book and changing the title. That's the bad end of publishing – someone can screw you for 40 per cent and your own publisher can bring out your book and change the title without even asking you."

The cheap, sleazy nature of the film might have even worked in its favour were it not for the absurd romantic subplots and leaden, predictable script. Robert Clouse is, at best, a hack director, and here he fails to produce any excitement from Charles Eglee's torpid screenplay, so the film is ultimately a vapid, enervating experience, devoid even of the occasional atmospheric touches and mysterious "qualities" of *The Survivor*. While these two catastrophic movies have disappointed Herbert, they haven't soured him completely . . .

New twist on an old story . . . A well-wrought, if slightly over-enigmatic thriller with a powerful ending.

– from *Science Fiction Film Source Book* (1985)

Golden Harvest presents A Filmtrust Production

THE RATS *(aka* DEADLY EYES*)*

Directed by ROBERT CLOUSE
Screenplay by CHARLES EGLEE
Based on the novel The Rats *by* JAMES HERBERT *and a screenplay by*
LONON SMITH
Produced by JEFFREY SCHECHTMAN *and* PAUL KAHNERT
Co-Producer CHARLES EGLEE
Executive Producer J. GORDON ARNOLD
Music by ANTHONY GUEFEN
Editor RON WISMAN
Director of Photography RENÉ VIRZIER
Art Director NINKEY DALTON
Special Effects MALIVOIRE PRODUCTIONS INC.
Special Make-up Effects and Animal Prosthetics by
MAKEUP EFFECTS LABS

Paul Harris	SAM GROOM
Kelly Leonard	SARA BOTSFORD
George Foskins	SCATMAN CROTHERS
Dr Louis Spenser	CEC LINDER
Trudy	LISA LANGLOIS
Martha	LESLEH DONALDSON
Mel Dederick	JAMES B. DOUGLAS
Tim Harris	LEE-MAX WALTON
Matt	JOSEPH KELLY
Hoserman	KEVIN FOXX

"There are two ways to look at it. One's Steve King's way – let 'em make the movie because it's good for you, it makes you a household name. The cinema audience is so massive, you get all the spin-offs, the advertising. . . So there's some benefit whether the film's good, bad or indifferent. People who don't read books still get to know your name.

"The other aspect is pride. The books are your children and you don't want to see them spoiled or corrupted. I find that hard to take, which is why I've been very choosy after *The Rats* and *The Survivor*. I've turned down offers because I've known they'd turn out to be sheer rubbish."

If many of the potential deals offered to Herbert are ultimately reduced to artistic integrity versus commercial appeal, perhaps Herbert could assure himself of a controlling interest by assuming a position of, say, executive producer?

"I couldn't do that, I'm a writer. I have actually been asked to act as producer. I was asked to be financial director on

Shrine, but it's something I wouldn't touch. There are too many hassles making movies, too many fingers in the pie, which is why I've also resisted writing screenplays. I know I'd need to make changes and it would all be very laborious, and all the fun would go out of writing. You end up taking a brief from others on your own work, and I think that's bad. The stuff the screenwriter of *Shrine* has had to put up with – he's had to sit here and take notes and have everyone telling him what to do. There's no way I could ever do that.

"When I left advertising I told myself I'd never get involved in organising. I try to keep as much influence as I can without actually getting involved in the business side."

In spite of the many nightmares (past and present) attendant in his dealings with the film world, Herbert has four projects in the offing, though he harbours few illusions by now about the chances of their imminent production.

"These are films that *may* be made. The options have been bought, screenplays have been written, but until that moment when you actually see it on the screen you can't say, this is going to be my movie. But things look good at the moment."

Of these projects, one (*Haunted*) has evolved from a particularly bitter experience at the hands of the BBC while another (*Shrine*) has its roots in some interminable financial wranglings . . .

"*Shrine* started off years ago when a guy called Chris Sprague came out to the Channel Islands to see me. He was a producer who used to work for ITV, a very ambitious and enthusiastic guy. Three different scripts have been written over the years, none really up to scratch, but now we've got a writer called Andrew Montgomery who's producing the goods. The director is Ian Sharp, who's done some good movies but no horror. We've also got on board a producer called Robert Watts, who's worked on the *Indiana Jones* films, *Star Wars*, *Papillon* – a big deal producer, and he's determined to see it made. They've got two-thirds of the money, but they need the final third to come from a major studio in order to tie up distribution rights.

"Originally we were involved with a financier who was going to float shares on the open market. It was a new thing for British films where they would get the man in the street to put up money in return for a certain percentage of the movie. I met this guy in Brown's Hotel . . . Very enthusiastic, a real high flyer, and it was he who introduced us to Robert Watts. The way the scheme was structured was that there'd be a holding company which would have a subsidiary company, and the hold-

Studio publicists are keeping a tight lid on the story of and behind Deadly Eyes . . . *Though the film is scheduled for an April release, publicists are reluctant to reveal much about the dogs. "Just as Universal did with* Jaws," *we were told, "we would like to keep [the dogs] top secret." Presumably, audiences will believe giant rats were trained for the film, just as Robert Shaw was bitten in half by a real shark.*

– from "Deadly Eyes: It's a Dog's Life", *Cinefantastique*, Vol. 13, No. 4, April–May 1983

Best scene is set in a Bruce Lee retrospective, as director Robert Clouse trashes his own, finest moment. Slummy to be sure, but you could do worse.

– TIM LUCAS, *Cinefantastique*, Vol. 14, No. 2, December/January 1983–84

"The company gave me one of the big Muppet-type rats they used for the close-ups. It's really very effective but for the long shots they used dachshunds, little dogs. They furred them up, stuck tails on them and fangs in their mouths and it looks really good. One of the troubles they had was that when they were streaming down a corridor or subway tunnel or swarming all over this guy to tear his guts out, they'd come running down and they'd all be barking! And the director would be tearing his hair out and jumping up and down yelling, 'Don't bark! Don't bark!' There's actually one scene where they're ripping this guy apart and one of them is sitting up begging!"

– JAMES HERBERT, from "Gnawing at the Movie Screen" by Martin Coxhead, *Fangoria*, No. 32, January 1984

ing company would get the money and plough it into the film. I said to this guy, that's fine, but I want you to be on the board of directors, as I am. He said no, and the more he resisted the more I insisted that he be on the board . . . Eventually he agreed, but a few months later Chris Sprague rang me up and said 'Don't say "I told you so," but . . .' And of course this guy hadn't turned out to be what he said he was at all. I did run into him later, in Ireland, and he said, 'You're a hard man, Jim.' I said, no, I'm used to spotting people like you . . ."

The Magic Cottage is another nebulous project which might come to fruition some time.

"The producer is David Kirstner, who did *An American Tail* – he's an artist, a writer, a producer. He also did *Child's Play*. A friend of his read the book on a plane journey and rang him up and told him he just had to make a film of it.

"David sees it as a combination of state-of-the-art robotics and animation, which sounds fascinating to me. It's art, animation, plus robotics. He got Charles Edward Pogue to do the script, which was terrific, though there were some changes I wanted to have made. David listened and made notes and we actually sat down and discussed our options! It does stick pretty strictly to the book, which is what I like. Pogue's screenplay is literate and intelligent. The idea is to make the film in England with American stars, which is fine with me. I think some of my books could actually benefit from being filmed in the USA. In England there are no actors to play good leads – who is there? Sean Connery and Michael Caine! The ideal hero for me is Richard Dreyfuss – he's humorous, very much an anti-hero, very believable. We don't have a British equivalent of him . . . we have brilliant actors, but not the right kind of main star, no one who really grabs you. Bob Hoskins is terrific, but he wouldn't fit in with any of my stories . . . I think we have the talent here to do justice to my books – in fact do better than America could film-wise, but we just don't have the money, so the ideal situation for me is with David getting the money and some American stars and shooting here in England.

"After our initial discussions David left Twentieth Century-Fox to become president of Hanna-Barbera, who want to start a branch like Touchstone, making adult-type movies. Fox re-optioned the film for another year because all his projects were delayed when David left, and he still wants to do the film with Fox even though he's president of Hanna-Barbera. If he remains in charge then I'll have faith in it."

At this point *The Magic Cottage* appears to have survived the often fatal "studio-executive shuffle" syndrome, whereby projects begun by erstwhile employees are forgotten, sold, sabotaged, tied up in endless litigation or otherwise left to rot by the new executive who finds it necessary to prove his worth by trying to ruin the studio.

Haunted didn't survive Herbert's first attempts to bring it to the small screen, but it looks like a distinct possibility that a big screen version will materialise in the not-too-distant future . . .

"The BBC came to me when we were out in the Channel Islands and said they'd love me to do a screenplay for them, an original screenplay. I said no, absolutely not. But they wanted to set up a meeting, so when I came over to do a *Wogan* show the producers met me. They were extremely persistent, very nice and very flattering. So I said, I'm going on holiday in a couple of weeks and if I have an idea I'll do a very rough outline for you; if you like it we'll talk business, but don't hold your breath. Anyway, I woke up one day from a bad dream about a haunted house, and in that transient stage between sleep and waking the dream continued, floating from my subconscious to my conscious, and I carried it on from there. I jumped up and filled five sheets of paper with the outline – it was the first time I'd ever done anything like that. So I rang up the BBC and told them to meet me and discuss the idea. As soon as I saw they were hooked it made me really enthusiastic. They went wild and asked me to do it as a proper treatment and a screenplay. I said okay – financially it was nothing at all, at the BBC it's peanuts, so it has to be a labour of love. Because I had so much to do at the time the only way I could work was to write the book and the screenplay simultaneously. I actually finished the book first.

"The BBC producer was a guy called Evgeny Gridneff. He and his partner pointed out things that needed doing, which were things that I'd had feelings about myself but was too much of a coward to face up to and didn't want to rework, but knew in my own mind were wrong. So in a way it was good for me – it made me a lot tighter, made me listen to other people. A lot of points I did argue and wouldn't change, but it was a good experience. It was then shown to Jonathan Powell, who was then head of BBC dramas and serials. The intention was to run it as a two-hour TV movie at Christmas, and there was a real buzz at the BBC about it.

"The contracts department then rang me up – they wanted to publish the book! Then they wanted a share of the royalties! I said, no, you're getting a screenplay, the rest is my territory. They said, 'Can't we just have a nominal share of the royalties,

"You can't make a real rat look all that fierce," says the film's Toronto backer, Gordon Arnold. "At first glance, rats look cute and cuddly." (Oh really?) "We'd have to use special effects and with rats it would have been difficult." He means: too expensive . . . "Dogs are easier," says Gordon Arnold . . . It's a bit like making Jaws III *with a goldfish.*

– TONY CRAWLEY, from "You Dirty . . . Dogs!", *Starburst*, No. 46, June 1982

Overgrown rats on the warpath, with science teacher Groom and health official Botsford to the rescue. You've seen it all before.

– Leonard Maltin's *TV Movies and Video Guide* (1986)

say one per cent . . . ?' The answer was still no. Jonathan Powell's idea was to do the movie then turn it into a series, each episode about fifty minutes long. I said I was agreeable but I couldn't do the screenplays, only outlines, and they'd have to bring in other writers. That weekend I sat down and within about forty-five minutes I had seven outlines. They got a script-writer, Stephen Volk (who wrote *Gothic*), and it wasn't quite to my liking, but things could have been changed. So it all seemed very good and I was happy with the people I was dealing with.

"But then nothing happened, and that went on for a couple of years. Eventually Jonathan Powell had been moved upstairs and a new guy had come in – Mark Shivas – who didn't like horror. Evgeny's contract wasn't renewed and all his projects walked out with him. No one rang me or wrote to me. Finally my agent had to phone them up and asked them to confirm whether it was going to happen or not. They just said, 'No, it isn't.' No apology or anything. I thought, if they can treat me like that then what are they doing to the people who depend on them for a living? I was quite disgusted. The folly of it was so great that I just couldn't see their way of thinking – there they had a book which they knew would come out in hardback and paperback and they knew would have a pretty wide readership; they knew the public is crying out for a good ghost story – particularly on TV around Christmas. They'd had it for next to nothing, yet they didn't want to use it – it wasn't just that they'd have a two-hour movie that they could sell worldwide, but the books, hardback, then paperback, had both gone straight to number one when they came out. It's inexplicable to me – no wonder the BBC gets into trouble.

"I got the rights back, and as soon as people realised it was available I had a few enquiries. Zenith looked at the script but they didn't want to do it. Then my agent said, 'There's someone who's really keen, he's an actor and a producer.' It turned out to be Anthony Andrews. When I started work on *Haunted* my image for the hero was Gabriel Byrne, a good, dark, brooding actor who's never had the chance to live up to his potential. I said I didn't think Anthony was quite right because I had Gabriel Byrne in mind. What I had against Anthony was that he was too good looking and too debonair, but the more we talked about it the more I was convinced that he could do it. I started thinking about how he'd looked in *Brideshead Revisited* when he was really out of it. In the end I said yes and he bought the option; he was really enthusiastic and charming. He has my script from the BBC which he wants to open out and put a lot more money into. He's going to produce it and star, and he's currently raising money for it in the USA."

The last of the "on the boil" projects is *Fluke*, perhaps the most unlikely candidate of Herbert's books for big screen adaptation, but in the twisted world of cinema nothing is impossible . . .

"I thought *Fluke* was almost a crackpot scheme at first. The producer, Carlo Carlei, is Italian and speaks very little English. But he wanted to make the film of the book, and nobody else had made any offers on it – I'd always thought it was unfilmable. The only way I could ever see it done was by animation with a Michael Caine voice-over.

"Anyway, Carlei bought the option and did a script which was awful – it had a fox hunt going through Lewisham and Peckham, and dog-catchers were chasing dogs with guns. It was crazy! He did another that was better, then got someone in Philadelphia to do it. Originally it was going to be shot in England, but they've moved it to the USA. The last screenplay I saw (April 1990) was very good, but at this stage they're still raising money."

Besides the four potential movies and the two extant disasters, there are a couple of unrealised projects. Again, it's surprising that neither of the books in question made it to the screen.

"*The Fog* was optioned shortly after *The Survivor* and I went to Pinewood to meet the producer, a guy called Greg Smith. The first thing he said was, 'I can promise you one thing, Jim, we're going to make this movie.' Then I read the screenplay, written by Chad Hall – in my old advertising days he'd been a big-deal photographer. The screenplay was *awful*. It was like 'James Bond meets The Fog'. The hero was an American played by Gene Hackman. As soon as I saw the line 'Get over here, Kowalski!' I thought, oh no . . . that summed it up – one cliché after another. *Any* film where you see the name Kowalski you know is *bad* news. So I was very disappointed, and quite relieved when it never got any further . . . But the option's run out, and it's one I'd really love to see made. I still think that one day it will be made.

"Then of course John Carpenter's film came out. I'm not making any allegations here, but this is the story I heard about *The Fog* (the movie). He (Carpenter) was in England and he said that the inspiration for the film came when he was driving across Salisbury Plain and saw a fog rolling across the countryside. It just happens that in *my* story that's where it begins – with a fog rolling across Salisbury Plain! It's a shame that

Herbert was also disappointed that the BBC seemed to be getting cold feet about his proposed television series: "It is still going ahead, but I said initially that they should not be scared and they seem to be slipping a bit on that," he explained with a laugh. "The last thing I heard was that they were thinking of making it a two-hour TV movie for Christmas, which is what I suggested in the first place!"

– STEPHEN JONES and JO FLETCHER, from *Science Fiction Chronicle*, Issue 90, March 1987

The book dealt with very intelligent issues of magic. Not in the sense of parlour tricks, but in the sense of real magic, like the Celtic and Druid mysticism that has been forgotten about over the last thousand years. Also, I thought the concept of a modern-day fairy tale within the context of a horror film was wonderful.

– DAVID KIRSCHNER, Producer, *The Magic Cottage*, from *Cinefantastique*, Vol. 20, No. 1/2, November 1989

Carpenter used the title because it's a bit misleading. In his film it's a sea mist, not a fog. But I think Carpenter would actually do a good job of making *The Fog* – it needs a director who could portray continuous murder and mayhem. It could be very action-orientated or it could be quite sci-fi. Russell Mulcahy would also be a good director for it, or John McTiernan.

"The other project that never came to fruition was *The Dark*. John Hough was going to do it, and I would have loved him to, but I drove such a hard bargain that it just wasn't feasible. I never saw any screenplays – I know he had some written, but he never showed them to me. He was going to use them to convince me to do the movie, but he was too embarrassed to let me see them. It was never actually optioned – I never signed any deals.

"I *want* films – I'm very keen to have films. For me it's the next step – I've done the books and now I want something a bit different. Primarily when I get involved with the film material it's on the basis of the people themselves. I do get money out of it – the options aren't cheap, but it's a nominal sum compared to how much I get if the cameras do actually roll. But at the initial stage it's the attitude of the people I'm dealing with that matters to me and the fact that they're not talking cheap horror. So much of the horror film scene these days is just sheer exploitation.

"But I'm very good at sussing people out and I make a point of speaking to them first and finding out if their intentions are good. What can obviously happen is that you get others involved who you haven't met or vetted.

"But that's a chance you just have to take sometimes . . ."

Jenny Agutter and Robert Powell in The Survivor *(1980)*

260

FROM RATS TO RICHES

Dave Hughes

THIRTY ONE

J AMES HERBERT, with thirteen novels behind him, is one of the few truly talented writers currently working in the field of horror. If his name is unfamiliar (certain extraterrestrials may not be familiar with his work), check your bookshelves; you're sure to find a dog-eared copy of *The Rats* or *The Fog* from the seventies lurking between the Harold Robbins and the Dick Francis books. Horror critic Douglas E. Winter calls him "one of the most influential and widely imitated horror writers of our time". He was recently named "the Godfather of splatterpunk".

I met him at his London flat, a gorgeous apartment which he uses for London business (his home is in Sussex), two weeks before the paperback publication of *Haunted*, halfway through his fourteenth novel, *Creed*, and about to move back into his Sussex home, which he is having extended. I asked him how he is currently spending his time.

James Herbert: Waiting to move back home! It's almost impossible for me; I'm halfway through the new book, but I've ground to a halt. I can't get into a flow because I've got architects and builders coming over all the time, interrupting.
Dave Hughes: What about the publicity for *Haunted*? That must be cranking up now–
Herbert: Yeah, it's starting. The day after I move back home I'm going to Dublin for a few days. I'm meeting some film people there; we're thinking of doing *Shrine*. We actually sat in this room thinking of where to set it, the obvious place being Sussex

which is where the book is set, but somebody came up with the bright idea of filming it in Ireland, because the book is about Catholics and so you can get that whole tradition. It makes good financial sense, as well.

Hughes: Is it a big-screen movie project?

Herbert: Oh yeah, it's serious. The executive producer is Robert Watts, who was one of the producers on the *Indiana Jones* movies, *Star Wars*, *Roger Rabbit*, etc. I'm very lucky to have him on the team.

Hughes: How involved are you with the project?

Herbert: Very much involved, although I'm not doing the screenplay – they asked me but I said no – but I'm involved. I'm a director of 'Shrine: The Movie Ltd', but I turned down Chris Sprague's [the producer] offer to be financial director. I want to write; I don't want to be involved in the business side. I suppose that once the director comes on the scene, my involvement might change . . .

Hughes: Any idea who that might be?

Herbert: I just turned down Wes Craven because I don't want it to be his sort of movie. I've seen the *Nightmare on Elm Street* films – the first two were enough for me – and I admire the technique, but it's usually all "slash-the-teenager" and I'm not into that.

Hughes: A group of teenagers go to a mysterious house, they take their clothes off and then get killed . . .

Herbert: Yeah, it's that sort of format, and I just didn't want that for *Shrine*. I also felt that the stars we were after would be frightened off by the name Wes Craven. What we want to do is a good quality horror movie, one that's going to be expensive to do but one that'll appeal not just to horror fans but to the general interest; a mainstream movie. You see, what the British film industry does is either *The Mission* or *My Beautiful Launderette*. There's nothing in between. You've got to have something that gets people out into the cinema.

Hughes: Entertainment.

Herbert: Exactly. I'm not into blood and gore, believe it or not. It really turns me off. I like it when it's well done, but you can't make a whole movie just on blood and gore. That might sound funny coming from me, but it's true. I don't read horror, either. I read Steve [King] but that's it.

Hughes: If blood-and-guts movies aren't your cup of tea, what sort of films are? Is *Indiana Jones* more your thing?

Herbert: :Oh yeah! In fact, my three favourite films are all Spielberg's: *Jaws, Close Encounters* and *Raiders of the Lost Ark*. I like others; in my top ten are films like *Twelve Angry Men*

Without doubt a bestseller has to be a good story. It also has to be readable and that's not as easy as it sounds.

People think there is a magic bestselling formula that will make lots of money. There isn't. You have to write from instinct.

Each of my books has a different style or concept so that the reader never quite knows what he'll get each time. There is no one ingredient you should include; once you start that you are writing too self-consciously. You can't even formulate the scary bits for horror, it has to flow naturally.→

with Henry Fonda, and *The Sweet Smell of Success*, which had Burt Lancaster and Tony Curtis as gossip writers. They were just out-and-out drama, though. So there's a lot of areas there that I'm into, but I must admit that I'm a sucker for *Indiana Jones* and things like that. So anyway, we hope to get *Shrine* going. *The Magic Cottage* looks good and *Haunted* should be next, so of those three if one or two of them come through, that'll be great.

Hughes: Which of those three would you most like to see filmed?

Herbert: Of all of them, *The Magic Cottage*. It'll be an American production, but we're trying to get it shot over here. It'll have American stars, which I don't mind because there aren't any English ones! [*laughs*] Apart from Connery and Caine, who else is there?

Hughes: Who would you choose for the lead of *The Magic Cottage*? Was there a role model for Mike Stringer?

Herbert: Well he was always based on a combination of three people. One – naturally enough – me. You can't avoid that, particularly when you're writing in the first person. Two, a friend of mine: a rock musician by the name of Bob Young. And third, Richard Dreyfuss. Now Dreyfuss is also one of a long line for *Shrine*.

Hughes: He's also in *Jaws* and *Close Encounters*, two of your favourite films!

Herbert: Yeah, I loved him in those. He's my kind of hero. A bit of an anti-hero.

Hughes: He's not the best looking guy in the world, and he doesn't get it right all of the time . . .

Herbert: Exactly. And the guy I'm using as a hero at the moment, because he fits the picture for the new book [*Creed*] so well, is Mickey Rourke. He's a real sleaze, this character.

Hughes: Yeah, I can just see Rourke as Joe Creed.

Herbert: It's great that you can get that image. He's wicked. When he gets frightened, he faints! None of this phony heroic stuff. He just faints! It's irritating to me not to be able to get on with the book because I'm actually enjoying this one, whereas *Haunted* was a tough one, and *Sepulchre* was a mean book. That was very difficult to enjoy. This one's wicked; black humour. Creed's the kind of guy you love, 'cause he reminds you of yourself.

Hughes: When you aren't writing, what are you reading? The last time I saw you, you were reading *The Catcher in the Rye*. Have you finished it?

Herbert: Yeah. I'm now reading *Einstein's Monsters* by Martin

Amis. I've just got around to reading *Jig* by Campbell Armstrong. I've had *A Brief History of Time* for about a year and I'm up to about page 8 [*laughs*] – I read some and realise I haven't read it at all. I'm not reading as much as I'd like to. I've just endorsed Steve King's new one, though.

Hughes: For the English market, presumably?

Herbert: And for the American market, too.

Hughes: That's good, because James Herbert has never been as popular there as King is here.

Herbert: My stuff has always sold well in the States, and I've always outsold Steve in this country (and he won't mind me saying that!), but people have always thought that Steve was the biggest seller, and he never has been. And in America I have the same kind of problem that Steve had here. Because I'm very English, and he's very American – very Norman Rockwell-ish. Do you know Norman Rockwell?

Hughes: The artist? Into brand names, like King?

Herbert: That's it. I've never had the breakthrough over there, and although I've had a couple of movies – *The Rats* and *Survivor* – it's just never happened. That's how King made it over here: with the movies. Now he's number two over here, and I guess Clive [Barker] must be number three. It's strange in this country, though: there's so many writers around – good ones, like Ramsey [Campbell], Brian Lumley, Stephen Gallagher, and that young writer who wrote *Roofworld* . . .

Hughes: Chris Fowler.

Herbert: Chris Fowler, yeah. I can't understand why they're not more successful.

Hughes: I think a lot of it's due to the publishers.

Herbert: Well, yeah; I feel quite selfish in a way because I've enjoyed the position all these years, you know. And I'm all for pulling up the ladder [*laughs*]! No, no; just joking. I mean, I'm very much an outsider as far as horror goes. I'm not in the club. I liked what I saw and who I met at the 1988 World Fantasy Convention, but I see books that are hyped and movies that are reviewed seriously, and they're rubbish. Now I know that the horror genre has got to self-generate, but there's a lot of stuff that shouldn't be taken seriously. I'm a bit bemused by it all. I wish it was more mainstream, to be honest. Horror writers are so defensive. They are all on about why horror isn't more acceptable to the media, etc., but it's never been a problem for me.

"The other day I had a letter from a girl who'd won a Duke of Edinburgh award for her studies on my books. She even sent a photo of herself and Prince Philip to prove it. I also found out Fluke *– about a man who suddenly finds he's turned into a dog – is recommended reading at Leeds University. Isn't that something?"*

– James Herbert, from "Spine Chilling Success" by Bonnie Estridge, *Girl About Town*, Issue 413, December 1, 1980

Salman Rushdie and James Herbert at the Author of the Year party, Hatchards, Piccadilly (circa 1992)

JIM MEETS GRAY

Graham Masterton

THIRTY TWO

HORROR history was made on a wild and windy day in mid-October when I met bestselling British author James Herbert for the first time. We got together at his home in Sussex to sign title pages for Stan Wiater's forthcoming collection of horror-author interviews *Dark Dreamers*.

Jim is one of the most affable and approachable blokes that you could hope to meet, but it's not particularly surprising that both of us have been toiling in the blood-spattered vineyards of horror writing for over fifteen years (and living no more than half-an-hour apart) without bumping into each other.

Although we like and appreciate our fans, especially the Horrific Order of the Brothers of the Immense Jeans, who faithfully attend every horror/fantasy bunfight going, neither of us are great attenders of conventions or panels, and neither of us feel an urgent need to discuss the implications either of our own work or anybody else's. We share a feeling that if a book can't speak for itself, then it must at best be deficient and at worst incomprehensible. We also happen to enjoy our homes and our families, and the idea of spending three days in a fog of cigarette-smoke talking about Zogbat of Plongo somehow doesn't come close to strolling across the autumnal English countryside with one's dear ones, a cocker spaniel and a Purdey shotgun, in search of a brace of pheasant and a warm and oak-beamed hostelry.

For me, however, one of the sadder consequences for horror writers who aren't inclined to appear at every conceivable convention is that their work is invariably ignored by those dedicated cliques who decide on the various horror/fantasy awards and prizes. I could be thoroughly objectionable and mention several bowel-binding short stories and novels which could only have been awarded honours because of cliquery (or because the judges simply hadn't read any others). I could also mention several worthy and brilliant short stories and novels which could only have been passed over for prizes because their authors weren't members of one of the charmed circles.

I expressed the opinion to Kelley Wilde not long ago that horror awards such as the Stoker were both irrelevant and divisive. Not that I really give a damn. But if they *are* going to be awarded, let them be awarded expansively and generously and with an open mind. Let them be awarded once in a while to those writers who have lifted horror out of the rut of category fiction and widened its general appeal . . . writers who have done a service to all of us not by stretching the boundaries of disgust or the outer limits of incomprehensibility, but by winning widespread public popularity.

James Herbert won't particularly thank me for saying this, because he's too modest and he doesn't actually care about it that much, but considering that he's been topping the British bestseller lists consistently for years, and writes bloody good books that his readers really enjoy, it's absolutely astonishing that he hasn't won one single horror/fantasy award.

Anyway, we spent a pleasant few hours together, toyed with a little Chablis, and talked about Jim's latest work-in-progress, *Creed*, which he promised would feature one of the most objectionable heroes in modern horror. We decided that Stan Wiater had done a good job of his interviews, apart from his habit of inserting [*laughs*] whenever his interviewee expresses mirth. Every horror writer I've ever met [*laughs*] differently. Some have completely different ways of reacting, which Stan has omitted. One writer I know [*falls off chair sideways*].

One interesting thing about James Herbert is that he looks just like James Herbert. So many writers don't look like themselves at all. Ramsey Campbell only sometimes resembles himself, and then you have to catch him in the right light. I always think I look like a moderately prosperous second-hand car dealer.

Perhaps that's the secret of Jim's success: that he's always himself, whether he's sitting at home with his friends or whether he's setting out to defeat the Forces of Darkness. He has a complete absence of what used to be called "side".

Another interesting thing is that – for a writer – he's terrifyingly tidy. I never met such a tidy man in my life. His huge

"Money? Yes I love it. If you come from a poor background like me you know just how important the stuff is."

– JAMES HERBERT, from "Jim Rates Riches of the Rat Race" by Tom Moore, *Argus Weekender*, August 12, 1989

"I pay a lot of tax, but if Britain is okay for Paul McCartney and Elton John, who pay even more, then it is all right for me."

– JAMES HERBERT, from "From a Coin Booth in High Holborn to the Supernatural", *Sunday Telegraph Magazine*, January 30, 1983

*"People regard
someone like me
paying taxes as a
punishment."*

– JAMES HERBERT,
from "I Have Always
Wanted Shirts Made
by Turnbull and
Asser" by Natalie
Graham, *Today*,
August 18, 1987

greenish altar of a desk has scarcely anything on it, and the
pale-coloured study in which he sits to write (by hand!!!) has
almost nothing in it. After I met him, I felt like writing a horror
story called *Tidy,* about an incredibly disorganised writer who
makes a deal with Beelzebub to make him fold his socks away
properly. I didn't like to ask him, but I'll bet Jim files his canned
food in alphabetical order. Spam before Sugar.

We found a camera in order to record the historic Herbert/
Masterton meeting, but unfortunately we didn't have any film
and nobody felt like walking down to the local Post Office to
buy any. So it was commemorated with self-drawn cartoons on
one of the title-pages of the long-suffering Stan's new book.

270

DARK DREAMER

Stanley Wiater

THIRTY THREE

"**P**EOPLE** expect us to look like Christopher Lee and wear a black cape, don't they?" James Herbert wondered out loud as his wife handed him a drink in his barren study. Of course, his huge study was not in its usual working order, as he explained that the office equipment hadn't arrived since adding a new wing to his country home in Sussex. Regardless, Herbert appeared quite comfortable sitting within a most ornate, and unusual-looking, chair. ("It's the first time I've sat in it, so it may give me some good vibes.") A chair which once belonged to the infamous Aleister Crowley (1875–1947), an occult writer and reputed sorcerer who was once termed "the most evil man in the world".

"People who have only read the first books don't know what I'm about."

– JAMES HERBERT, from "Animal Calm" by Neil Gaiman, Today, June 1, 1986

Herbert doesn't even look moderately evil, and in fact has a lovely wife and three daughters to prove that he is just an ordinary husband and father. Of course, he is much better known as one of the world's bestselling horror writers. The author of such novels as *The Rats, The Fog, The Survivor, Lair, Fluke, The Dark, The Spear, Shrine, The Jonah, Moon, The Magic Cottage* and *Sepulchre*, he commands a popularity in his native England that is second to no one – not even Stephen King.

As Herbert was one of the first contemporary writers in the genre to "tell it like it is", he was initially condemned by the critics as going too far over the edge with his particularly grim and violent visions. Yet whatever the critics might say, the public has always embraced his work, as evidenced by how all fourteen of his novels remain in print with more than 20 million copies of his works published worldwide.

Born in the East End of London on April 8, 1943, Herbert is now surrounded by the material wealth he never imagined he would have as a youngster growing up in poverty. Although he repeatedly prefaced his remarks with the hope that he wasn't speaking too pompously or self-consciously, I found James Herbert to be a genial yet always direct man who believes he has worked hard, and now is simply enjoying the fruits of his labour as a dark dreamer.

Stanley Wiater: In spite of the present condition of your study, what's your daily writing schedule like?

James Herbert: I'm a late riser. I'm one of those people that for me to go to sleep, it's like another day's work. I dream very heavily, in full Technicolor. But I get into the study at ten, and I work through to lunchtime, at one o'clock. I'll have lunch, read the morning newspaper, and get back to the study about half-past two, and then I'll work through to six o'clock in the evening, and if it's going well, until seven. But that's my deadline; I never work beyond that. Sometimes it's seven days a week, but generally it's six days a week.

Wiater: You mentioned to me earlier that your wife does the physical typing of your manuscripts. So you prefer to write in longhand?

Herbert: I do. I use a medium-thick Pentel pen and a jumbo exercise pad, and I've worked that way from day one. It seems to work for me. You know at the moment I'm working on a desk – it's not even a desk, it's one of those coffee tables which has a strange hydraulic system where you can have it high or low – and it's the table that I did *The Rats* on, my very first book. And *The Fog*, years ago. Because at the moment I'm waiting for my office equipment to come in, I'm actually working on this old table again.

Wiater: Well, between the table and the Crowley chair, some sparks of inspiration had better occur!

Herbert: The thoughts that must be ingrained in that table – it must be quite remarkable by now. [*laughs*]

Wiater: You mentioned your dreams as being particularly vivid. When you're writing, have you already visualised the entire novel in your mind, or is each day a new adventure for your imagination?

Herbert: Each day is a new adventure. I sit there and just let it pour out. If I'm lucky, it pours out!

Wiater: After fourteen novels, do you find that the horror genre still fascinates you? Or are you growing tired of it?

"There's those that like The Rats, and you know that all they really want is horror, blood and gore. And they're probably a bit disappointed in James Herbert now that there's not so much blood and gore."

– JAMES HERBERT, from "Haunted by Rats" by Dave Hughes, *Skeleton Crew* II, 1988

Herbert: It is *endlessly* fascinating. But there's a lot of humour in my books as well. So both ends fascinate me: humour and horror. And they often walk hand in hand. To put it more basically, I just find that you can write about a very mundane situation, and you can get into that; but after a while, it can become tedious for a writer – and certainly for a reader. When you find that boredom is approaching, you can take that mental leap – and invite the reader to take it with you – and take that one bound into horror that transcends everything you've written before that. You know, it really stops you getting bored with what you're doing.

You're only limited by your own imagination. So you can – I don't know. So you can . . . dig into areas that nobody else wants to dig into. Or they didn't use to want to – now everybody wants to! [*laughs*] You see what I mean? It gives you a lift. It gives you a metaphorical erection, if you like. It just gets the blood flowing and the thoughts flowing. It's wonderful.

Wiater: But how seriously should we take horror? For some writers, it's just a series of scary scenes, while for others, it's what they seem to be literally born to do with their lives.

Herbert: I know what *I'm* doing, and I know that Steve King knows what *he's* doing, and Peter Straub knows what *he's* doing, whether anyone else can understand what we're doing is another matter. I find one of the dangers nowadays is that we can get very pompous about what we do. It's almost a defence mechanism. When people want to put down horror, we tend to try and explain it too much, and give too much motivation for what we're doing.

I think we do it by instinct alone. One critic said of me a few years back, that "James Herbert could make Scarborough on a wet, dreary afternoon seem interesting." Now Scarborough is one of our dreariest, worst towns. So that was a great compliment for me. It's something that's within us . . . I have great difficulty explaining what I do. I work by instinct. Others are very articulate about this, but I try not to be. I really try not to be. Because I don't want to open that box. I don't want to see the mechanics of it.

Wiater: But if you could think of yourself as a magician, shouldn't you know better than anyone in the audience how the mechanism, or the tricks, operate?

Herbert: But see, I don't know how the tricks work! And I'm determined to keep it that way. I'm a magician by instinct. To me, it *is* magical. In the true sense. Writing is not a mechanical thing; it's not trickery. And as soon as you analyse, and as soon as you give reasons, and as soon as you get pretentious about it, or try to explain it, I think it evaporates. It disappears. You know? Or at least it dissipates.

Wiater: So what you're saying is that true horror writers cannot be manufactured, that you have to be born with this fascination for the dark side?

Herbert: I firmly believe they are born this way. The trouble with the genre at the moment is that there are too many horror writers who are manufactured; not natural horror writers. It's a booming industry, it's an exciting industry, and a lot of these guys don't work by instinct, they work by process, if you like. They've read a lot of good horror over the years, and a lot of *bad* horror over the years, and they emulate it. It doesn't come from deep within. With me, there must be some twisted side of my nature that just *loves* horror. And I think that's true of the best of us. There's something within us that is, I think, a bit warped, and you're born with that. It's not manufactured.

Wiater: What are your fans like? Obviously your work has a broad appeal for you to be considered a "mainstream success".

Herbert: Yes, it's a very, very broad spectrum – from eleven-year-old kids to eighty-two-year-old grannies. It's right across the board. And, in a way, that's where I think I'm lucky. It's not just one "market" if you like, or just one age group. Which makes the books more mainstream than just horror. If anything, I guess that's the secret of why I do pretty well over here. It's because it's not just the horror lovers who buy them. I would say the main market for me is between – I guess – the ages fifteen to forty to forty-five.

I've also found my audience to be way down the middle, between male and female. Which is interesting, you know? You'd think it would be more male-orientated than female. But I have found with my stuff it's straight down the middle. In fact, one of the women's magazines over here has already serialised two of my books: one was *The Magic Cottage*, and one was *Haunted*. So it must have that female attraction.

Wiater: John Saul and Stephen King reportedly have a large female following. Any idea how that works for certain horror authors, and not for others?

Herbert: I must confess I don't. It could be my books are just more accessible to women than a lot of other horror books. I fear to say it's because I show a lot more sensitivity, because some of the stuff that both Steve and I do is pretty hard to take! [*laughs*] But I don't really want to speculate about it, in case I discover what it is – and I get self-conscious about it.

Wiater: It's been reported that you're so successful you're no longer the leader of the pack. Rather, you're in a pack all your

Herbert is not a bad novelist; he is simply regarded as one by fantasy fans who've not read his work.

– STEPHEN KING, from *Danse Macabre* (1981)

own. People will buy anything that has your name on it, whether they're horror fans or not.

Herbert: Yes, that's one of the secrets to my success that I was referring to earlier. It's not just those horror aficionados – my books attract the whole range of readership. People that you'd be amazed would ever pick up a horror book – but they do! I think Steve King and I are both now in that bracket, and probably Peter Straub and Dean Koontz as well. I think that well-written horror can sell. I can only speak for myself here – I don't know what the situation is over in the States – but there are many very talented horror writers over here, and yet they can't seem to break out of that genre market.

Wiater: What are your thoughts on the recent trend in horror films, more specifically, the so-called "splatter movies"?

Herbert: I hate them. I really detest them. It's self-conscious horror, isn't it? It's just going out to *shock*. And we all want to shock – but they do it on such a very *low* level: "How many ways can you kill a teenager?" I just hate that – there's no real story to them; there's no real characterisation to them. It's just sensationalism for the sake of it. Now, we've all done a bit of that – but we do back it up with good plots, and good characterisations and, occasionally, a fine bit of writing. Just occasionally. But these films, they don't do that – and they don't even *attempt* to do it. And it's damaging, not just to society as a whole . . . I mean, I've got young daughters, and I hate them seeing those films – but it's damaging to us, in regards to the genre. So I really loathe and detest them – and yet, I would never say, "You mustn't do that." These films will find their own level. I think the kids will grow up, and they'll get sick of them as well. They're a passing phase.

Wiater: Back in the 1970s you were one of the first modern horror writers purposely not to restrain yourself in terms of scenes of explicit sex and violence. Now you're no doubt aware that many writers have surpassed you in both areas. What are your thoughts on that subject?

Herbert: At the 1988 World Fantasy Convention, Charles L. Grant said to me, "Really, Jim, you're the Godfather of splatter-punk." I was a bit taken aback by that! [*laughs*] Then I understood what he was saying. And it is true. It's a reputation I've had a lot of trouble shaking off over the years because when people think of *nasty* horror, they do think of *The Rats* and *The Fog*. Now these books were written fourteen, fifteen years ago, and my style has changed. There's still the same ingredients; but the more you do something, you have to improve.

One of the problems I have with America is that the critics

"I've wanted to be taken seriously from the beginning. From The Rats. *The trouble is that when I'm not actually working, I'll joke about it. I don't want to get intellectual about the books, because what I've put into the books is there in the books themselves.*

"I love what I'm doing and I always strive for something better than went before. I sweat blood and tears over the books. I could just churn them out, but they wouldn't be any good. And because my books are readable, and people can go through them pretty fast if they want to, people think, 'Oh he just dashed it straight off.' It doesn't work that way; to make *it so readable you've got to work hard-hard-hard . . . but I shouldn't be telling you that. That's my job."*

– JAMES HERBERT, from "James Herbert: Growing Up in Public" by Neil Gaiman, *Gaslight & Ghosts* (1988)

James Herbert stock-car racing (circa 1988)

still think I'm doing that sort of stuff; they don't think I've changed. What happened was they picked up a few of the earlier books, and not bothered to read the later ones. So they can't see how I've developed as a writer. They just think of me as "splatterpunk", if you like. Whether I'm responsible now for those kind of books, I don't know. I really don't. Do you think I am?

Wiater: I would say you were more or less responsible for the sub-genre of "creature" books that appeared after *The Rats*. Stories dealing with monstrous bugs, slugs, and various slimy members of the lower orders gone suddenly homicidal.

Herbert: [*laughs*] That is true, but it goes way beyond that. Think of how certain scenes in *The Fog* and *The Dark* have been copied over the years.

Wiater: Some writers believe it's their duty to try and go beyond what's been previously done before. To make the shocks even greater than ever before. What do you think of that concept?

Herbert: That's the mistake they make. "Let's go farther; let's go way over the edge." When I did my first books – yes, I did know I was breaking new ground – but it was a natural thing for me to do. It wasn't me self-consciously saying, "I'm going to be outrageous. I'm going to do things that nobody's ever done before." It was a very subtle thing – I was aware that I was doing it, but it wasn't a conscious decision to do it. It just happened that way.

Wiater: I know that in England you've had the opportunity to design the entire package: artwork, typography, and so forth, that go into the physical production of one of your books. If you were asked to design the cover for something called, say, *Dark Dreamers: Conversations with the Masters of Horror*, do you have any ideas how you would go about it?

Herbert: Absolutely! I'd have a *huge* photograph on the front of James Herbert. And it would be the most dominant name, "James Herbert", as well. That's how I would do it.

Wiater: And I suppose everyone else's name in half the size.

Herbert: What? Do they have to be even half size? [*laughs*]

Wiater: If you had to choose, could you tell someone which three of your novels they should read first?

Herbert: Oh, very difficult! Very difficult! I'm not allowed four?

Wiater: All right, four. But no more.

Herbert: I would say *The Fog* certainly, because that's sheer madness and mayhem. And to me, rather than *The Rats*, that's the book that knocked down the boundaries of horror. After

STANLEY WIATER

that, I would say *Shrine*, which technically was probably the best book I've written. In terms of profundity, probably the best I've written. Another must would be *The Magic Cottage*, because it's the one I'm most pleased with. The choice for me next is a bit more difficult because I would love for everybody to have read *Fluke*. On the surface it's such a simple book, but in fact it's such a deep book, as far as I'm concerned.

On the other hand, I would love for everybody to have read *Haunted*, because that takes you through the whole spectrum of what I've done, from *The Fog* to *Shrine* to *The Magic Cottage* to *Haunted*. Which is a reversion to the Gothic horror story – the old manor house ghost story. So with that four you have a very broad spectrum of horror – it would encompass the whole genre, to me. But in a few years time I would hope to have another four to choose from.

Wiater: Over the past few years, many critics have had to do an about-face regarding your work, and now you're recognised as a true master of the genre. Any specific instances which have been especially gratifying?

Herbert: My books have been used in exams, they've been used in universities – and not just here, but in Europe as well. [*long pause*] People are actually being educated in some way by my books. It's another reward for me. It's nice to be appreciated in your own lifetime. I mean, having said that, I'm still knocked all the time, particularly by teachers with young students, because I know the younger kids just want the blood and gore. There's not too much of that in my later books, you know, so some of them must be disappointed.

But for instance, I was invited to Oxford University, to give a talk to the students. Now, no amount of money can actually equal that! Just the joy of actually being asked, let alone doing it. To speak to the Art Society was for me – remembering my background from the East End of London – it's a *tremendous* compliment. And I can't help but feel very proud of that. So it is doing other things than just "entertaining the masses". There *is* another level to what we're doing, and that's important.

Wiater: Some of your books are quite bleak and unrelenting, such as *Sepulchre*. While others, like *The Magic Cottage*, are noticeably lighter and more humorous in tone. Is there any reason to believe that one type of horror novel is easier to write than another?

Herbert: They're all difficult, though some appear to be less difficult than others. For me, *The Magic Cottage* was a breeze. *The Fog* wrote itself. Books like *Domain* were very, very difficult because there was so much research. *Sepulchre* was very,

I do get a bit tired of journalists who keep, you know, going back to The Rats *and* The Fog *as though that's all I've ever done and as though I'm still at that stage in the writing. You know 'cause* The Rats *was a first story – and I've progressed from then. You learn your craft – the more you do something the better you get – and I put a lot more into the books now – so yes, it is a bit frustrating when they keep harking back on that.*

– JAMES HERBERT, from *Danse Macabre*, No. 8, January 1986

very difficult because it was so dark, and I had to keep myself in that mood all the time. I didn't want to enjoy myself while I was doing it. I had to remain very dark and sinister, so I could give myself no relief with humour or sheer enjoyment. The research aspects come into it as well – it's very difficult to stop your imagination from running away and just collate all those facts that you have, and make sense of them.

So it does vary from book to book. The one I'm doing at the moment I'm finding easy to write, because again it's very humorous, though it's very wicked humour. It's not written in the first person, though it very well could have been. I'm making the reader very conscious of the narrator. I'm telling it in a very, very relaxed tone of voice –

Wiater: Almost as if you were writing in an Aleister Crowley chair and getting these particular vibes . . .

Herbert: Yes, I'm still trying to get relaxed, but it's just not working! [*laughs*]

Wiater: How wrapped up do you get emotionally with your characters while you're writing? Do you laugh when they laugh? Cry when they must die?

Herbert: I don't cry when they die, but I do get totally wrapped up in the characters, the plot, the whole thing. It's a very draining experience, yet I do have control over it. It takes a *lot* to frighten myself nowadays. When there's a scary moment – yes, I'm very, very tense. I find I'm more scared if I relate that scary moment in that book when I'm talking to people.

For instance if I was in a pub, and was asked "What did you write today?" I would actually go through this scene of horror. *That's* when I would find the hair on the back of my neck standing up – when I'm doing it verbally. That's when I get that chill. When I'm writing it, I get a certain kind of chill, but I'm in control. But when I'm describing it, it's like I've reverted back to Jim Herbert – not James Herbert the writer – and it's almost like me telling a scene from a movie I've just seen or from a story I've just read. The audience part of me comes to the fore, not the author part. It's quite a weird thing, actually, but it does happen.

Wiater: To what degree do you use your own personal fears or real-life experiences in your fiction?

Herbert: You have to remember that the hero of the book is usually the author's alter-ego, so therefore your hero is thinking thoughts that you, the writer, would think. You can't avoid that, and your worst sort of phobias and fears come out. One phobia I do avoid is anything happening to children. It's one of the areas that Steve King and I differ on – he would always write about

"You've got very few limitations when you're writing horror or supernatural, and that's what I like about it. It excites me. And it's a fascinating area anyway, the supernatural. To try and guess what is out there or up there or down there . . . it's wonderful just to think about it – and to be paid *to think about it is even more wonderful."*

– JAMES HERBERT, from "Bloody Good Storyteller" by Lisa Tuttle, *The Twilight Zone Magazine*, Vol. 4 No. 5, November/ December 1984

STANLEY WIATER

horrible things happening to kids. It's Steve's way of exorcising those fears. And I try to avoid that because it's too meaningful for me, you know? I'd rather run away from it. I've got three daughters, and I find it too painful to write about nasty things happening to kids. I have done it – and I've regretted it afterwards.

I did try once, with a book called *Moon*. The hero had a daughter who was, at that time, the same age as my daughter. And the whole story was leading up to something really terrible that was going to happen to this child. And I couldn't do it! So the dreadful thing that happened, happened to her best friend next door. The reader never got to meet her, and nor did I as a writer – it had to be once removed. It was too horrific. I couldn't get into that terrible emotion of writing about the hero's daughter, because it would have been my daughter. And so I just avoided it. Very cowardly – but it was for a reason; it was too much to take.

Wiater: I know your religious upbringing was as a Catholic. Does a writer truly have to believe in the concepts of Good and Evil to write effectively about them?

Herbert: I can only answer for myself: I do. I really do believe in Good and Evil. I asked a priest once, "Do you think Evil is an actual force?" And he said, "Yes. Undoubtedly – it is an actual force." Of course, being a Catholic, you're brought up with the supernatural. Because if you believe in God, it's as a supernatural being. It's instilled in you. I find it very valuable now as a writer in our genre. Of course, the Catholic Church is supposed to frown on the sort of thing that I do, but it's given me so much information and insight on the supernatural! [*laughs*]

Wiater: Do you think you've ever reached the true "heart of darkness" in your work? To fully explore and perhaps ultimately understand the pitch-dark core that is the heart of evil?

Herbert: I've never even scratched the surface. [*long pause*] It's just beyond us all. I thought I had in a number of books. Certainly with *The Dark* I thought I got pretty close. Again, with *Sepulchre* I thought I was very near. But I've come to realise I've never even scratched it. There's so much going on – yes, people like me have more of an imagination than the majority. And so we can either rise to great levels or sink to deep levels. I feel that I've sunk about as low as anybody. [*laughs*] But I still haven't even scratched the surface.

Whether that remains an ambition for me to do just that, I don't know. Maybe that's the next step for me, to *really* get as far as I can in presenting Evil as it really is. Evil is such a

I know what I do and how important it is to me, and I don't actually believe you should foist that on other people just to up the horror genre, to make it sound more important than it is. It's important to me, it's important to all of us, but you can't keep insisting on that to other people who don't want to know. It comes across as very pompous. Stephen King is down to earth when he talks about horror – not the glamour of horror, but about why it actually is good. He's great at that.

– JAMES HERBERT, at *Fantasycon XIV*, October 7, 1989

tenuous thing; in some sense it's very, very subtle, and in other ways it's very obvious and very overt. It's a wonderful, mysterious, mystical area. And that's why we do it. That's why we keep striving to reach for that understanding.

Rick Wakeman and James Herbert working together on a record album (circa 1991)

THEY DON'T LIKE US

James Herbert

THIRTY FOUR

I have to admit I'm totally biased as far as Stephen King is concerned. We were both published around the same time, King with Carrie, *me with* The Rats, *and I think it's reasonable to say that this was probably the beginning of horror fiction's renaissance in the UK and the USA. It was also when I became a solid fan of his work.*

We met a little later when he was in England on a publicity jaunt, and we shared an after-dinner speaking engagement. If not quite hostile to horror, our middle-aged, middle-class audience was certainly not →

I KNOW there'll be trouble the moment I go through the door. Some bars don't mind you – hell, cash is cash, no matter where it comes from – but others put up the shutters as soon as they see you approach.

They don't like us, see? We're not their kind. In fact, to *them* we're not even people. It makes life . . . it makes things . . . difficult. To say the least.

Anyway, this time I step into the place – shit, a rat-hole if ever there was one – and take a coupla seconds to blink out the darkness. There's cobwebs like dirty rags in the corners, the wood floor needs scrubbing, the mirrors need scraping. The dive is full of low-lives. You'da thought one more would'na made no difference. But then there's always the bigots. Christ on a Crutch, them are everywhere.

H'mn. They say the same about us.

One of my kind is over there in a corner, making like he don't see me as he brushes dirt from one part of the floor to another. He ignores me, and man, I ignore him. No bro' he, think I.

The buzz that's been going on stops awhiles, like they all waiting for me to make my move to the bar. I make that move and things start up again, tho' I can tell many an interested eye is still on me.

It's hard to walk well when you cold – cold and thirsty. I need some fire in me, and brother, this is the place, this is the place I'm gonna get it. I've taken enough of their shit.

I got money, the gov'mint gives me money. It don't like my

JAMES HERBERT

kind, but there's too many Bleeding Hearts in the country for them in power to ignore their vote. 'Sides, we got the vote too. Every man is equal, right? Some is more so, is all.

It's a long hike to that old chipped bar counter, but I've taken longer ones. A bear scrapes back his chair and stands in front of me as I get near – you can always count on a redneck to make his feelings plain. I guess the idea is to stare me down, but hell, I don't even look. I've learned better by now. I shuffle round him.

He gives a kinda snort, hitches up his belt, and stomps out to the back room, probly to piss up the wall. Better than up me, right? Yeah, that's been done too.

So here I am, finally at that dusty old bar, thirsting so hard, man, my throat is kinda seized up. Raw like. Scorched.

It ain't easy to talk that way.

"Whu . . ." I try. I swallow, and fuck, that hurts like hell. "Whisky." It's a rasp, but he knows what I mean all right.

"This ain't the place for you, boy," the barman tells me, like it's fresh news.

I repeat the order. "Whisky . . . uh, please." The more you talk, the easier it gets, but we don't get much chance for conversation, y'know?

"You harda hearin'?" the fat man, this pig of a barman, says to me.

I put the money – I've counted the 'xact amount outside, and Christ, that took some time – on the bartop. "Whisky," I say for the – what was it? Oh yeah, the third – for the third time.

So he reaches down for his baseball bat under the bar and brings it up for me to see. He shows it off, and to make sure I understand he says, "See." Then he points it at my head.

It's not the pain that matters – that don't matter at all. Nor the indignity. It's the fuckin' dent, man.

"Hey, give the zook a drink," comes a voice from behind. I don't turn. No, I keep my eyes on that bat.

"Ain't nunna your bisness, mister," the barman says back.

I swear I hear that brush moving faster over there in the corner. My bro' is trying to dig hisself a hole.

A chair behind me scrapes the floor again. Different one this time, I'm sure of that. Footsteps approach. Someone moves round me, leans on the bartop.

"These guys got enough problems without you givin' 'em crap," he tells the barman. He's a big one, big shoulders, big fuckin' hands. Even the bat looks uneasy.

"I gotta respect'ble jointa run," says the barman, but it's a

comfortable with it. However, mainly due to King's relaxed and good-humoured manner, together with his special ability to communicate, by the end of the evening we had managed to win them over.

Now, although a relatively small event, it was an important one, for that audience comprised booksellers and wholesalers – the "Trade". In their hands was the power to make or break a book (in this case, read "book" as "genre"). To my mind it was a significant step towards the general acceptability of the horror novel in the British market place.

In his work, as in his approach to that evening in Surrey, Stephen King lacks pomp and pretension. He has humour. He has depth. He knows how to strike at the heart.

I've often referred to him as the Norman Rockwell of American literature. Like Rockwell, whose brilliant paintings of "Americana" were often reviled by certain bloodless critics, King →

sorta whine. His weapon ain't gonna do much to this ol' boy.

"Yeah, you must be 'spectin' the President any minute," says my man. I don't feel much these days, but I'm kinda warming to him. "Now gimme a whisky and make it another for my buddy here. I getta little upset when my throat's dry, unnerstand what I mean?"

The barman, that fat slimebag, seems to unnerstand pretty well. He puts two glasses on the counter, neither one of 'em too clean, tho' that don't bother me none, and I can tell my new friend's not fussed. The barman pours and if it woulda done any good, the look he gives me woulda killed.

"Down the hatch, zook," the good guy says.

"Tha–th–th . . ." says I.

"Thanks?" he asked. "Fuck you," he adds.

I try a nod, but my neck's stiff from too long out in the cold. Mainly my attention is on that half-full glass on the bar. I reach for it and it seems awful hard to pick up. I make it tho', oh man, I do pick it up, and my hand's shaky as I bring it to my dry old lips.

But someone smashes the glass from my paw and I watch it shatter on the wood top, that lovely liquid spilling out like treacle on brown bread. I just look at it.

The big guy turns and I know, shit I know, it's the other big one, the bear, behind me.

"They don't drink with us," I hear his grizzly voice say.

"Ain't no fault he's like he is," my buddy says back.

"No, but it's your fuckin' fault he's drinkin' here," comes the reply.

A big hand – a mighty big hand, bigger'n the one resting on the bar 'side me – grabs my shoulder and hauls me round. The bear drops his hand away and looks at it like he's disgusted at what might be there. He wipes that nothingness away on the backside of his 501s. Then he smashes my face.

I don't groan, I don't hurt. It's just like – numb. No more'n that. But then I'm so cold I'm numb all over anyways. That's why I like the whisky, see, the ol' firewater.

Well I don't know why – who can tell? – but this upsets my pal and he takes a swing at the bear. Bear don't like that, but on his knees it's like he accepts it. He shakes his head, just like a stunned grizzly, and reaches for something stashed in his shirt pocket. There's a *click*, and then there's the blade.

I don't like blades, never did like 'em. Maybe they're the way I am, I forget.

My friend at the bar won't wait, he goes for the kneeling man. Then they're in a heap, rolling round the dirty floor, cussing and hollering, kicking and squealing. It don't take long – funny how these things never do – the Big Disease never did, it came fast, took what it wanted, then spread in other ways. But that's not the main topic right now. Not really, anyways.

So there comes one helluva scream and both of 'em lie still, leaving the rest of us wondering who's gonna get up. Luckily, my pal does. Only he looks at me and I can tell we're not friends anymore. Shit, he's outa there like a bat outa hell.

The bear gives a groan, but it's a tired one, you know, like his last. If I could smile, I'd do that. Instead I just gawk.

Man, he's dead, and everyone there knows it. And they don't like it much. They know what's gonna happen before too long. None of 'em want to rush, so they kinda drift out, in twos and threes, conversation pretty dull-like and their "so-longs" a little half-hearted. Even the slimebag barman fades away.

So there's only three of us left. Me, the new corpse, and the bro' sweeping the floor. He's standing there resting on the broom, watching us from his corner, those big zook eyes white and staring outa his black face. (We all turn a nasty shade of black eventually, and no one's figured out why. Leastways, nobody's bothered to explain it to us.)

The process takes half an hour, mebbe forty minutes, and I got time to wait. I got all the time in the world. I just kinda stand there and look down on the dead old bear.

Could be he'd been half-dead already – some folks are, you know, like their souls have left their bodies long before the flesh is ready to give itself up – well, anyways, it don't seem like but ten minutes before he stirs, twitches a little. Another five and he's sitting up, looking round, wondering what the fuck he's doing there and feeling nothing.

It's the Big Disease, I could tell him, but he wouldn't appreciate it right now. Wouldn't understand. Part of the old brain cells go with the death, see? It's why we're stupid, some more so'n others. Ain't gonna mean nothing to him to say something in the air don't let us die no more, we just kinda rot away.

That's why people don't like us. It ain't the stink – we get sprayed regular nowadays – it's the sight of them lumps falling off us. If it weren't for the Bleeding Hearts we'd all be dumped somewhere. But then, we all got family, don't we?

So we roam, become a general nuisance, and remind people what's in store should they die before their natural time. It ain't no fun, but it beats nothing. I think.

Anyways, here's our boy, Mr Grizzly, all glassy-eyed and slack-jawed, the knife's hilt still sticking out his chest, lumbering to his feet.

"Poor authors have given everyone connected with the genre a bad name. I have actually acquired a bad reputation in some quarters because people equate my name with trash written by others."

– JAMES HERBERT, from "Herbert's Not Such a Horrible Hack" by Keith Newbery, *Portsmouth News*, June 19, 1986

THEY DON'T LIKE US
287

"Whu . . . whisk . . . y?" I ask, bearing no malice now he's one of us.

And he looks at me like he don't know what I mean. I won't say it – tongue don't work too well all swollen and black – but I'd like to tell him he won't get much chance to drink with a buddy anymore. I show him the glass instead, the one the other big guy had been drinking from, and shit, ain't his skin turning dark already? This zook – you know, zombie-spook – is a classic. Like I said, mebbe he was half-dead already.

So I drink the hot stuff for him. Then I leave. And you know, he follows, like he's scared to be without me. He'll get use to wandering alone, tho'. He'll soon get to know that nobody likes you when you're dead, not even your own kind.

He won't feel it, tho'. No, he won't feel it at all.

NOTES TOWARDS A REAPPRAISAL

Ramsey Campbell

THIRTY FIVE

"JAMES HERBERT," Stephen King writes in *Danse Macabre*, "is held in remarkably low esteem by writers in the genre on both sides of the Atlantic." I was one of the writers he had in mind. A thorough reading of Herbert's work has convinced me I was wrong, and I've begun to wonder if Herbert is disliked by some writers because he challenges the class bias of English horror fiction.

English horror fiction is almost entirely middle-class, either in its overt attitudes or its assumptions. As the world outside this perimeter becomes increasingly difficult to ignore, writers react in various ways: Dennis Wheatley blamed everything that threatened his way of life on Satan, Basil Copper retreats consciously to the Victorian era and writes, as one reviewer aptly put it, "as if he lived in a timeless void of writing". Compared with the American tradition, English horror fiction is singularly lacking in working-class characters, and too many of those it presents are caricatures: for example, Brian Lumley's criminals (one of whom manages to call a character both "guv" and "recluse") ring as false as Russell Wakefield's. All too often the working class in English genre fiction seem based on versions of the working class received from English genre fiction. Not so with James Herbert, whose first novel *The Rats* (1974) is based solidly in the real world.

In this novel a mutant strain of rats bred in the East End of London emerges from a derelict house to hunt human beings. The threat is eventually contained by government intervention, though not, as the sequel *Lair* makes clear, for very long. Herbert himself was born and bred in the East End, in a street which had been left half derelict by bombing, and which was overrun by rats. The protagonist of the novel, a teacher called Harris, has a background that resembles Herbert's. "How colourful," an art student remarks about Harris's East End background; perhaps it was this kind of comment that encouraged Herbert to show the area as it really was.

The Rats announces at once that he won't be confined by the conventions of English macabre fiction. The first chapter is a sympathetic portrait of an alcoholic who has become outcast because of his homosexuality, while the fifth portrays one of several derelicts who meet on a bomb site. This latter chapter has savage power that recalls *Last Exit to Brooklyn*, and as in Selby's novel, aesthetic objections to the savagery are beside the point: it would be dishonest of both writers to try to soften their material so as to spare the reader. In Herbert's case, given that he was working in the mid-seventies in a genre often dictated to by the audience's expectations, his refusal to mince the squalor is all the more admirable.

The rats "were the system", Herbert said in an interview for *Fangoria* magazine. "That's why it was open ended, the system still goes on." They clearly also represent neglect personified. "What disgusted him more," Harris the teacher reflects, "the vermin themselves – or the fact that it could only happen in East London?" But Harris continues, "It was no good becoming over-wrought with authority, for he knew too well that apathy existed on all levels . . . Wasn't that what Original Sin was supposed to be about? We're all to blame . . ." That the book can discuss its underlying themes so directly without becoming pretentious – a trap into which several contemporary American writers in the field have fallen – is one of Herbert's strengths. The hint of Catholicism is developed in later books, while the flaws of "the system" are explored in more detail in his next book, *The Fog* (1975).

The fog is a bacteriological weapon, stored underground when its development was discontinued, released by the army's testing explosives. Herbert uses the situation of a potentially nationwide disaster for two purposes: to show its effect on ordinary people and how they respond (as in the science fiction novels of H. G. Wells and, later, John Wyndham) and to illuminate flaws in the Establishment, particularly in terms of the way they deal with the crisis (a tendency in Herbert's writing which recalls the Quatermass stories of Nigel Kneale). In Herbert's world, however, the "ordinary" person is generally lonely and

"There are so many dilettantes who think they can churn out a horror novel. They're basically all the same: the babysitter did it; the baby did it. They're just stringing together a bunch of ways to kill people. There's no depth to them . . . It's because people don't use their own imaginations any more. It takes more and more to titillate them. Like snuff movies. Or killer slugs. It's taking more and more blood."

– JAMES HERBERT, from "Smilin' Jim is the Horrormaster of Them All" by Susan Kastner, *Sunday Toronto Star*, September 11, 1988 often deeply flawed. Portraits of loneliness are central to almost all his novels (some of the most extreme appearing in the early chapters of *The Rats*), and the typical Herbert hero is an outsider who develops a strong, usually sexual, relationship in the course of the novel.

Where *The Rats* had its characters doing their best to cope with a crisis, *The Fog* shows its characters invaded by the threat, a "fog" or gas which causes insanity. (In this it resembles Charles Platt's pornographic novel *The Gas*, but Herbert's novel is altogether more controlled.) The book has been criticised for the consequent scenes of violence, and Stephen King quotes Herbert as saying that his approach in writing it was, "I'm going to try to go over the top, to see how much I can get away with" (a comment reminiscent of Straub's statement that he meant *Ghost Story* to "take the classic elements of the horror novel as far as they could go"). But *The Fog* contains remarkably few graphic acts of violence, though two (one in a gymnasium, and the other in the bedroom of a Chief Superintendent of Police) are so horrible and painful, at least for this reader, that they pervade the book. Herbert concentrates rather on painting a landscape of (occasionally comic) nightmare, and most of the human episodes are of terror rather than explicit violence: the pilot of a 747 goes mad at the controls, and in the most disturbingly ironic scene a would-be suicide who has thought better of making away with herself is caught up in a lemming-like exodus from the seaside town of Bournemouth. Herbert triumphantly reverses the usual method of building terror in a novel: where traditionally this is achieved by a gradual accumulation of events, *The Fog* is all the more nightmarish for its breathless pace. Its final image (prefiguring that of the film *Alien*) is, appropriately, of restful sleep.

The Fog was a bestseller, but Herbert's next two books show that he won't play safe. *The Survivor* (1976) – later filmed, insipidly and obscurely, by David Hemmings – is the pilot of a 747, the only person to survive its crash, who proves to have been sent on a mission by the spirits of its victims. Though the book rises to heights both of horror (an infernal scene in a college chapel) and ecstasy, it's weighed down by too much spiritualistic discussion, as hindering to Herbert as it was to Algernon Blackwood. Perhaps at the time Herbert's preoccupation with the afterlife, or his doubts about life after death, were so great that the theme got the better of him. For most of its length *The Survivor* (an ironic title) is among his bleakest books, not least because the pilot's lover has been killed in the crash.

"*Everybody else jumped on the bandwagon, so you had writers coming along – they saw, yes, this was the new market, and this guy Herbert is actually describing things that nobody's described before. And they did it. But unless you do it with the right intent, and, to use a pompous word,* integrity – *you know, you've actually got to do it for a good reason, and show motivation as well – unless you do it that way, then you're a bad writer and you're just exploiting. And there's a huge prejudice against me because of the mass of books that came out in the wake of* The Rats *and* The Fog.*"

– JAMES HERBERT, from "Hot Rats!" by William Leith, *New Musical Express*, January 10, 1987

RAMSEY CAMPBELL

Fluke (1977) returns to the subject of the afterlife, but with great stylistic and narrative confidence. Of all his books, this divided his admirers most sharply; none of his books conforms less to the expectations of his fans. Fluke is a man reincarnated as a dog, much to the dismay of Herbert's British publishers, who would have preferred the dog at least to be rabid. It is Herbert's only first-person narrative so far, and it may be this unaccustomed voice that reveals new qualities – a greater generosity towards his characters, an unexpected lyricism. Significantly, it's his favourite among his novels. Not that the book is inconsistent with his other work: again the protagonist (in many ways the typical Herbert hero) is sent on a quest whose outcome proves to be ironic. A greater belated irony may be that the entire book-length monologue goes unheard by its chosen audience, a dying tramp. However, this image of extreme loneliness gives way to a finely suggestive last line.

His next book *The Spear* (1978) – an action thriller about neo-Nazism and the resurrection of Himmler – is more immediately commercial; nevertheless it's courageous of Herbert to address the theme of British fascism through a genre which, like sword and sorcery, attracts fascist mentalities. (One of the most blatant statements of this appears at the end of Dennis Wheatley's non-fiction coffee-table book, *The Devil and All His Works*, where Wheatley declares that anti-apartheid demonstrations are the devil's work and that it is the job of the governments to govern.) *The Spear* scores as a thriller, especially in its set-pieces (a Herbert speciality, perhaps most skilfully and expressively employed in *The Fog*), but its anti-fascist message was clear enough to earn Herbert the hatred of the National Front, the British fascist party. Because the supernatural is only hinted at in the course of the novel, the climactic manifestation is the more disturbing.

Herbert sees *Lair* (1979), the sequel to *The Rats*, as a relaxation after *The Spear*. It attacks the apathy of officialdom with renewed vigour, and contains one of the most terrible death scenes in all his work, the death of a priest who is losing his faith. This points forward to the more explicit horrors of *The Dark*.

The Dark (1980) is necessarily his most violent novel. Whereas the possessing force in *The Fog* was unmotivated, the dark is evil embodied and deliberately invoked. The book is about the rejection of God, whatever God may be. Proving the non-existence of God is seen as the ultimate insanity; rejection of faith leads straight to breakdown and the asylum. *The Dark* conveys a greater sense of helplessness than Herbert's earlier

"Another thing I don't do is knock other writers publicly, even though I'm always being pressed to comment particularly on authors such as Guy N. Smith, Shaun Hutson and the like. As far as I'm concerned we all do it for a living and we each choose our own way. Enough said."

– JAMES HERBERT, from "For God's Sake, Don't Leave This On Aunt Edna's Chair", *Pieces of Mary*, No. 4, 1987 work; the little organised response to the threat is largely ineffectual. It's to his credit that he doesn't use the theme of possession as an alibi for his characters (which is to say, to allow the reader to feel that evil has nothing to do with us). The novel's most terrifying scene, an outbreak of football hooliganism, hardly needed possession to explain its cause.

The Jonah (1981) restates this theme in passing: a character dismisses the supernatural as "something people have invented to suit their own tiny minds, something that helps them put troubles and misfortunes into tiny little boxes". As in *The Spear*, the supernatural is kept largely offstage until the final chapters. The "jonah" is a policeman haunted by something that brings disaster to those involved with him and which he finally confronts while investigating drug smuggling. It's an oddly contradictory book: one character gives a speech against drug abuse so impassioned that it's reasonable to conclude (particularly since her partner in argument hardly gets a word in) that Herbert endorses her feelings, yet a later description of an LSD trip is as lyrical as it is terrifying. Presumably Herbert's imagination is stronger than his doubts. Still, *The Jonah* is his most lightweight book.

Shrine (1983) is an overtly Catholic novel, about a child who claims to have had a vision of the Virgin Mary, but who is in fact inspired by the Devil. The first half of *Shrine* is as compelling as any of his novels, and leads to a stunning setpiece that is rounded off by a breathtaking supernatural image.

Untypically, the second half slows down enough to let the reader spot inconsistencies: symptoms of possession which the reader can't help but recognise seem to trouble the religious characters far less than they should (though this might be one of Herbert's objections to the way the Catholic Church responds to the child's visions). Once again, Herbert uses the conventions of the genre more responsibly than many of his peers: there is no suggestion that the child herself is evil. Despite its flaws, *Shrine* is deeply felt, and clearly was a book Herbert had to write; some of its effects show a new deftness and subtlety. Some readers have found the final apparition ambiguous, but presumably Herbert is being true to his own doubts.

Domain (1984) is one of his most vividly imagined novels. It pits man against mutant rat in a London devastated by nuclear bombing. As in several of his novels, there are vignettes of character at the moment of disaster; those in *Domain*, and the insights they convey, are especially bleak. A scene in which characters try to clear an escalator piled with corpses has a nightmare absurdity, while the novel's sense of suffering is appropriately more intense than that of any of its predecessors. One chapter in which an injured man is dragged back from drowning is as disquieting as anything Herbert has yet given us. *Domain* is really only nominally a novel about the rats; it's a clear-eyed view of a future that may be uncomfortably close, a praiseworthy attempt to give readers what they may not think they want.

It seems to have been too uncomfortable for the American editor who worked on the book and who suggested omitting some of the character vignettes. Herbert, already at work on his next novel, told him to go ahead as a preamble to telling him and the publisher where to go, and so some chapters from *Domain* have appeared as self-contained stories in America.

Moon (1985) is a suspense novel which is gradually invaded by the horrific. Its theme recalls that of Thomas Harris's *Red Dragon* – in both novels the protagonist is able to help the police track down serial murderers by sharing their mental processes – but Herbert pushes the psychic theme further, to an especially disturbing conclusion when the process becomes mutual and the murderer to whose consciousness the psychic Jonathan Childes is intermittently linked begins to feed off Childes' own memories of atrocities which Childes has vicariously experienced. Herbert's sojourn in the Channel Islands lends the book its setting. As the island is invaded first by Childes' visions of atrocities and then by the murderer herself, so the book is invaded by terse savage chapters from the mainland, the most disorientating of them no more than a sentence in length. The growing horror is kept under severe restraint until the very end, when psychical and physical horror meet in a finale whose outrageousness both delivers what the novel has been threatening throughout and passes beyond it into a kind of spectral surrealism.

The Magic Cottage (1986) – which would have been called *The Enchanted Cottage* if Hollywood hadn't got there first – is a personal favourite of the author's. As in *Fluke*, the first-person voice makes for relaxed narration, but the book abounds with details which suggest that it will repay a careful reading: the names of characters – Flora Chaldean, Eldrich P. Mycroft, the Reverend Sixsmythe – sound as if Herbert is both having fun and scattering enigmatic clues through the book, so that when the narrator Mike Stringer claims that "when luck is on your side numbers don't come into it", this reader's immediate reaction is to look suspiciously at the phone number of the estate agent handling the cottage – Cantrip 612, a six and two more sixes – and to begin to wonder about that name Sixsmythe.

"There are lots of other good up and coming horror writers, you have to stay on your toes."

– JAMES HERBERT, from "Quiet Man Behind the King of Horror" by Angela Carless, *Northampton Chronicle & Echo*, August 15, 1989

I think Clive [Barker] is going to do extremely *well. I really do – because he's a quality writer,* very *original – and I think he'll be mass-appeal as well. I don't think he'll fall by the wayside at all.*

– JAMES HERBERT, from *Danse Macabre*, No. 8, January 1986

After all, the book is sufficiently playful to accommodate a walk-on out of *Fluke*. Even without all this, the ambiguities are plentiful. In particular the magic of which the cottage proves to be a focus is presented as a powerful but neutral force, much like the mushrooms which sprout in place of the cottage at the end of the novel. Though the book contains its share of warnings about the allure of the occult it also celebrates its appeal to the imagination, and so the scenes of magical confrontation are unexpectedly, if entirely appropriately, reminiscent of Bulwer-Lytton, "The House and the Brain" in particular. Despite its gentleness or quite possibly because of it, *The Magic Cottage* also builds up a considerable sense of horror, though underlying this effect there generally tends to be a deeper meaning. There's even a scene of batty birth to appal conservationists.

"Why should I want to try anything different? The sort of books I write allow me to diversify . . . so there is no way I shall want to try anything that represents a major departure."

– JAMES HERBERT, from "Herbert's Not Such a Horrible Hack" by Keith Newbery, *Portsmouth News,* June 19, 1986

The Magic Cottage can be read as an expansion of the last line (also the last chapter) of *Moon. Sepulchre* (1987) – with its subtitle "A conflict of evils" and its epigraph "There are no absolutes" – reads like a further exploration of the moral ambiguities of its immediate predecessor. It's perhaps the grimmest of Herbert's novels which begin as thrillers and turn nastier; though at least one of his imitators has accused him of toning his books down in order to court a wider audience, that is clearly not the case here. While the central relationship between the crazed psychic Kline and Halloran, the man apparently chosen to protect him from kidnapping and worse, is as ambiguous as the protagonist Halloran himself, the darkest sections of the book trap the reader in the minds of several monstrous characters, as disturbing an experience as it evidently was for Herbert to write them. The book is something of a return to the raw horror of his early books, but it may be said to reach back further, however inadvertently or coincidentally. Of all Herbert's novels it's the one which most recalls the pulp horrors of the thirties: in passages of writing ("They did their best to ignore the squishy gurgling of the sinuous island as it heaved itself from the water"); in its use of an ancient Sumerian evil; perhaps most strikingly, in the titles of chapters – "Return to the Death Hut". The scene in which the heroine is tied up and whipped by an obese hairy bodyguard offers a combination of bondage and horror the like of which has scarcely been seen since the days of the spicy horror magazines.

After *Sepulchre, Haunted* (1988) is yet another change of direction and simultaneously a further exploration of earlier themes. It's possible to mourn the non-existence of the BBC film which would have been based on Herbert's original script, but then, had the film been made we might not have had the

RAMSEY CAMPBELL

novel, his most atmospheric to date; we would certainly not have had the seance scene, which was written to bulk out the novel and which is one of his most affecting set-pieces. Also particularly effective, as in *The Magic Cottage*, is the image of the haunted building whose fabric gradually betrays what it hides. Herbert's return to the area he first explored in *The Survivor* is all the more welcome for the greater control he brings to the material, and especially for his increasing ability to communicate a sense of supernatural terror. What else the book conceals I leave for its readers to discover.

Creed (1990) is his best book since *The Magic Cottage*, and it strikes me as one of his most personal. In some ways it sums up aspects of his work to date: it rediscovers the eroticism of his early books, and revels in its macabre set-pieces – a nightmarishly comic episode in which paparazzo Joseph Creed is pursued across a London pond by a paddling Nosferatu, a demonic masked ball, a descent into the bowels of an especially hellish rest home. It also stars his sleaziest protagonist yet, who nevertheless compels the reader's reluctant involvement. Like *The Magic Cottage*, it feels relaxed, though in fact the circumstances under which it was written were hardly conducive to relaxation. It easily incorporates gags aimed at the fans of the genre (there's even one about *The Rats*) and an intermittent commentary by the author himself, which seems almost Victorian. This willingness to comment, and the serious theme underlying all the gags, suggests to me that *Creed* may be read as a kind of statement of the author's beliefs about his genre – his creed, dare I say. Mind you, in an interview in *Fear* Jim declares that the book is his *Abbott and Costello Meet Frankenstein*, so perhaps he may give my interpretation a raspberry. Let me content myself by saying that I believe it is a perfect companion volume to the book you are holding.

Herbert writes bestsellers, but he doesn't manufacture them. Rather than compete with his imitators in terms of escalating violence (a trap into which such as John Carpenter and the EC comics of the fifties have fallen), he has opted for restraint. His sex scenes are sometimes prolonged, but they range from the tender to (particularly in *Shrine*) the grotesquely comic to an accumulation of awkward detail which is the opposite of pornographic. Some of his novels contain no sex at all. It may be his Catholicism, or the puritanism that seems to underlie *The Jonah*, which leads him to suggest that any kind of sexual deviation is bound for grief, but in other ways his work is less reactionary than much of the genre. While he sometimes stumbles stylistically, there's a developing sense of language in

"I don't want to be the literary equivalent of the Carry On *films, I want to try to do something different each time."*

– JAMES HERBERT, from "Heavy Stuff" by Tony Eyers, *Isis*, March 1989 his effects. In *Danse Macabre*, in the course of an appreciation of Herbert, King describes him as coming at the reader "with both hands, not willing to simply engage our attention; he seizes us by the lapels and begins to scream in our faces. It is not a tremendously artistic method of attack, and no one is ever going to compare him to Doris Lessing or V. S. Naipaul – but it works – he is what he is and that's all that he is, as Popeye would say."

To be fair, King has more to say for him than that, yet I wonder if some of King's readers may have gained the impression that Herbert's work is cruder than in fact it is. Herbert is an unmistakably English, and unmistakably contemporary, writer who refuses to conform to what's expected of him or to stop questioning what he sees and feels.

I look forward to many more surprises from him, not to mention some of the most attractively designed novels in the British bookshops.

James Herbert and family after signing session at London's Forbidden Planet (circa 1983)

JAMES HERBERT: AFTERWORD

Clive Barker

THIRTY SIX

W HEN Mr Jones, the editor of the volume in your hand, invited me to add a few words of my own to this collection, I turned over the options several times. Should I write about Jim the affable conversationalist, whose wry asides on his contemporaries so winningly mingle sting and affection? Or James Herbert the publishing phenomenon, whose name is enough to guarantee his books the number one slot on the bestseller lists before the reviews and the puff-pieces have even appeared?

Both seemed predictable, and while I won't let this opportunity slide by without assuring you that Jim is as entertaining in the flesh as he is on the page, there's another element of his personality which I'd like to speak of, and that's the seam of paradox in him.

There is a tendency, whenever books of analysis or celebration are written about artists, for the authors of such books to attempt a reconciliation of elements, and drive out the contradictions. In my opinion this is highly regrettable, because such contradictions, though they can be uncomfortable for the artist and critic alike, are very often extremely illuminating.

I offer, for example, the brief substance of an exchange I had with Jim while he and I were sharing a festival podium with Peter James, speaking to a lively audience about the fiction we write. In such circumstances, I should explain, Jim has a posture for which I've become a useful foil: that of the plain man who'll have no truck with talk of subtext, metaphor or allegorical intent. Whenever such words stray on to my lips (and, *mea*

CLIVE BARKER

culpa, they often do) he takes great delight in refuting my high-flown claims with jocular but well-argued replies, stating clearly that he believes all such analyses are poppycock.

Or such had been the case until this particular afternoon, when, quite without prompting, Jim told the audience that his novel *Shrine* contained a number of observations about the workings of the Catholic Church and the vulnerability of faith which were of no little significance to him.

Subtext? I said; surely not! Jim grinned. Yes, he confessed, it was indeed subtext.

Now please don't get me wrong. I don't doubt that Jim's phenomenal commercial success is based upon his instincts as a storyteller, and his undoubted skill at orchestrating his scenes to generate the maximum *frisson*. But the fiction of the *fantastique* is seldom successful simply because it tells a chilling tale. At some point in the narrative, something other than the pulse is quickened, and something more than the urge to be thrilled satisfied.

It's my hope that this book will attract to Jim's fiction the kind of close scrutiny it deserves, and that such scrutiny will uncover these layers of meaning. When that happens I'm certain that all kinds of symbolism, metaphor and subtext will be found. Nor do I doubt that when that happens Jim will politely say that his tales are pieces of entertainment, and only that.

But I suspect that a smile will not be far from his lips while he makes these protests, and that, delightful paradox that he is, it will give him a kind of pleasure to have the whispers beneath the beguiling voice of Jim Herbert, Master Storyteller, discovered and heard.

You never know what you're going to get from me next, and this is one of the things that confounds the critics. They figure they've got me boxed, and then I do something completely different.

– JAMES HERBERT, *Box Office* (Channel 4-TV, 1990)

JAMES HERBERT: A WORKING BIBLIOGRAPHY

Introduction

i. This checklist is designed to give collectors and dealers an idea of the wealth of James Herbert material available – in both English and foreign-language editions. In order to keep it relatively simple, we have decided not to include such usual bibliographic details as book size, page count, cover artist, etc. This listing covers publications from 1974 to 1991 and is, by necessity, incomplete (even the author does not have copies of many of his own volumes). We welcome all corrections and additions, and hope to update the information in any subsequent versions of this work.

ii. A brief explanation of the following abbreviations and symbols may be required:

a. (hc):   hardcover
b. (pb):   paperback
c. (tp):   trade paperback
d. *:   entry has been seen
               and inspected
e. [   ]:   alternative title

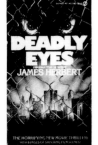

A NOVELS

Includes a chronological listing of all books written by James Herbert.

A1

THE RATS

a. _____, New English Library, London, UK, 1974 (hc)*
    Price: £1.95
    ISBN: 45001867–9
b. _____, New English Library, London, UK, 1974 (pb)*
    Print run: 100,000 copies
    Price: 0.40p
    ISBN: 0–450–02954–9
c. _____, New American Library/Signet, New York, USA, 1975 (pb)*
    Price: $1.50
    ISBN: 0–451–W6460–150
d. [as *Deadly Eyes*], New American Library/Signet, New York, USA, 1983 (pb)*
    Price: $2.95
    ISBN: 0–451–12246–1
    (Note: 8th printing. "The Horrifying New Movie Thriller!/With 8 Pages of Shocking Film Scenes!")
e. _____, Filofiction/Octopus, London, UK, 1988
    Price: £4.95
    ISBN: 1–871307–03–1
    (Note: Loose-leaf version for use with Filofaxes)

302   JAMES HERBERT:

f.   _____, Hodder & Stoughton, London, UK, 1991 (hc)*
     Price: £14.99
     ISBN: 0–340–52366–2
g.   [as *Rattorna*], Ryslig Midnattslasning, Norway, 1974 (pb)*
     Translator: Alf Agdler
     ISBN: 91–32–40847–1
h.   [as *La Invasión de Las Ratas*], Editorial Planeta, Barcelona, Spain, 1975
     (hc)*
     Translator: Miguel Torres
     ISBN: 84–320–1432–X

i.   [as *The Rats*], Sankei, Japan, 1975 (pb)*
     Price: 800 Y
     ISBN: 0097–075443–2756
j.   [as *De Ratten*], Uitgeverij Luitingh-Laren N.H., Holland, 1976 (tp)*
     Translator: L. Koopman-Thomas
     ISBN: 90–245–0293–4
k.   [as *I Topi*], Sonzogno, Milan, Italy, 1976 (tp)*
     Translator: Natalia Coppini
     Price: 2,000 Lire
     CL–52–1306–1
l.   [as *Rattboet*], Ryslig Midnattslasning, 1979 (pb)*
     ISBN: 91–32–50550–7
m.   [as *Die Ratten*], Heyne, Germany, 1988 (pb)*
     Price: 007.80 DM
     ISBN: 3–453–02544–X
n.   [as *Les Rats*], Librairie Des Champs-Elysées, Paris, France, 1989 (pb)*
     ISBN: 2–266–02825–1

A2

THE FOG
a.   _____, New English Library, London, UK, 1975 (hc)*
     Price: £3.95
     ISBN: 4500–26078
b.   _____, New English Library, London, UK, 1975 (pb)*
     Price: 0.65p
     ISBN: 0–450–02918–2
c.   _____, New American Library/Signet, New York, USA, 1975 (pb)*
     Price: $1.50
     ISBN: 0–451–W6708–150

d.   _____, New English Library, London, UK, 1988 (hc)*
     Print run: 3,000 copies
     Price: £12.95
     ISBN: 0–450–02607–8
     (Note: Hardcover edition to celebrate one million copies sold in the UK.
     Contains new "Foreword" by the author)
e.   _____, New English Library, London, UK, 1989 (pb)*
     Price: £3.50
     ISBN: 0–450–03045–8
     (Note: Same text as "A2(d)")
f.   _____, Sankei, Japan, 1976 (pb)*
     Price: 880 Y
     ISBN: 0097–076499–2756

URANIA
I ROMANZI
NEBBIA
James Herbert   MONDADORI

1-1-1976
QUATTORDICINALE
lire 600

g. [as *Nebbia*], Arnoldo Mondadori Editore, Milan, Italy, 1976 (tp)*
    Translator: Bianca Russo
    Price: 600 Lire
    (Note: Part of the *Urania* series, published every other week)
h. [as *La Niebla*], Editorial Planeta, Barcelona, Spain, 1978 (tp)*
    Translator: José Luis Bozzo
    Price: 300 ptas
    ISBN: 84–320–4124–6
i. [as *Dodelijke Nevel*], Uitgeverij Luitingh-Laren N.H., Holland, 1985 (tp)*
    Translator: Jan de Meester
    ISBN: 90–245–0397–3
j. [as *Unheil*], Heyne, Germany, 1990 (pb)*
    Price: 008.80 DM
    ISBN: 3–453–03676–X

A3

THE SURVIVOR

a. _____, New English Library, London, UK, 1976 (hc)*
    Price: £4.50
    ISBN: 45003067–9
b. _____, New English Library, London, UK, 1977 (pb)*
    Price: 0.75p
    ISBN: 0–450–03241–8
    (Note: NEL "Open Market" edition available three months earlier)
c. _____, New American Library/Signet, New York, USA, 1977 (pb)*
    Price: $1.75
    ISBN: 0–451–07393–2
d. _____, Charnwood, Leicester, UK, 1984 (hc)*
    ISBN: 0–7089–8165–8
    (Note: Large print edition)
e. [as *Wraak van de Overlevende*], Phoenix, Holland, 1976 (tp)*
    Translator: Ruth Liebenthaler
    ISBN: 90–6879–006–4
f. [as *Il Superstite*], Arnoldo Mondadori Editore, Milan, Italy, 1977 (tp)*
    Translator: Beata della Frattina
    Price: 700 Lire
    (Note: Part of the *Urania* series, published every other week)
g. [as *Celui Qui Survit*], Librairie Des Champs-Elysées, Paris, France, 1978
    (pb)*
    Translator: Dominique Mols
    ISBN: 2–7024–0785–4
h. [as *The Survivor*] Sankei, Japan, 1978 (pb)*
    Price: 880 Y
    ISBN: 0097–781554–2756
i. [as *El Superviviente*], Editorial Planeta, Barcelona, Spain, 1979 (tp)*
    Translator: César Armando Gómez
    Print run: 5,000 copies
    ISBN: 84–320–4140–8
j. [as *Le Survivant*], Presses Pocket, Paris, France, 1990 (pb)*
    Translator: Dominique Mols
    ISBN: 2–266–03480–4

A4

FLUKE

a. _____, New English Library, London, UK, 1977 (hc)*
   Price: £4.50
   ISBN: 4500–34321
b. _____, New English Library, London, UK, 1978 (pb)*
   Price: 0.80p
   ISBN: 0–450–5033–5
c. _____, New American Library/Signet, New York, USA, 1978 (pb)*
   Price: $1.95
   ISBN: 0–451–16490–3
d. [as *Chamba*], Editorial Planeta, Barcelona, Spain, 1979 (tp)*
   Translator: César Armando Gómez
   Price: 300 ptas
   ISBN: 84–320–4136–X
e. [as *Fluke*] Sankei, Japan, 1979 (hc)*
   Translator: Yukio Sekiguchi
   Price: 1,300 Y
   ISBN: 0097–791663–2756

A5

THE SPEAR

a. _____, New English Library, London, UK, 1978 (hc)*
   Price: £4.95
   ISBN: 4500–4040–2
b. _____, New English Library, London, UK, 1980 (pb)*
   Price: £1.00
   ISBN: 0–450–04300–2
   (Note: Missing the prologues found only in "A5(a)")
c. _____, New American Library/Signet, New York, USA 1980 (pb)*
   Price: $2.50
   ISBN: 0–451–E8650

A6

LAIR

a. _____, New English Library, London, UK, 1979 (hc)*
   Price: £4.95
   ISBN: 4500–4111–5
b. _____, New English Library, London, UK, 1979 (pb)*
   Price: 0.95p
   ISBN: 0–450–04546–3
c. _____, New American Library, New York, USA, 1979 (pb)*
   Price: $2.25
   ISBN: 0–451–08650–3
d. _____, Hodder & Stoughton, London, UK, 1991 (hc)*
   Price: £14.99
   ISBN: 0–340–52365–4
e. [as *El Cubil*], Planeta, Barcelona, Spain, 1981 (pb)*
   Translator: Josefina Guerrero
   ISBN: 84–320–4182–3
f. [as *Het Rattenleger*], Elsevier, Amsterdam/Brussel, Holland/Belgium, 1981 (tp)*
   Translator: Rob Van Moppes
   ISBN: 90–10–03810–6

g. [as *Le Repaire des Rats*], Presses Pocket, Paris, France, 1989 (pb)*
    Translator: Anne Crichton
    ISBN: 2–266–03163–5

A7

THE DARK

a. _____, New English Library, London, UK, 1980 (hc)*
    Price: £5.95
    ISBN: 0–450–04738–5
    (Note: Book Club edition same as "A7(a)" but without price on jacket.)
b. _____, New English Library, London, UK, 1980 (pb)*
    Price: £1.50
    ISBN: 0–450–04970–1
c. _____, New American Library/Signet, New York, USA, 1980 (pb)*
    Price: $3.95
    ISBN: 0–451–15542–4
d. _____, New English Library, London, UK, 1988 (hc)
    Print run: 2,000 copies
    Price: £11.95
    ISBN: 0–450–34582–9
e. [as *Uit de Afgrond van de Hel*], Elsevier, Amsterdam/Brussels,
    Holland/Belgium, 1983 (tp)*
    Translator: Henny Corver
    ISBN: 90–10–04442–4

A8

THE JONAH

a. _____, New English Library, London, UK, 1981 (hc)*
    Price: £6.50
    ISBN: 0–450–04855–1
b. _____, New English Library, London, UK, 1981 (pb)
    Price: £1.50
    ISBN: 0–450–05316–4
c. _____, New American Library/Signet, New York, USA, 1981 (pb)*
    Price: $2.95
    ISBN: 0–451–11066–8

A9

SHRINE

a. _____, New English Library, London, UK, 1983 (hc)*
    Price: £7.95
    ISBN: 0–450–04894–2
b. _____, New English Library, London, UK, 1984 (pb)*
    Print run: 450,000 copies
    Price: £2.25
    ISBN: 0–450–05659–7
c. _____, New American Library/Signet, New York, USA, 1984 (pb)*
    Price: $3.95
    ISBN: 0–451–12724–2

A10

DOMAIN

a. _____, New English Library, London, UK, 1984 (hc)*
   Price: £8.95
   ISBN: 0–450–06076–4
b. _____, New English Library, London, UK, 1985 (pb)*
   Print run: 400,000 copies
   Price: £2.50
   ISBN: 0–450–05822–0
   (Note: Also issued as an "NEL Open Market Edition", March 1985)
c. _____, New American Library/Signet, New York, USA, 1985 (pb)*
   Price: $3.50
   ISBN: 0–451–13471–0
d. _____, Book Club Associates, London, UK, 1985 (hc)*
   Title code: CN9856
e. _____, Hodder & Stoughton, London, UK, 1991 (hc)*
   Price: £15.99
   ISBN: 0–340–52364–6
f. _____, Heyne, Germany, 1987 (pb)*
   Price: 009.80 DM
   ISBN: 3–453–00702–6

A11

MOON

a. _____, New English Library, London, UK, 1985 (hc)*
   Print run: 15,000 copies
   Price: £9.95
   ISBN: 0–450–06088–8
b. _____, New English Library, London, UK, 1986 (pb)
   Print run: 350,000
   Price: £2.95
   ISBN: 0–450–38999–5
c. _____, Chivers Press, Bath, UK, 1986 (hc)*
   ISBN: 0–86220–168–3
   (Note: Large print edition)
d. _____, World Books Edition, London, UK, 1986 (hc)
   Title code: CN4995
e. _____, Crown, USA, 1986 (hc)*
   Price: $14.95
   ISBN: 0–517–56278–2
f. _____, New American Library/Onyx, New York, USA, 1987 (pb)
   Price: $4.50
   ISBN: 0–451–40056–9
g. [as *Luar*], Editora Best Seller, Brazil, 1986 (tp)*
   Translator: Else Piacentini Medeiros Fortunato
   ISBN: 85–85091–17–7
h. [as *Moon*], Bastei Lubbe, West Germany, 1986 (tp)*
   Price: 019.80 DM
   ISBN: 3–404–28155–1
i. [as *La Pietra della Luna*], Romanzo Armenia, Milan, Italy (hc)*
   Translator: Vittorio Curtoni
   Price: 22.000 Lire
   ISBN: 88–344–0263–3

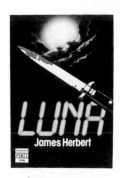

j. [as *Luna*], Plaza & Janes, Barcelona, Spain, 1987 (tp)*
    Translator: Alicia Steimberg
    ISBN: 84–01–32225–1
k. [as *Luna Sangrienta*], Emecé Editores, Buenos Aires, Argentina, 1987 (tp)*
    ISBN: 950–04–0689–6
l. [as *Pierre de Lune*], Albin Michel, Paris, France, 1987 (tp)*
    Translator: Evelyne Chatelain
    Price: 79,00 F
    ISBN: 2–226–03097–2
    (Note: Also issued with outer wrapper: "Spécial Fantastique")
m. [as *Pierre de Lune*], Editions J'Ai Lu, France, 1987 (pb)*
    Translator: Evelyne Chatelain
    ISBN: 2–277–22470–7
n. [as *Priesteres van het Kwaad*], Uitgeverij Luitingh-Utrecht, Holland, 1987 (tp)*
    ISBN: 90–245–1672–2
o. [as *Mane Offer*], Hjemmet, Denmark, 1988 (pb)*
    Translator: Thor Dag Halvorsen
    Price: 34,000 Kr
    ISBN: 82–7315–841–1
p. [as *Moon*], Bastei Lubbe, West Germany, 1990 (pb)*
    Price: 009.80 DM
    ISBN: 3–404–13249–1

A12

THE MAGIC COTTAGE
a. _____, Hodder & Stoughton, London, UK, 1986 (hc)*
    Print run: 25,000
    Price: £9.95
    ISBN: 0–340–39066–2
b. _____, Book Club Associates, London, UK, 1986 (hc)
    Title Code: CN6889
c. _____, New English Library, London, UK, 1987 (pb)*
    Print run: 400,000
    Price: £2.95
    ISBN: 0–450–40937–6
d. _____, New American Library, New York, 1987 (hc)
    Price: $17.95
    ISBN: 0–453–00574–8
e. _____, New American Library/Onyx, New York, USA, 1988 (pb)*
    Price: $4.50
    ISBN: 0–451–40106–9
f. [as *Os Visitantes da Noite*], Editora Best Seller, Brazil, 1986 (tp)*
    Translator: Jurandy Bravo Nogueira Junior
    ISBN: 85–7123–071–4
g. [as *Det Magiska Huset*], Bonniers, Stockholm, Sweden, 1987 (hc)*
    Translator: Eva Larsson
    ISBN: 91–0–047206–9
    (Note: "Original title *The Magic House*")
h. [as *Het Vervloekte Huis*], Uitgeverij Luitingh-Utrecht, Holland, 1987 (tp)*
    ISBN: 90–245–1993–4
i. [as *The Magic Cottage*], Hayakawa, Japan, 1987 (pb)*
    Translator: Yukio Sekiguchi
    Price: 420 Y
    ISBN: 4–15–040455–0

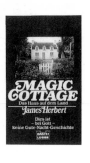

JAMES HERBERT:

j. [as *La Casa Maledetta*], Armenia Editore, Italy, 1988 (hc)*
Translator: Mario Monti
ISBN: 88–344–0308–8

k. [as *Magic Cottage*], Bastei Lubbe, Germany, 1988 (tp)*
Price: 019.80 DM
ISBN: 3–404–28163–2

A13

SEPULCHRE

a. _____, Hodder & Stoughton, London, UK, 1987 (hc)*
Print run: 30,000 copies
Price: £10.95
ISBN: 0–340–39472–2

b. _____, Guild Publishing, London, UK, 1987 (hc)
Title Code: CN1456

c. _____, New English Library, London, UK, 1988 (pb)*
Print run: 500,000
Price: £3.50
ISBN: 0–450–42668–8
(Note: Special "Open Market" edition also produced with same ISBN)

d. _____, Putnam, New York, USA, 1988 (hc)*
Price: $17.95
ISBN: 0–399–13365–8

e. _____, Jove, New York, USA, 1989 (pb)*
Price: $4.95
ISBN: 0–515–10101–X

f. [as *Kryptan*], Bonniers, Stockholm, Sweden, 1988 (hc)*
ISBN: 91–0–047541–6
(Note: "Original title *Sepulchre, A Conflict of Evils*")

g. [as *Die Gruff*], Heyne, Germany, 1989 (pb)*
Translator: Helmut Degner
Price: 008.80 DM
ISBN: 3–453–03281–0

h. [as *Il Sepolcro*], Sperling & Kupfer, Milan, Italy, 1989 (hc)*
Translator: Bruno Amato
Price: 24,900 Lire
ISBN: 88–200–0884–X

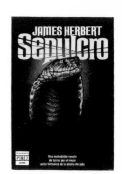

i. [as *Kryptan*], Bladkompaniet, Oslo, Sweden, 1989 (tp)*
Translator: Jan Schei
ISBN: 82–509–2232–8

j. [as *Sepulcro*], Plaza & Janes, Barcelona, Spain, 1989 (tp)*
Translator: Julio F. Yanez
ISBN: 84–01–32286–3

k. [as *Tentakels van het kwaad*], Burna, Holland, 1989 (tp)*
ISBN: 90–5154–201–1

l. [as *Sepulcro Maldito*], Emecé Editores, Buenos Aires, Argentina, 1990 (tp)*
Translator: Eduardo Ruiz
ISBN: 950–04–0934–8

A14

HAUNTED

a. _____, Hodder & Stoughton, London, UK, 1988 (hc)
There are two variants of this edition: a trade edition and a limited edition.
   i. Description: trade state*
      Print run: 35,000 copies
      Price: £10.95
      ISBN: 0–340–41616–5
   ii. Description: signed, boxed and numbered state*
      Print run: 250 copies
      Price: £40.00
      ISBN: 0–340–49367–4
      (Note: Issued in black cloth box, with no dust jacket)

b. _____, Guild Publishing, London, UK, 1988 (hc)
Price: £7.95
Title code: CN3744

c. _____, Stoddart/Hodder & Stoughton, Canada, 1988 (hc)*
Price: £10.95
ISBN: 0–7737–2226–2

d. _____, Magna Print Books, Long Preston, UK, 1989 (hc)*
ISBN: 1–85057–652–1
(Note: Large print edition)

e. _____, New English Library, London, UK, 1989 (pb)*
Print run: 510,000 copies
Price: £3.50
ISBN: 0–450–49355–5

f. _____, Putnam, New York, USA, 1989 (hc)*
Price: $18.95
ISBN: 0–399–13486–7

g. _____, Magna Print Books, Long Preston, UK, 1989 (pb)*
ISBN: 1–8505–653–X
(Note: Large print edition)

h. _____, Berkley/Jove, New York, USA, 1990 (pb)
Price: $4.95
ISBN: 0–515–10345–4

i. [as *Yön aaveet*], Gummerus, Helsinki, Finland, 1989 (hc)*
Translator: Tarmo Haarala
ISBN: 951–20–3370–4

j. [as *Ondskans Hus*], Bonniers, Stockholm, Sweden, 1989 (hc)*
Translator: Eva Larsson
ISBN: 91–0–047762–1

k. [as *Ztoixeiwuevo*], Harlenic Hellas, Greece, 1990 (pb)*

l. [as *Dis-moi Qui Tu Hantes . . .*], Presses de la Cité, France, 1990 (tp)*
Translator: Thierry Arson
Price: 130 F
ISBN: 2–258–02923–6

A15

CREED
a. _____, Hodder & Stoughton, London, UK, 1990 (hc)*
    Price: £12.95
    ISBN: 0–340–50909–0
    (Note: Cover artwork and frontispiece by the author)
b. _____, New English Library, London, UK, 1991 (pb)
    Price: £4.50
    ISBN: 0–450–54743–4
    (Note: "Open Market Edition". Frontispiece by the author)
c. _____, New English Library, London, UK, 1991 (pb)*
    Price: £4.50
    ISBN: 0–450–54743–4
    (Note: Frontispiece by the author)

B OMNIBUS EDITIONS

Includes those books that collect together more than one James Herbert volume.

B1

MOON, SHRINE, THE DARK, FLUKE, Octopus, London, UK, 1988 (hc)*
Price: £9.95
ISBN: 0–7064–3808–6

B2

JAMES HERBERT, Guild Publishing, London, UK, 1988 (hc)*
Price: £7.95
Title code: CN2496
(Note: Contains *The Rats*, *The Dark* and *Fluke*)

C SHORT STORIES AND NON-FICTION

Includes fiction and articles by James Herbert published in magazines, newspapers and books. Stories are capitalised and non-fiction works are in italics.

C1

THE SPEAR, Signet, New York, USA, 1980 (booklet)*
(Note: 12 page promotional booklet with excerpt from novel. "An Exciting Preview of a Sensational New Diabolical Chiller!")

C2
a. **THE MAGIC COTTAGE**
    in *Woman*, UK, 1986 (magazine)*
    (Note: Serialised condensed form of the novel over four issues dated May 10, 17, 24 and 31, 1986)
b. _____, in *Woman's Day*, Australia, 1986 (magazine)*
    (Note: Serialised condensed form of the novel over four issues in November 1986)

C3

Comic Relief
in *She*, UK, July 1987 (magazine)*

C4

a. **MAURICE AND MOG**
   in *Masques II*, Maclay Associates, Baltimore, USA, 1987 (hc)
   Edited by J. N. Williamson
   (Note: Excerpt cut from US edition of *Domain*)
   There are two variants of this edition: a trade edition and a limited edition.
   i.   Description: trade state*
   Price: $19.95
   ISBN: 0–940776–24–3
   ii. Description: boxed and numbered state, bound in gold cloth and
   signed by the editor. Limited to 300 copies*
b. _____, in *The Best of Masques*, Berkley, New York, USA, 1988 (pb)
   Edited by J. N. Williamson
   Price: $3.50
   ISBN: 0–425–10693–4
c. _____, in *Masques Two*, Futura, London, UK, 1989 (pb)*
   Edited by J. N. Williamson
   Price: £3.50
   ISBN: 0–7088–4285–2
d. _____, in *Masques Two*, Severn House, London, UK, 1989 (hc)
   Edited by J. N. Williamson
   Price: £10.95
   ISBN: 0–7278–4004–5

C5

Foreword
in *Swamp Thing*, Titan Books, London, UK, 1987 (tp)*
by Alan Moore, Steve Bissette, John Totleben
Price: £5.95
ISBN: 0–907610–88–9

C6

Foreword
in *The Fog*, New English Library, London, UK, 1988 (hc)*
Price: £12.95
ISBN: 0–450–02607–8

C7

HAUNTED
in *Woman*, UK, 1988 (magazine)*
(Note: Serialised condensed form of the novel over four issues dated July 30,
August 6, 16, and 23, 1988)

C8

Bowled over by the Beast
in *The Sunday Times*, UK, September 18, 1988 (newspaper)*

C9

a. **HALLOWE'EN'S CHILD**
in *Gaslight & Ghosts,* 1988 World Fantasy Convention/Robinson, London, UK, 1988 (hc)*
Edited by Stephen Jones and Jo Fletcher
Print run: 1,500 copies
Price: £9.95
ISBN: 0–951389–26–3
(Note: Excerpt from short story)

b. _____ in *Male & Femail* UK, October 29, 1988 (magazine)*
(Note: Colour supplement for the *Daily Mail.* Contains the full text of short story)

c. _____, in *The Complete Masters of Darkness*, Underwood-Miller, Lancaster, USA, 1991 (hc)
Edited by Dennis Etchison
There are two variants of this edition: a trade edition and a limited edition.
i. Description: trade state*
Price: $39.95
ISBN: 0–88733–116–5
ii. Description: limited edition*
Price: $160.00
ISBN: 0–88733–117–3
(Note: "Special leatherbound edition. 350 numbered copies. This lavish deluxe edition is bound in English pigskin and German silk cloth, with hand marbled Japanese endpapers and linen traycase." Signed by many of the contributors including Herbert)

d. _____, in *Masters of Darkness III*, Tor Books, New York, USA, 1991 (pb)
Edited by Dennis Etchison
Price: $3.95
ISBN: 0–812–51766–6

C10

a. **BREAKFAST**
in *Scare Care,* Tor Books, New York, USA, 1989 (hc)*
Edited by Graham Masterton for the Scare Care Trust
Price: $19.95
ISBN: 0–312–93156–5
(Note: Excerpt cut from American edition of *Domain*)

b. _____, in *Special Report*, USA, August-October 1989 (magazine)*

c. _____, in *Scare Care*, Tor Books, New York, USA, 1990 (pb)
Edited by Graham Masterton for the Scare Care Trust
Price: $4.95
ISBN: 0–812–51097–6

d. _____, in *Scare Care*, Severn House, Wallington, UK, 1990 (hc)*
Edited by Graham Masterton for the Scare Care Trust
Price: £13.95
ISBN: 0–7278–4113–0

e. _____, in *Scare Care*, Grafton Books, London, UK, 1991 (pb)*
Edited by Graham Masterton for the Scare Care Trust
Price: £4.99
ISBN: 0–586–21123–3

C11

Book Choice: James Herbert
in *Waterstone's Catalogue 1989/90* (magazine)*

C12

a. **_The Mangler Introduction_**
in _Dark Voices: The Best from The Pan Book of Horror Stories_, Pan Books, London, UK, 1990 (hc)*
Edited by Stephen Jones and Clarence Paget
Price: £13.95
ISBN: 0–330–31565–X
(Note: Simultaneous with "C12(b)". A book club edition was produced for The Leisure Circle, same as "C12(a)" except for no bar code on the back cover and the correct spelling of Dennis Etchison's name on page 162. This was a second printing, although there is no indication of such in the preliminary pages)

b. _____, in _Dark Voices: The Best from The Pan Book of Horror Stories_, Pan Books, London, UK, 1990 (pb)*
Edited by Stephen Jones and Clarence Paget
Price: £3.99
ISBN: 0–330–31100–X
(Note: Simultaneous with "C12(a)")

C13

a. **CREED**
in _Fear_, UK, No. 20, August 1990 (magazine)*
(Note: Excerpt from novel)

D PROOF COPIES

Includes proofs and advance reading copies of books by or including James Herbert

D1

DOMAIN, New English Library, London, UK, 1984 (tp)*
ISBN: 0–450–06076–4

D2

MOON, New English Library, London, UK, 1985 (tp)*
ISBN: 0–450–06088–8
(Note: "Uncorrected Book Proof")

D3

THE MAGIC COTTAGE, Hodder & Stoughton, London, UK, 1986 (tp)*
ISBN: 0–340–39066–2
(Note: "Proof Copy")

D4

SEPULCHRE, Hodder & Stoughton, London, UK, 1987 (tp)*
ISBN: 0–340–39472–2
(Note: "Presentation Page Proofs")

D5

HAUNTED, Putnam, New York, USA, 1989 (tp)
(Note: "Uncorrected proof copy")

D6

DARK VOICES: THE BEST FROM THE PAN BOOK OF HORROR STORIES, Pan Books, London, UK, 1990 (tp)*
Edited by Stephen Jones and Clarence Paget
ISBN: 0–330–31565–X (cased)
　　　　 0–330–31100–X (paper)
(Note: "Uncorrected proof copy"/"First World Hardcover". Contains "Introduction" (to *The Mangler*))

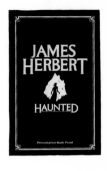

D7

CREED, Hodder & Stoughton, London, UK, 1990 (tp)*
ISBN: 0–340–50909–0
(Note: "Uncorrected page proofs". Cover artwork and frontispiece by the author)

E MISCELLANEA

Includes other James Herbert items that do not fit into the previous categories

Unique Editions:

E1
a. **THE FOG**, New English Library, London, UK, 1975 (hc)*
　　Description: Author's presentation copy from the publisher, bound in dark red leather with gold lettering on the spine.
b. ————, New English Library, London, UK, 1988 (hc)*
　　Description: Author's presentation copy from the publisher, bound in pale red leather with gold lettering on the spine, decorative boards and matching endpapers.
c. ————, New English Library, London, UK, 1989 (pb)*
　　Description: Author's presentation copy from the publisher, encased in silver box engraved with the cover of the book, to celebrate 1,000,000th printing.

E2

THE SURVIVOR, New English Library, London, UK, 1976 (hc)*
Description: Author's presentation copy from the publisher, bound in dark red leather with gold lettering on the spine.

E3

FLUKE, New English Library, London, UK, 1977 (hc)*
Description: Author's presentation copy from the publisher, bound in dark red leather with gold lettering on the spine.

E4

THE SPEAR, New English Library, London, UK, 1978 (hc)*
Description: Author's presentation copy from the publisher, bound in dark red leather with gold lettering on the spine.

E5

LAIR, New English Library, London, UK, 1979 (hc)*
Description: Author's presentation copy from the publisher, bound in dark red leather with gold lettering on the spine.

E6

THE DARK, New English Library, London, UK, 1980 (hc)*
Description: Author's presentation copy from the publisher, bound in dark red leather with gold lettering on the spine.

E7

DOMAIN, New English Library, UK, 1984 (hc)*
Description: Author's presentation copy from the publisher, bound in pale red leather with gold lettering on spine, decorative boards and matching endpapers.

E8

a. **MOON**, New English Library, UK, 1985 (hc)*
    Description: Author's presentation copy from the publisher, bound in pale red leather with gold lettering on spine, decorative boards and matching endpapers.
b. , Crown Publishing, USA, 1986 (hc)*
    Description: Author's presentation copy from the publisher, bound in black leather with gold lettering on spine, decorative boards and matching endpapers.

E9

a. **THE MAGIC COTTAGE**, Hodder & Stoughton, UK, 1986 (hc)*
    Description: Author's presentation copy from the publisher, bound in pale red leather with gold lettering on spine, decorative boards and matching endpapers.
b. _____, Hodder & Stoughton, UK, 1986 (hc)*
    Description: Tooled white leather binding with gold inlay lettering on front and spine and gold page edging. Two presentation copies produced by *Reader's Digest* as "The Special James Herbert Award" for the "1988 Young Illustrator's Competition". One copy in the collection of the author.

E10

SEPULCHRE, Hodder & Stoughton, UK, 1987 (hc)*
Description: Author's presentation copy from the publisher, bound in pale red leather with gold lettering on spine, decorative boards and matching endpapers.

E11

HAUNTED, Hodder & Stoughton, UK, 1988 (hc)*
Description: Author's presentation copy from the publisher, bound in pale red leather with gold lettering on spine, decorative boards and matching endpapers.

JAMES HERBERT:

AUDIO TAPES

E12
THE FOG, Octopus Books, UK, 1987
Read by Christopher Lee
(Note: Abridged, 2 cassettes)

Tape Aids for the Blind

E13
THE RATS (1974)

E14
LAIR (1979)

E15
DOMAIN (1985)

E16
MOON (1986)

E17
THE MAGIC COTTAGE (1987)

E18
SEPULCHRE (1987)

Computer Game

E19
THE RATS, Hodder & Stoughton Software, Sevenoaks, UK, 1985
Price: £7.95

Unpublished Screenplay

E20
HAUNTED (1986)

ACKNOWLEDGEMENTS

"James Herbert: Introduction", copyright (c) 1992 by Stephen King.

"A Category to Himself", copyright (c) 1992 by Stephen Jones.

"A Life in the Day of James Herbert", copyright (c) 1983 by Times Newspapers Limited. Originally published in *The Sunday Times Magazine*, September 11, 1983. Reprinted by permission of the publisher.

"Bowled Over by the Beast", copyright (c) 1988 by James Herbert. Originally published in *The Sunday Times*, September 18, 1988. Reprinted by permission of the author and the author's agent.

"At Home With James Herbert", copyright (c) 1989 by Dave Hughes. Originally published in *Fear*, No. 8, August 1989. Reprinted by permission of the author.

"Doing It With Style", copyright (c) 1985, 1990 by Douglas E. Winter. Originally published as "James Herbert" in *Faces of Fear*. Reprinted by permission of Pan Books Limited and the author.

"Comic Relief", copyright (c) 1987 by James Herbert. Originally published in *She*, July 1987. Reprinted by permission of the author and the author's agent.

"Castaway", copyright (c) 1992 by Mike Ashley.

"My Ten Favourite Books", copyright (c) 1989 by James Herbert. Originally published in *Waterstone's Catalogue, 1989/90*. Reprinted by permission of the author and the author's agent.

"The Craft", copyright (c) 1992 by Neil Gaiman.

"Breakfast", copyright (c) 1984, 1989 by James Herbert. Reprinted by permission of the author and the author's agent.

"Season of the Rat", copyright (c) 1992 by Adrian Cole.

"Horror of *The Rats*", copyright (c) 1985 by John Gilbert. Originally published in *Farnborough News & Mail*, October 4, 1985. Reprinted by permission of the author.

"*The Fog*", copyright (c) 1988 by James Herbert. Reprinted by permission of the author and the author's agent.

"The Curious Case of *The Spear*", copyright (c) 1992 by Jo Fletcher.

"Maurice and Mog", copyright (c) 1984, 1987 by James Herbert. Reprinted by permission of the author and the author's agent.

"James Herbert and Science Fiction", copyright (c) 1992 by Michael A. Morrison.

"The Dark Domain", copyright (c) 1988 by John Fraser. Originally published as "James Herbert: A Profile" in *Horrorstruck*, Vol. 1, No. 5, January/February 1988. Reprinted by permission of the author.

"Breaking the Mould", copyright (c) 1992 by Stephen Laws.

"The Eidetic Image", copyright (c) 1987 by Michael A. Morrison. Originally published as "The Unreal Estate" in *Washington Post*, September 9, 1987. Reprinted by permission of the author.

"A British Phenomenon", copyright (c) 1988 by David J. Howe. Originally published in slightly different form in *Starburst*, No. 121, September 1988. Reprinted by permission of the author.

"Herbert, *Haunted*, and the Integrity of Bestsellerdom", copyright (c) 1992 by Stephen Gallagher.

"Haunted by Success", copyright (c) 1988 by John Gilbert. Originally published in *Fear*, No. 2, September–October 1988. Reprinted by permission of the author.

"Selling a Bestseller", copyright (c) 1988 by Hodder & Stoughton Publishers. Reprinted by permission.

"In the Hall of the Monster King: Music and the Maestro of Horror", copyright (c) 1992 by Edwin Pouncey.

"Hallowe'en's Child", copyright (c) 1988 by James Herbert. Reprinted by permission of the author and the author's agent.

"Swamp Thing", copyright (c) 1987 by James Herbert. Originally published as "Foreword" in *Swamp Thing*. Reprinted by permission of the author and the author's agent.

"The Devil You Know", copyright (c) 1990 by John Gilbert. Originally published in *Fear*, No. 20, August 1990. Reprinted by permission of the author.

"*Creed*: The Advertisement", copyright (c) 1990 by David J. Howe. Originally published in *Starburst*, No. 145, September 1990. Reprinted by permission of the author.

"Big Climaxes and Movie Bullshit", copyright (c) 1992 by Stefan Jaworzyn.

"From Rats to Riches", copyright (c) 1989 by Dave Hughes. Originally published in *G.M. Magazine* No. 8, October 1989. Reprinted by permission of the author.

"Jim Meets Gray", copyright (c) 1990 by Graham Masterton. Originally published in slightly different form in *Mystery Scene*, No. 24, January 1990. Reprinted by permission of the author.

"Dark Dreamer", copyright (c) 1990 by Stanley Wiater. Originally published in slightly different form in *Dark Dreamers: Conversations with the Masters of Horror*. Reprinted by permission of the author.

"They Don't Like Us", copyright (c) 1992 by James Herbert. Reprinted by permission of the author and the author's agent.

"Notes Towards A Reappraisal", copyright (c) 1985, 1988, 1992 by Ramsey Campbell. Originally published in slightly different form in *Fantasy Review*, No. 76, February 1985, and *The 1988 World Fantasy Convention Progress Report Three*, October 1988. Reprinted by permission of the author.

"James Herbert: Afterword", copyright (c) 1992 by Clive Barker.

"James Herbert: A Working Bibliography", copyright (c) 1992 by Stephen Jones.

"Waiting . . ." copyright (c) 1991 by James Herbert. Originally published in *Now We Are Sick*. Reprinted by permission of the author and the author's agent.

ILLUSTRATIONS ACKNOWLEDGEMENTS

Page 1 – Photo Credit: Bob Knight
Page 7 – Artist Credit: Bill Gregory (*Sepulchre*)
Page 17 – Artist Credit: Zehra Arabadji
Page 18 – Photo Credit: Bob Knight
Page 28 – Artist Credit: Bill Phillips (*The Rats*)
Page 32 – Artist Credit: Bill Gregory
Page 35 – James Herbert & his home swimming pool Photo Credit: Bob Knight (circa 1991)/ James Herbert relaxing at home (circa 1987)/James Herbert signing *The Dark* (circa 1980)
Page 37 – Artist Credit: Howard Shaw (*The Magic Cottage*)
Page 38 – James Herbert in Jersey (circa 1984)
Page 42 – Artist Credit: Keith Pointing (*The Rats*)
Page 46 – James Herbert and Fluke (circa 1984)/James Herbert signs for a very unusual fan (circa 1987)
Page 48 – James Herbert aged 10/James Herbert aged 12/ James Herbert aged 16
Page 57 – James Herbert's grandfather, Peter Riley/ James Herbert's mother, Kitty Herbert/James Herbert and his mother (circa 1991)
– James Herbert's wife, Eileen, on their wedding day (26/8/67)
Page 62 – James Herbert at the Hornsey Art College dance (circa 1961)
Page 63 – Artist Credit: Keith Pointing (*Lair*)
Page 64 – James Herbert at home
Page 67 – Artist Credit: Warren Tufts (*Casey Ruggles*)
Page 68 – Sample drawing from James Herbert's graphic novel, *The City*, to be published in 1993. Artist Credit: Ian Miller.
Page 74 – Artist Credit: Zehra Arabadji
Page 74 – Artist Credit: Howard Shaw (*The Magic Cottage*)
Page 78 – James Herbert and family at home, Christmas 1983
Page 86 – Selected advertising campaigns art directed by James Herbert
Page 92 – James Herbert behind the camera for a Harp Lager TV commercial (circa 1976)
Page 97 – Artist Credit: Keith Pointing (*The Survivor*)
Page 98 – James Herbert (circa 1970s)
Page 107 – Artist Credit: Gerry Grace (*The Rats*)
Page 108 – Artist Credit: David Kearney (*The Fog*)
Page 111 – James Herbert takes the controls (circa 1960s)
Page 112 – Photo Credit: Otto Georg Prachner. Copyright © Meyer Wien VI (*The Spear*)
Page 122 – James Herbert
Page 131 – Artist Credit: Chris Brown (*Fluke*)
Pages 132–135 – Artist Credit: James Herbert
Page 136 – Extract from James Herbert's story board for graphic novel, *The City*, to be published in 1993
Page 148 – Jeffrey Archer and James Herbert (circa 1991)/ Denis Healey and James Herbert at a literary lunch (circa 1989)/James Herbert signs a book for actress Rula Lenska (circa 1989)/James Herbert interviewed by Brian Hayes on LBC News Radio (circa 1987)
Page 150 – Artist Credit: Bill Gregory (*The Spear*)
Page 159 – Artist Credit: Bill Gregory (*The Magic Cottage*)
Page 160 – Artist Credit: James Herbert
Page 164 – Design roughs by Bill Gregory (*Sepulchre*)
Page 167 – Artist Credit: David O'Conner (*The Magic Cottage*)
Page 168 – Border Design (*The Magic Cottage*)
Page 179 – Photo Credit: Chris Holland
Page 180 – Artist Credit: Larry Rostant (*Moon*)
Page 187 – Stephen King, David Tate and James Herbert (circa 1984)
Page 188 – Artist Credit: Howard Shaw (*The Magic Cottage*)
Page 196 – Eileen Herbert/Kerry Herbert/Emma Herbert/ Casey Herbert
Page 200 – James Herbert (circa 1988)
Page 208 – James Herbert at home (circa early 1980s)/ James Herbert in a musical mood
Page 216 – Artist Credit: Bill Gregory (*Sepulchre*)
Page 229 – Artist Credit: Keith Pointing (*The Fog*)
Page 230 – James Herbert at home. Photo Credit: Bob Knight
Page 233 – Artist Credit: Stephen Bissette/John Totaleben. Swamp Thing Copyright © 1987 by DC Comics, Inc. Courtesy of Titan Books Ltd.
Page 234 – Photo Credit: Bob Knight
Page 241 – Artist Credit: Larry Rostant (*Haunted*)
Page 242 – Bob Flag as Nosferatu in *Creed* TV advertisment (circa 1990). Photo Credit: David J. Howe
Page 247 – Artist Credit: Clifford Webb (*Creed*)
Page 248 – The rats strike in *Deadly Eyes* (1983). Copyright © 1983 by Warner Bros., Inc.
Page 260 – Jenny Agutter and Robert Powell in *The Survivor* (1980). Copyright © 1980 RIACI Investments/Hemdale.
Page 266 – Salman Rushdie and James Herbert at the Author of the Year party, Hatchards, Piccadilly (circa 1992). Photo Credit: Copyright © 1992 by Richard Young.
Page 270 – Artist Credit: James Herbert (*Creed*)
Page 277 – James Herbert at home. Photo Credit: Bob Knight (circa 1991)/James Herbert stock-car racing (circa 1988)
Page 282 – Rick Wakeman and James Herbert working together on record album (circa 1991)
Page 288 – James Herbert and his famous pair of white sneakers (circa 1986). Photo Credit: James Herbert
Page 298 – James Herbert and family after signing session at London's Forbidden Planet (circa 1983)
Endpaper-Lionel Jeans (*Moon*)
All other artwork and illustrative material Copyright © James Herbert. All rights reserved.

JAMES HERBERT

WAITING

James Herbert

So here I lie beneath the bed
One eye upon the clock
The other's somewhere close by too
Wrapped in a smelly sock.
An arm, I think, is in the loo
Next to the toilet cleaner
The fingers make a scouring brush,
Though lately they've worn leaner.
A leg is in the wardrobe,
Still in its leather boot,
The other's a draught excluder.
I'd protest but my tongue is mute.
A hand has become an ashtray
On the dusty mantelshelf,
The fingers curled hold cigarettes
(Remember, these are bad for health!)
My torso's over there, sitting in a wicker,
No arms, no legs, no head, no life,
Can you imagine anything sicker?
Also absent is my heart,
Spleen, kidneys, and liver too.
By now I expect you've already guessed
Just who likes meaty stew.
The only blessing I suppose –
And this might make you think –
I'd hate the smell of rotting flesh
But my nose is in the sink.
So here my head lies in the dark
Listening with half an ear,
Those nibbling maggots at my brain
Will soon stop thoughts I fear.
And here he comes, that crazed axeman
All chuckles and sniggers and leers
To put me all together again –
Christ! This could go on for years.

Written for NOW WE ARE SICK, An Anthology of Nasty Verse.